STRUCTURE, MEANING & RITUAL
IN THE NARRATIVES OF THE SOUTHERN SAN

The Khoisan Heritage Series

Series Editor: David Lewis-Williams

Other titles in the Khoisan Heritage Series,
published by Wits University Press

*Contested Images: Diversity in Southern African
Rock Art Research*
Edited by Thomas A Dowson and David Lewis-Williams

Customs and Beliefs of the /Xam Bushmen
Edited by Jeremy C. Hollman

Rock Engravings of Southern Africa
by Thomas A Dowson

*Voices from the Past: /Xam Bushmen and the
Bleek and Lloyd Collection*
Edited by Janette Deacon and Thomas A Dowson

*Women Like Meat: The Folklore and Foraging Ideology
of the Kalahari Ju/'Hoan*
by Megan Biesele

STRUCTURE, MEANING & RITUAL
IN THE NARRATIVES OF THE SOUTHERN SAN

ROGER HEWITT

WITS UNIVERSITY PRESS

Wits University Press
1 Jan Smuts Avenue
Johannesburg
2001
South Africa
http://witspress.wits.ac.za

First published 1986 by Helmut Buske Verlag, Hamburg, Germany.
This second edition published 2008 by Wits University Press.

ISBN 978-1-86814-470-9

Cover photograph by Anthony van Tonder, The Media Bank, africanpictures.net
Cover design by Hybridesign
Layout and design by Acumen Publishing Solutions, Johannesburg.
Printed and bound by Creda Communications

For Georgia

Contents

Acknowledgements

My first thanks are, undoubtedly, to Pippa Skotnes, who managed to blow a trumpet in my ear from what seemed a very long way away to wake me up and let me know about the developments in the Bleek and Lloyd Archive in recent times and to invite me to Cape Town. She gave me such positive encouragement to re-publish this book, and pointed me in exactly the right direction. She is a very special person to whom I owe a great debt of gratitude.

I would also like to take this opportunity to make an acknowledgement that would have been in the first edition, had its birth not been such a casual and chaotic affair. David Lewis Williams was a fellow at Cambridge working on his earliest ideas concerning the San rock paintings he had been so meticulously recording and analysing when we somehow came into contact at the start of my doctoral research. We had many fascinating conversations and debates in London over the published Bleek and Lloyd materials at a time when it was hard to find a soul who even knew of their existence. He also gave very ungrudgingly of his time to translate from the Afrikaans for me a number of the von Wielligh texts of |Xam narratives, the whole four volumes of which I had somehow assembled myself a photocopy version but could not read. I would like to thank him, somewhat belatedly, for his generosity and company at that time.

Others who were the effective *dramatis personae* of that period and with whom I had really fruitful dialogue were Megan Biesele, Sigrid Schmidt and Alan Barnard who started his doctoral research at the London School of Oriental and African Studies in exactly the year I started there. I still have some of the letters he sent me, somewhat sandy, from the Kalahari, while he was doing his fieldwork. Each of these scholars was all in different ways important to me in the development of my own thinking.

Finally, of course, I would like to acknowledge again the work of the staff at the University of Cape Town Library, who tolerated and then responded so well to my unexpected and at the time obscure request that they search to see if the Bleek and Lloyd notebooks were with them. Little were they to know at the time that that was just the beginning and that over 30 years later their office would be caught up in a tsunami of Bleek and Lloyd digitalisation.

In the production of this book, I have been fortunate to have the services of Fiona Potter as proofreader, Margie Ramsay as indexer, Karen Lilje of Hybridesign as cover designer and Acumen Publishing Solutions as book designers.

Introduction

This new edition of *Structure, Meaning and Ritual in the Narratives of the Southern San* comes some 20 years after its initial printing and 30 after the text, with few differences, was presented as a doctoral thesis to the School of Oriental and African Studies, University of London. Since then there has been a great deal of excellent scholarship that has explored the Bleek and Lloyd collection of |Xam texts, housed mainly in the library of the University of Cape Town (UCT), or has added substantially to what we know of the historical context of that collection and its content. At the time of my thesis, however, not only was the location or, indeed, the continued existence of Lucy Lloyd's |Xam transcriptions – the largest part of the collection – unknown, but the content of Bleek's own notebooks also remained unexplored and the notebooks themselves barely catalogued. Thus it was with something of a gamble that I embarked on a thesis designed to be based alone on those as yet 'undiscovered' notebooks. Luckily for me my optimistic digging was rewarded[1] and the work that produced this book was able to commence. Naturally the existence of the notebooks did not remain a secret for long, and much useful scholarly work, largely by South African researchers, started to flow.

Much has changed in the intervening years. Even between the presentation of the thesis in 1976 and 1986, when editors from Helmut Buske publishers in Hamburg approached me to ask if they might publish the work, there had grown a greater sensitivity around nomenclature applied to peoples customarily studied by anthropologists. For many years the term 'Bushmen' had been used to describe the hunter-gatherers whose click language was closely related to that of the Khoi herders with whom they also shared much of the Cape. Both Wilhelm Bleek and Lucy Lloyd referred to theirs as a collection of 'Bushman folklore'. By the late 1970s, however, the Khoi word 'San' became widely adopted to describe the various language groups evident amongst the hunter-gatherers, as well as the people themselves. While anthropologists familiarised the reading public with the specific names of some of these – principally the !Kung, made internationally famous by the Marshall expeditions to the Kalahari desert in the 1950s – the term 'San' became preferred by many in seeming not to have the derogatory connotations that 'Bushmen' might be thought to possess. It was not long, however, before it was pointed out that 'San' itself was often a derogatory term applied to the hunter-gatherers and was often used simply to mean 'thief'. The best nomenclature was clearly not to be found in these terms for the general category, but those used by each specific group to refer to itself. For this reason, as most of the texts collected by Bleek and Lloyd were from one large group of hunter-gatherers, the |Xam, it was possible to use that term in accounts of that people and their language. However, for anyone except for a very small circle of academics, the name '|Xam' meant nothing. Hence the general terms were often attached, giving 'the |Xam Bushmen' or '|Xam San' and it has not been until very recently that '|Xam' has acquired greater popular currency – certainly within South Africa if not elsewhere – so that it can now be used without explanation. Too late, alas, for the title of this book, which, being republished more or less as it stood, has for the sake of transparency to carry its original title. Similarly, the text throughout uses both 'San' and '|Xam' in different contexts, reflecting the initial academic need to identify the people within the widest anthropological frame and at the same time be specific. The need to do so continues to be shared with most authors today, and we find the words 'Bushmen' and 'San' in common use alongside '|Xam' in even the most recent texts.

It would be very time-consuming and possibly pointless in the end also to allow the text of this book now to benefit from all the scholarship that has followed – tempting though that might be. This is particularly so because the work is fundamentally an analysis of narratives in relation to their specific ethnographic context insofar as that context is reconstructible from the ethnographic record in many of the texts collected by Bleek and Lloyd and from writings by early travellers, missionaries, local officials and so on. There is a strong argumentative thread – heavily structuralist – to this book, and its virtues – if virtues it has – will not lie in the comprehensiveness of its scholarship, but in the persuasiveness of its analysis and the logic of its arguments. Furthermore, that scholarship that has emerged since it was written speaks for itself.

Hardly in mitigation of the slow genocidal process by which the |Xam had ceased to exist, but in a miraculous parenthesis to its final stages, the written record of |Xam culture, belief and oral tradition was constructed by the co-operative efforts of several |Xam people – five men and one woman – and the two Europeans, Lucy Lloyd and Wilhelm Bleek. The constructed texts were subsequently explored, written about and partially published by

Lucy Lloyd herself, then Dorothea Bleek, but by few others (see below). Between 1936 and 1973 they more or less disappeared from view. From the 1980s onwards, however, there was a gradual scholarly awakening to the power and uniqueness of the collection. The most important work to appear at that time was by archaeologist Jeanette Deacon, whose scrupulous research produced an outstanding paper that identified the exact location of the homes of Bleek and Lloyd's collaborators: '"My place is Biterpits": The home territory of Bleek and Lloyd's |Xam San informants'.[2] Other papers by Deacon followed, culminating in a milestone edited book with T.A. Dawson in 1996.[3]

That publication followed on from an important conference on the collection at UCT in the previous year, and also coincided with an exhibition of art, artifacts and other materials curated by Pippa Skotnes – now director of the Lucy Lloyd Archive, Resource and Exhibition Centre at the Michaelis School of Fine Art, UCT – that confronted the difficult moral and political dimensions of the relationship between the |Xam and the other inhabitants of South Africa and was entitled: 'Miscast: Negotiating the Presence of the Bushmen'. It also involved the production of a book of the same name.[4] One of the most important chapters in that book was the one by Tony Traill on the condition of the |Xam language in the last quarter of the 19th century.[5] Given the inherent problems of the socio-linguistic reconstruction of that period and place, this was a deeply insightful and scholarly account that has, thankfully, been reproduced in Skotnes' more recent, lavishly illustrated book on the collection, *Claim to the Country*.[6]

There has been much work that made excellent use of the collection. Amongst the earliest was David Lewis-Williams' ground-breaking book *Believing and Seeing: Symbolic Meanings in Southern San Rock Paintings*,[7] as well as his more recent popular edited reproductions of many of the |Xam texts: *Stories that Float from Afar*.[8] His early knowledge of the published work originally derived from the collection and subsequently of the collection itself was second to none, and his contribution to scholarship in the field has been immense. Mathias Guenther also drew on the collection in his comparative study of Nharo and |Xam oral traditions.[9] Creative writers too have made use of the |Xam texts, and amongst these Alan James' beautiful and informed engagement in *The First Bushman's Path* stands out above the rest. It is, perhaps, the historians who have recently shed the most light on the important context of the |Xam texts. Firstly, there is Nigel Penn, whose excellent theorisation of the economic and social relations between the |Xam and the colonists in his *The Forgotten Frontier*[10] provides a frame within which to understand the larger processes that brought about the ugly realities of |Xam extinction. Secondly, there is Andrew Bank's brilliant and painstaking research into the minutest details of the relations between Bleek and Lloyd and each of the |Xam individuals who also brought the texts into being. His book, *Bushmen in a Victorian World,*[11] is a masterpiece of detection and exposition.

Perhaps the greatest contribution to the future investigation of the |Xam, however, has been made by the tireless efforts and commitment of Pippa Skotnes and her staff at UCT. Thanks to their work, the entire Bleek and Lloyd collection is available on the Web as well as on DVD,[12] permitting a whole new generation of researchers to explore this extraordinary and unique archive.

In 1855 Wilhelm Bleek arrived in Natal to compile a Zulu grammar for J.W. Colenso, first Anglican bishop of Natal. A few years earlier Bleek had received his doctorate from the University of Bonn for a thesis on grammatical gender in African languages (W.H.I. Bleek 1851). Bleek remained in Natal for nearly two years and during that period began to develop an interest in the San and their language. This interest persisted for many years, but it was not until 1870, while he was employed as curator of the library of Sir George Grey in Cape Town, that he was presented with an opportunity to study a San language in depth.[13] In that year 28 |Xam prisoners were sent to work on the breakwater in Cape Town harbour. By then Bleek had published two volumes of his *Comparative Grammar of South African Languages*, but, interrupting further work on this grammar, he turned his attention to the study of |Xam. His daughter, Dorothea Frances Bleek, has reported:

> Father asked whether he might work among the Bushmen kept prisoners at the Breakwater. He had discovered, however, that the surroundings of prison were by no means helpful in persuading these people to talk. He asked whether it might be possible to allow some of the Bushmen to work for our family, so that he could interview them in the peace of our own home at Mowbray. This was approved by Sir Philip [Wodehouse, the governor], and we then had a few of them as servants. You can imagine that a Bushman, who has not even learnt to live in a house, and who knows

nothing about cultivating soil, did not make a particularly good house-boy, but this did not worry Father. What he wanted was to hear their language (Rosenthal & Goodwin 1953:12f).

Bleek's first informant was a young man called |A!kungta, who was soon joined by ||Kabbo, a much older man. In the 'Report of Dr. Bleek concerning his researches into Bushman language and customs, presented to the ... House of Assembly ...' of 1873, Bleek wrote of these informants:

> Both are still with me. Their term of penal servitude expired in the middle of the year 1871 and they have since remained of their own free will. In order to achieve the object of these enquiries (a thorough knowledge of the Bushman language and literature) the presence of these men (or other Bushmen) is necessary for several years; at least four; two and a half of which have already expired.
>
> What has been written down from the lips of the Bushmen, consists of more than four thousand columns (half pages quarto) of text, besides a dozen genealogical tables, and other genealogical, geographical, and astrological, &c, notices (Bleek & Lloyd 1911: 443f).

In October 1873 these informants returned to their homes near the Strontbergen in the northern Cape (lat. 30 S., long. 22 E.), but in the following months were replaced by ǂKasing and Dia!kwain from the Katkop Mountains north of Calvinia. In June 1874 !Kweiten ta liken, ǂKasing's wife and Dia!kwain's sister, and her children also came to Bleek's house at Mowbray. In 1875 Bleek wrote in his second report:

> The amount of native Bushman literature collected, has increased since our last report from more than 4,000 to about 6,000 half-pages or columns (in seventy-seven volumes of quarto); of which more than one-third has been written down by myself. A large portion of these Bushman texts has been translated with the aid of the narrators.

In a footnote Bleek added:

> As the printing of this report (handed to the Government in February last) has, through press of business been delayed to the present month (May), we are able to state that the total amount of Bushman native literature

collected is now about 7,200 half-pages, in eighty-four volumes (W.H.I. Bleek 1875b: 5).

During this period, Bleek was still working at the Grey Library and leaving the collection of |Xam oral literature mainly to Lucy C. Lloyd, his wife's sister. Indeed, the major part of the total collection was made by Lloyd, while Bleek worked on compiling a dictionary of the language and studying the grammar.

In August 1875 Bleek died, at the early age of 48, having been troubled with very poor health for many years. Lloyd was then appointed to the staff of the South African Public Library, Cape Town, editing material collected by Bleek. However, with the aid of other informants, she continued the work of collecting San texts until 1884. In 1887 she retired to North Wales and later Berlin. In 1889 a 'Third report concerning Bushman researches, presented to both Houses of the Parliament of the Cape of Good Hope ...' was published by Lloyd under the title, *A Short Account of Further Bushman Material Collected* (Lloyd 1889). This report followed the format of Bleek's second report and contained, in fact, a very detailed account of everything that had been collected since that date. This, like Bleek's report, provided an inventory not only of the oral literature, but also of the very many texts that dealt with customs and beliefs, and other matters of ethnographic interest. Together, Bleek's report of 1875 and Lloyd's of 1884 form a published index to all of the material collected between 1870 and 1884, a collection that amounts to some 13,000 pages of text and folio sheets.[14]

In 1911 Lloyd published a selection of the collected material in a volume entitled *Specimens of Bushman Folklore* (Bleek & Lloyd 1911) which contained |Xam texts and translations. An appendix to *Specimens of Bushman Folklore* also contains a few !Kung texts gathered by Lloyd between 1879 and 1882 from two adolescents from the northeast of Damaraland. This volume was the first major publication of the collected material. Lucy Lloyd died in 1914, after which Bleek's daughter, Dorothea Bleek, who had been only two years old when her father died, took up the task of publishing parts of the collection, as well as carrying out fresh research into other San groups and their languages.

In 1910 Dorothea Bleek made the first of her many expeditions when she visited the surviving |Xam living near Prieska. She later wrote:

In 1910 and 1911 when I travelled through Prieska and Kenhardt districts, I found just a handful of old people left here and there, some of them relatives of our former men. From them and from the farmers whose parents had settled here in the sixties, I received corroboration of what our Bushmen had told long before (D.F. Bleek 1923: viii).

She had already studied |Xam life and languages under her aunt, Lucy Lloyd, and helped in the preparation of *Specimens of Bushman Folklore*. In 1923 she published *Mantis and His Friends* (*ibid.*) containing translations of a number of narratives collected by her father and Lucy Lloyd concerning the trickster |Kaggen. Other original works were also published by her in the following years, but between 1931 and 1936 she edited a series of texts entitled 'Customs and beliefs of the |Xam Bushmen; from material collected by Dr. W.H.I. Bleek and Miss L.C. Lloyd between 1870 and 1880', which appeared in the journal *Bantu Studies*.[15]

In 1936 she also published, in the same journal, a further selection of the material, this time of narratives and fragments of narratives with texts, entitled 'Special speech of animals and moon used by the |Xam Bushmen'.[16] Apart from these publications of the collections, Dorothea Bleek also published part of a |Xam grammar (D.F. Bleek 1929c); an account of |Xam kinship terms (D.F. Bleek 1924); a volume of copies of rock paintings made by G.W. Stow together with a commentary by her containing interpretations and comments on the copies by her father's informants (Bleek & Stow 1930); and a good but brief sketch of |Xam oral literature in a paper called 'Bushman folklore' (D.F. Bleek 1929a). Finally, *A Bushman Dictionary* by Dorothea Bleek was published in 1956, eight years after her death, based on the work of many writers, including her father, Lucy Lloyd and her own researches (D.F. Bleek 1956).

The oral literature collected by Bleek and Lloyd comprises approximately one hundred different narratives, many of them in several versions; nearly eighty very short songs; and a few formal addresses to supernatural entities. Eleven of the songs were published in *Specimens of Bushman Folklore*, and a further selection, together with their melodies written down in musical notation, was published in 'A study of Bushman music' by Percival Kirby in 1936 (Kirby 1936a). Recent printed publications of parts of the collection include most notably David Lewis-Williams' *Stories that Float from Afar*, mentioned above, and Neil Bennun's *The Broken String: The Last Words of an Extinct People*.[17]

The texts were taken down by hand, sometimes by Bleek, more often by Lloyd. These were later roughly translated with help of the informants, most of whom spoke English and Afrikaans. In some cases the job of translation was left to a much later date, when other informants assisted in the translation, and a few of the texts were never translated. This process was excavated in detail in Andrew Bank's *Bushmen in a Victorian World*. Bleek and Lloyd had six main informants, five men – |A!kungta, ||Kabbo, ǂKasing, Dia!kwain and |Hang ǂkass'o – and one woman – !Kweiten ta ||ken. In addition to these, a few other informants assisted the collectors for brief periods. |A!kungta was with Bleek and Lloyd from August 1870 until October 1873; ||Kabbo from February 1871 until October 1873; Dia!kwain from December 1873 until March 1876; and ǂKasing from November 1873 until January 1875, when he left with his wife, !Kweiten ta ||ken, who had been at Mowbray since June 1874. |Hang ǂkass'o assisted Miss Lloyd from January 1878 until December 1879.

With the exception of |A!kungta, these informants were from two families. Dia!kwain, his sister !Kweiten ta ||ken and her husband ǂKasing were all from the Katkop Mountains, while ||Kabbo and his son-in-law, |Hang ǂkass'o, lived near to the Strontbergen, about a hundred miles east of Katkop. There were very slight differences in dialect in the language spoken in these two areas. In terms of custom, belief and narrative tradition, however, there were no major differences between the |Xam in these areas that can be detected from the information given in the texts.

All of the informants had had some contact with Europeans since the northwest of the Cape was penetrated by settlers after 1850, and most of the men had worked for European farmers at times. Indeed, it is clear from various comments in the texts that the old patterns of |Xam life had been considerably eroded by the settlers, who simultaneously took much of the land and carried out violent raids on the |Xam. The lives led by these informants were only partially traditional as they were increasingly forced to seek employment on farms. In consequence of European settlement they were also greatly endangered both by starvation and by the violence of the settlers.[18]

Beside the researches of Bleek and Lloyd, little work was done on the |Xam language. M.H.C. Lichtenstein, who travelled in the northern Cape in the years 1803–06, published a fragment on the language (Lichtenstein 1930: Vol. II, 463–475) and in 1888 Fr. Müller's brief paper 'Die sprache der |Kham Buschmänner' (Müller 1888) appeared, the material for which was given further scrutiny by W. Planert in 'Ober die sprache der Hottentotten und Buschmänner' (Planert 1905). In 1929 P. Meriggi's 'Versuch einer grammatik des |Xam-Buschmannischen' (Meriggi 1929) examined the texts published by Lloyd in *Specimens of Bushman Folklore*. These and Dorothea Bleek's own 'Bushman grammar' (D.F. Bleek1929c) comprise the bulk of the earliest work concerning the language. The best recent overviews are to be found in Traill.[19]

A large collection of |Xam narratives collected by Gideon Retief von Wielligh in the late 19th century was published in four volumes between 1919 and 1921 (von Wielligh 1919–1921). Many of these were collected from |Xam speakers north of Calvinia, and this collection represents an often illuminating supplement to the Bleek and Lloyd collection. However, von Wielligh was a popular writer who sought to encourage poor Afrikaners to read. His simplified stories, published in Afrikaans, were remodelled by him to these didactic ends and, unfortunately, cannot be taken as reliable versions of |Xam narratives.

This book examines the narratives at several levels, analysing the ways in which the organisation of narrative materials (plots, themes, motifs, etc.), together with the values and norms expressed through them, was frequently influenced by conceptual templates traceable in other aspects of the culture, including belief and ritual.

The collection is described in groups distinguished by content; plots, themes and motifs being related to their ethnographic context and situated as deeply with |Xam culture as the data allow.[20] Particular versions of narratives are also discussed in terms of the tradition that they display and as examples of the way in which common narrative materials were moulded by the personal interests and skills of individual narrators.

The group of narratives concerning the trickster and supernatural being, |Kaggen, constitute by far the largest thematically and structurally definable group in the collection. As such it is of special interest and particularly amenable to a wider range of analytical procedures than can be applied to other groups. Its discussion forms the largest part of the study and relates the beliefs and ritual practices concerning |Kaggen to the narratives and to |Kaggen's character and actions in them. In this way the associations that this character had for |Xam audiences are probed and his role qua trickster elucidated within a very specific ethnographic context.

By situating individual narratives within their narrative tradition, and that tradition within a cultural context extending from the material world to the conceptual frameworks evinced in custom and belief, this book attempts to demonstrate some of the many levels at which |Xam narratives were capable of having significance for their audiences, and to provide a basis for the comparative study of the oral literature of other San groups. Published texts have been referred to wherever possible. For the most part, summaries of narratives are employed, although important discrepancies between different versions of the same story are noted in every case.[21]

Orthography

Because the spelling in the manuscripts often varies considerably, the spelling of the texts quoted in this book has been standardised in accordance with the Bushman Dictionary (D.F. Bleek, op. cit.). As |Xam is a dead language it is impossible to know how accurately the texts represent the spoken language. Dorothea Bleek's statement that:

> Bushmen do not open their mouths much in speaking, it is therefore not easy to distinguish the vowels clearly. Slurred indefinite vowel sounds are in the majority and often vary slightly with individual speakers (D.F. Bleek 1929c: 82)

may account for many of the differences in spelling encountered in the manuscripts.

Long vowels are represented by a colon following the vowel. All vowels and diphthongs may be nasalised and this is indicated by ~. Where two vowels that occur together are sounded separately, ¨ is placed over the second.

Of the consonants, only few require a comment. A glottal closure is often encountered with k and g and is represented thus: k', g'. The letter r is slightly rolled and nasalised.

A glottal stop is indicated by ?; and a 'very loud plosive croak' (D.F. Bleek, 1929c: 83), often found as an initial sound, is represented by k', as in the Bushman Dictionary. Likewise, the five clicks found in |Xam are indicated by the following conventional signs: |, the dental click; !, the cerebral click; ||, the lateral click; ǂ the alveolar click; and ☉, the labial click.

Some |Xam words are distinguished from each other only by the tone in which they are uttered. There are three tones, high, middle and low. The middle tone is unmarked in the texts. The high tone is indicated by – placed before a syllable; the low tone by _. Words are usually accented on the first syllable, and always when the word begins with a click.

Finally, a brief note on the unabashed structuralism of the body of the analysis that follows. At the time of its writing the assault on structuralism was already under way – even if its consequences in deconstructionism were not yet apparent. My analytical choices were made in full awareness of available approaches, and although I am now a little alarmed by the monologic energy of my own argument in places, I reluctantly still find it persuasive and am happy to stand by it in republication.

Endnotes

1   See Pippa Skotnes. 2007. *Claim to the Country: The Archive of Lucy Lloyd and Wilhelm Bleek*. Cape Town: Jacana and Athens, Ohio: Ohio University Press, 160–167.

2   J. Deacon, ' "My place is Biterpits": The home territory of Bleek and Lloyd's |Xam San informants', *African Studies*, 45 (2), 1986, 135–155.

3   J. Deacon and T.A. Dawson. 1996. *Voices from the Past: |Xam Bushmen and the Bleek and Lloyd Collection*. Johannesburg: Witwatersrand University Press.

4   Pippa Skotnes (ed.). 1996. *Miscast: Negotiating the Presence of the Bushmen*. University of Cape Town.

5   Anthony Traill. 1996. '!Khwa-Ka Hhouiten-Hhouiten: The linguistic death of the |Xam', in *Miscast: Negotiating the Presence of the Bushmen*, edited by Pippa Skotnes, pp. 161–182. University of Cape Town.

6   Skotnes, 2007.

7   David Lewis Williams. 1981. *Believing and Seeing: Symbolic Meanings in Southern San Rock Painting*. London: Academic Press.

8   David Lewis Williams (ed.). 2000. *Stories that Float from Afar: Ancestral Folklore of the San of Southern Africa*. Cape Town: David Philip.

9   Mathias Guenther. 1989. *Bushman Folktales: Oral Traditions of the Nharo of Botswana and the |Xam of the Cape*. Stuttgart: Franz Steiner Verlag.

10 Nigel Penn. 2005. *The Forgotten Frontier: Colonist and Khoisan on the Cape's Northern Frontier in the 18th Century*. Athens, Ohio: Ohio University Press and Cape Town: Double Storey Books.

11 Andrew Bank. 2006. *Bushmen in a Victorian World: The Remarkable Story of the Bleek-Lloyd Collection of Bushman Folklore*. Cape Town: Double Storey Books.

12 Pippa Skotnes (ed.) (2005–2007), Lloyd and Bleek online, LLAREC: < http://www. lloydbleekcollection.uct.ac.za >, and on DVD in: *Claim to the Country*.

13 Biographical details concerning W.H.I. Bleek can be found in Bank (2006).

14 The collection is now contained in the UCT Library, the National Library and the Iziko South Africa Museum.

15 'Part I: Baboons', Vol. 5 (1931), 167–179; 'Part II: The Lion', 'Part III: Game Animals', 'Part IV: Omens, Windmaking, Clouds', Vol. 6 (1932), 47–63, 233–249, 323–342; 'Part V: The Rain', Vol. 7 (1933), 297–312; 'Part VI: Rainmaking', Vol. 8 (1933), 375–392; 'Part VII: Sorcerors', Vol. 9 (1935), 1–47; 'Part VIII: More about Sorcerors and Charms', Vol. 10 (1936), 132–162. Much of this is reproduced in J.C. Hollman (ed.). 2004. *Customs and Beliefs of the |Xam Bushmen*. Johannesburg: Witwatersrand University Press.

16 *Bantu Studies*, Vol. 10 (1936), 163–203.

17 Neil Bennun. 2004. *The Broken String: The Last Words of an Extinct People*. London: Viking.

18 See Skotnes (1996) and Penn (2005).

19 Traill, 1996; Anthony Traill. 2002. 'The Khoisan language', in *Language in South Africa*, edited by R. Mesthrie. Cambridge: Cambridge University Press.

20 While an ethnographic background to the texts is given in Chapter 1, further ethnographic data are contained throughout the book where this illuminates aspects of the narratives discussed. Further ethnography may also be found in Appendix A, which gives an account of girls' puberty observances, and Appendix B, which deals with the shamans of the |Xam.

21 In the following chapters, frequent reference is made to Bleek and Lloyd's manuscript notebooks. Reference takes the following form: the collector's name is indicated by the initial letter, B for Bleek or L for Lloyd, which is followed by a Roman numeral indicating either a particular notebook, in the case of the texts collected by Bleek, or a particular informant, in the case of the texts collected by Lloyd. The Roman numerals assigned to the six main informants were: I, |A!kungta; II, ||Kabbo; III, ‡Kasing; IV, Dia!kwain; V, !Kweiten ta ||ken; VIII, |Hang ‡kass'o. Where Lloyd's notebooks are referred to, this Roman numeral is followed by two Arabic numerals, the first, in brackets, indicating the initial notebook, the second indicating the page. In the case of Bleek's notebooks, the Roman numeral is the notebook number and the Arabic numeral that follows is, therefore, the page reference.

1

Ethnographic background

T he |Xam once occupied much of the Calvinia, Prieska and Kenhardt districts of the Republic of South Africa. Their language, with only slight regional differences, was spoken in many parts of the country west of Port Elizabeth and south of the Gariep River. It is likely, but not certain, that all of the speakers of this language called themselves the |Xam.[1]

All of these |Xam-speakers are now extinct; many thousands were killed off by white farmers and others, between the early 18th and late 19th centuries. By the first decade of the 20th century numbers were so depleted and their culture so eroded that extinction became inevitable. In the northwestern Cape this process had begun much later than elsewhere because the inhospitable climate and poor farming conditions discouraged white settlement. The northwestern Cape, therefore, formed a pocket in which the San survived longer than they did further to the east and south. However, after the mid-19th century, penetration by the farmers into even this arid country caused severe reductions in the numbers of game animals as farmers hunted with firearms. At the same time the farmers' cattle broke up the soil crust which supported the plant-life upon which the |Xam relied for much of their food. The livelihood of the |Xam was threatened and many were forced to seek employment on the farms.

By the 1870s the process of cultural disintegration was well under way. There is, unfortunately, no information of the extent to which traditional life in this area was maintained under the pressure of European penetration. The texts collected by Bleek and Lloyd often make reference to the beliefs and customs of the informants' parents, as though these were no longer current. On the other hand, some accounts of rituals, beliefs and social customs are also described as part of contemporary life. This may indicate that while the life of the |Xam in the Cape was being rapidly destroyed, much still remained intact at the time of collection.

By being both a record of current practices and beliefs, and also containing ethnographic data relating to the period before European settlement in the northwestern Cape, the Bleek and Lloyd texts are the primary source of ethnographic information relating to the |Xam. A number of official papers, and the writings of various missionaries and travellers also provide additional information on these and other |Xam-speaking San; most of this was written in the late 18th century and the first half of the 19th century. As the Bleek and Lloyd collection was made in the 1870s, the time-span covered by this body of data is approximately 100 years.

The area which was inhabited by |Xam-speakers consists, in the main, of semi-desert with a mean annual rainfall of below 5 inches in the northwest, to 15 inches in the east. The period of heaviest rainfall is between January and April when the monthly mean ranges between 0.5 to 3 inches from west to east. In the northwest the dominant vegetation is largely short bushes, grasses and occasional thorn trees poking from the pebbles, rock fragments and sand, which cover a thin layer of sandy loam. Dry river-beds, which flow for a few days during some rainy months, course this region in places but the main water sources are the 11 'pans' – shallow natural basins – which contain water for varying periods (Wellington 1955, Vol 1, 240ff, 278ff, 323, 374ff, 474ff).

Here the |Xam lived as hunter-gatherers, having little contact with other races except, in some areas, with the Khoe-khoen and, ultimately, the European farmers (Wilson & Thompson 1969, Vol 1, 63ff). They lived in small groups each of which shared the resources of a defined area within which they led a semi-nomadic existence, erecting simple hemispherical huts of branches covered with grass or reed mats, standing about three or four feet high (Barrow 1801, Vol 1, 275).

Social units

Estimates by early travellers of the size of |Xam bands, were entirely based on isolated sightings and did not take into account temporary fission, where a section or sections of the group might move to another part of the resource territory, or seasonal migrations, during which two or more groups might join together for a period of time either to share resources or for the purpose of defence. However, Dorothea Bleek, who visited the |Xam in 1910–11, reported that

> Three or four huts stand together, in one is the father, in others his married children. At most eight or ten huts of connections were dotted about within a radius of a few miles from the water, but this is an institution of later days (D.F. Bleek 1923: viii).

Many earlier writers also reported similar numbers of people living together. The most detailed of such reports come, unhappily, from the official accounts of those sent on expeditions to exterminate the San in certain areas. Thus the 'Report of the Field-Commandant Nicholas van der Merwe, of the Expedition performed against the Bushman Hottentots' which 'took the field on the 16th of August 1774' (Moodie 1960: 35ff) described the many San *'kraals'* which the expedition surrounded, as containing between eight and 30 people, men, women and children, whom they slaughtered. Other expedition reports give similar numbers (*ibid.*, 33, 38, 45). The reports of travellers in the late 18th and early 19th centuries tend to confirm these numbers (*ibid.*, 231; Campbell 1822: 17; Sparrman 1785, Vol 1, 202).

Larger groups were also sometimes reported. Often such groups were seen living near to farms or were defensive aggregations (Moodie 1960: 5f, 25, 34; Lichtenstein 1930, Vol 2, 62; Barrow 1801, Vol 1, 307). That different groups did occasionally share resources is suggested by J. Barrow the traveller, who writes:

> During the day vast numbers of the savages had appeared upon the plain digging up roots: that they came from different quarters and in so many groups that (local farmers) concluded there must be several hordes in the neighbourhood (Barrow 1801, Vol l, 271).

And again:

> Several little children came down upon the plain ... presently afterwards the women and young girls, to the number of thirty or forty (*ibid.*, 273).

Dorothea Bleek (1923: ix) also claimed that 'several family groups' sometimes joined together for a game drive.

When writing about dwellings, however, the majority of the early travellers describe only a few huts at each encampment. M.H.C. Lichtenstein (*op. cit.*, 61ff) reports that:

> A horde commonly consists of the different members of one family only and no one has power or distinction over the rest.

and that

> Very little intercourse subsists between the separate hordes: they seldom unite, unless in some extraordinary undertaking, for which the combined strength of a great many is required.

The picture which emerges, therefore, is that of a number of extended family groups of various sizes, probably related by blood or marriage and joining together at certain times mainly for economic reasons. The concept of 'the band', however, lacks both spatial and social definition in the absence of adequate data. It might have been the case that a band consisted of a number of extended families related to a core of siblings, sharing a defined territory which contained a number of water sources. These people would be related to members of neighbouring bands with whom they visited, exchanged gifts, and married. The picture, however, must remain vague.

According to Dorothea Bleek (1923: vii),

> The Colonial Bushman's property was the water. Each spring or pool in that dry country had its particular owner and was handed down from father to son with the regularity of an entitled estate. Many families owned more than one water, had summer and winter residences, to which they resorted as the growth of the field supplies or the movements of the game necessitated. However, the owners never lived near the spring, for that would prevent the game from using it. The huts were a good way off, perhaps an hour's walk and hidden by bushes. Their position was frequently changed.

Miss Bleek's observation that water resources were 'handed down from father to son' may have been based on a statement by ‖Kabbo, one of her father's informants, that his own territory – his !xoe – containing several water-holes, had belonged to his father's father, and, upon his death, had gone to his father, then to ‖Kabbo's elder brother, and, on his elder brother's death, to ‖Kabbo (Bleek & Lloyd 1911: 305ff). However, this is the only instance of such information being given. It is possible that inheritance may have been patrilineal in some cases and matrilineal in others. Such was certainly true of the !Kung-speakers of the Dobe area studied by Richard Lee (1972, Vol 1, 129).

The territory itself was defined by water sources and other natural landmarks. |Hang ǂkass'o reported that ‖Kabbo's !xoe had a name, ‖Gubo, and that it contained a number of named sites including water sources (Bleek & Lloyd 1911: 307). The precise nature of the relationship between the inheritor of a resource area and the rest of the group is unclear. Beside possibly being responsible for regulating the use of water-holes, and having unquestionable rights to food resources, there is no evidence that any special privileges attached themselves to the inheritor and, judging by reports of usage and descriptions of everyday life in the oral literature, the question of ownership did not arise or influence the collective use of water, game and *veldkos*[2] by the group. From the earliest to the last reports, all writers claimed that, except in times of warfare, the San had no leaders of any kind (Schapera & Farrington 1933: 75; Lichtenstein 1930: 61f; Moodie 1960: 34; Barrow 1801, Vol 1, 274).

Membership of the group was either by consanguinity or through marriage. The father and mother lived in one hut together with their young children until the children could feed themselves and 'talked with understanding' (Bleek & Lloyd 1911: 307), when they made their own huts next to their parents. In the other huts would live the married children with their offspring. Membership was not based on descent traced exclusively through either the male or the female line and both married sons and married daughters belonged to the same band. There is no evidence that bride service existed.

Kinship and marriage

Such kinship terms as were collected[3] are incomplete and based mainly on vocabulary sources rather than on any actual observations of kinship as a system of obligations and affiliations within the group. However, beside purely descriptive terms of relationship, some terms were collected which were applied to whole groups of different relatives and these might have indicated special social relationships. Siblings and both cross and parallel cousins had the same terms of address applied to them, ‖kā: (male), ‖kāxai (female). (Cousin marriages, however, were not forbidden, and did occur.) Similarly, the parents of a son or daughter-in-law, and the parents of a brother and sister-in-law were addressed by the same term, ‖k'en (male), ‖k'aiti (female). The terms for 'grandfather' and 'grandmother', !kõing and !kõite, were used in addressing any elderly relative or person distinctly senior to the speaker. The term xoakengu, 'mothers', was applied to older women of the group and was 'often used where we should say "the elder women" or "mother and her friends"' (ibid., 57). These women were especially responsible for the education of young girls in matters concerning puberty rites.

Beside these terms, there were others which indicate a special relationship between certain individuals. A woman called her father's parents her 'real' (kwokwang) grandparents, and her mother's parents her 'lent' (|xwõbe) ones. A man reversed this. His mother's parents were his 'real' grandparents. Another special relationship seems to be indicated between a woman's siblings and her sons, for a man addressed his mother's sister as Opwaxai, 'daughter', and his mother's brother as Opwõng, 'son', while they called him oä, 'father'. Dorothea Bleek admits that she is unable to give an explanation for these terms but, in the latter case, suggests that 'a particularly affectionate relationship is indicated' (ibid., 59). A joking relationship appears to have existed between alternating generations of co-sanguines but there are no extant details concerning this relationship.

The |Xam were strictly monogamous, although some early writers have suggested that occasionally a man might have two wives, one elderly and one much younger. This impression might have resulted from observers mistaking the wife's younger sister, who customarily helped in the married home, for a second wife (D.F. Bleek 1923: ix; Stow 1905: 95; Barrow 1801, Vol 1, 241ff). (After the death of his wife, a man was free to marry whoever he chose but there is no evidence to show if this was also true for women.) Marriage could be between any man and woman except between brothers and sisters, and tended to be between members of different groups, although marriage within groups also occurred. The marriage was marked by no ceremony and there were no special requirements, save the consent of both parties. Residence was a matter of convenience and could be with the parents of either party. Miss Bleek (1923: ix) writes:

> Sometimes the young couple build their hut near the bridegroom's father, sometimes near the bride's. They seem to keep the family groups fairly even.

The couple lived together in one hut with their young children and usually close to the huts of the rest of the family. Certain avoidances were practiced between the wife's parents and their son-in-law. A man would not usually talk to his mother-in-law but would address his comments to his father-in-law. However, sometimes the same man would address his mother-in-law and not his father-in-law. In this case his wife or his children would address his father-in-law on his behalf. There is no further information to indicate when these avoidances or the breaching of them occurred (Bleek 1924: 58).

Children

Nothing is recorded about child-bearing amongst the |Xam but it is known that naming was done by the child's parents. According to George Stow (*op. cit.*, 103), the child would be named either from the place where it was born, a cave, river, etc. or from some other thing which might distinguish it, such as a physical peculiarity of the child or one of its parents. In the Bleek and Lloyd material the name given to a child at birth was called its 'little name'. In later life, however, this name would be supplemented by another given, apparently in an informal way, by the community, and the name given at birth would fall from use. There is no record of name-giving being done in any formalised fashion (Bleek & Lloyd 1911: 101, 305, 367; also notebooks, L. VIII, (4) 6370 rev.).

Babies were not weaned until they were about three years old. They were carried in their mother's *karosses*[4] on food-gathering treks long after they could toddle, which they did at an early age. Children were soon expected to help with the gathering of *veldkos*, and large numbers of children would accompany the women to the food sources, and would work with the women. They were explicitly encouraged to be self-supporting and learn to gather, catch and cook food as an insurance for themselves against the sudden loss of both or either parent. Small boys were given miniature bows and arrows to practise with and would also be expected to help on a game drive by attending to many small but necessary tasks such as raising clouds of sand or planting the sticks used to guide the game. Again, they might be sent to discover the location of an antelope recently shot by a poisoned arrow and lying within a known area, or would watch out for game while the hunters slept during the day. Older boys would accompany their fathers when out hunting.

All children would help gather ants' chrysalids and fulfil certain constant duties like fetching water or collecting firewood. All were expected to learn cooking techniques, the girls helping their mothers on occasions and, well before puberty, should be able to catch various small creatures, such as tortoise and lizard, and cook them without assistance from adults. In these ways children were educated into a close knowledge of the world about them and taught to acquire the skills needed in adult life (Lichtenstein 1930, Vol 2, 290; Barrow 1801, Vol 1, 273, 287; W.H.I. Bleek 1875: 14, 19; Bleek & Stow 1930: text facing plate 34; Bleek & Lloyd 1911: 313, 337, 359).

The aged

Once a man became too old to hunt successfully a number of less demanding duties fell to him. He might be expected to do jobs such as gathering wood or guarding the fire at night when lions were known to be in the vicinity. Old women would probably continue to collect *veldkos* well after the age at which men ceased to hunt, but collecting *veldkos* was a task specifically for women and children, and the old men would not engage in this work (Bleek & Lloyd 1911: 185; D.F. Bleek 1931–36, Part II: 62, Part IV: 340, Part V: 306).

The old people were respected for their knowledge and wisdom and would support the hunters by suggesting and giving the appropriate food to be eaten prior to a hunt.[5] The old women were particularly responsible for helping with the children and were regarded as especially trustworthy consultants when children were ill.

While being valued members of the group, old people were, nevertheless, minimally productive in economic terms and could be a threat to the existence of the whole group when water supplies were low. At such times the old people might be left by the group and would usually die of hunger and thirst or be devoured by wild animals unless the rest of the group reached a water source in time to send someone to hurry back with supplies. An aged grandparent, or sometimes both grandparents, would be left in this fashion. Their children would do as much as they could towards the protection of their parents before leaving. They would close the sides of the hut and the door-opening with sticks from the other abandoned huts, thus giving a certain protection from beasts of prey, but they would leave the top of the hut open so that the occupants could feel the warmth of the sun. They would also leave a fire burning and extra firewood to frighten away dangerous animals, and a small supply of food and water if they could spare it (Lloyd, *op. cit.*, 22; Sparrman 1785, Vol 1, 358; Bleek & Lloyd 1911: 229).

Hunting

Hunting was done exclusively by the men, although women would occasionally assist during game drives. There were several methods of catching game. Usually animals were stalked with a bow and arrow, the hunters waiting not far from the waterholes or setting out to intercept predictable movements of game following rain. Springbok, for example, were always hunted after rain. Hunters worked either singly or in small groups but sometimes a large game drive would occur involving many of the men and some women and children. In springbok hunting a number of sticks would be planted in the ground at a distance from one another and ostrich feathers tied onto the top of each stick to make it more noticeable. These feathers would be made and owned by one of the men. A number of people would stand at strategic points and, while others drove the game toward the sticks, would make a great deal of noise and throw up sand to force the bucks along the line of sticks beyond which hunters would wait, arrows at the ready, and shoot the bucks as they passed by Bleek & Lloyd (1911: 285ff).

Springbok, duiker, gemsbok, rhebok, eland, quagga, zebra and ostrich were all hunted with bow and arrow but during the dry season when the game may have migrated, and at other times when there was little game about, smaller animals were also hunted. Anteater, porcupine, hare and dassie were all hunted, anteaters and porcupines being dug out of their holes with the use of a long barbed stick, while dassies and hares were often run to ground or killed with a thrown club. Most groups possessed a number of hunting dogs which were trained to total silence. Dogs were the property of individual hunters rather than of the group (*ibid.*, 251ff, 311; Lloyd, *op. cit.*, 16; W.H.I. Bleek 1875: 17; Moodie 1960: 231; Campbell, *op. cit.*, Vol 2, 18; L. II, (26) 2320–2504).

Several kinds of traps were also used in hunting. These included very deep covered pitfalls, often seven or eight feet in depth, containing sharpened stakes on which the animals would impale themselves. Sometimes water-holes were covered over with bushes and reeds, and shallow pits dug nearby which soon filled with water. These pits were poisoned with Euphorbia branches; when the animals came to drink they would die, usually after a very short time. Both of these kinds of pits were dug by the men using horn-tipped digging-sticks, and, in the case of pitfalls, must have involved an immense amount of labour (Stow, *op. cit.*, 81, 90ff; Campbell 1815: 215; 1822: 42; Barrow, *op. cit.*, Vol 1, 284f).

Fishing was practised wherever possible. Groups living close to the Gariep River used funnel-shaped traps of closely woven reeds, about 3 feet long and 18 inches to 2 feet wide, which narrowed towards the mouth. These were stretched across a shallow part of the river while several men drove the fish towards the baskets where they would be caught and thrown ashore. On other occasions larger fish were harpooned, the harpoon being of wood pointed with bone and fixed to a long sinew line (Barrow, *op. cit.*, Vol 1, 290, 300; Stow, *op. cit.*, 93).

All large game was cut up where it was killed. The unwanted contents of the stomach were buried on the spot and the meat carried home in sinew nets. Arrows were scored with a personal mark so that each hunter could gather his own arrows after the hunt. The hunter whose arrow was responsible for the kill would have possession of the skin, if he so desired, although this does not seem to have been the case with springbok hunting (Bleek & Lloyd 1911: 275ff, 361ff; D.F. Bleek 1931–36, Part II, 55).

The arrow poisons used by the |Xam were a mixture of animal and vegetable poisons, or sometimes a 'black rock' (Campbell 1822, Vol 1, 31; Barrow, *op. cit.*, Vol 1, 230) poison, probably a form of arsenic. The most frequently used ingredients were amaryllis juice (*Haemanthus toxicarius*) and snake poison, which were mixed together in a fragment of ostrich shell. This mixture was then boiled until it took on a thick jelly-like consistency. When required for use, part of it was heated in a tortoise shell and placed in a special 'poison stone', a small flat stone deeply grooved in the middle. The tip was pressed down into the groove and slowly turned. The poison did not take instantaneous effect, but usually the smaller the animal, the more rapid the action. With large game animals, the hunter would have to return to his camp and wait overnight for the poison to take effect. He would then go out on the following morning and track the animal (Stow, *op. cit.*, 78; Moodie, *op. cit.*, 401; Schapera 1925a).

Gathering

Gathering was the responsibility of women of all ages. They gathered roots, bulbs, berries, edible leaves, in fact any wild vegetable food that was in season. The range of *veldkos* collected seems, from innumerable references in the Bleek and Lloyd texts, to have been very great indeed. Some lists of plants used by the |Xam were collected, but in the absence of reliable botanical information or information on the relative quantities of each species used, no picture of the |Xam diet and its nutritional value can be drawn.

Small animals such as tortoises, snakes, lizards and locusts were also collected by the women if they happened to come across them but for the most part the women would concentrate on a specific *veldkos* source, gather there over a period of time until the source was exhausted and then move to another source. The women worked together in large numbers, accompanied by their children, using, where appropriate, a weighted digging-stick of about three feet long, sharpened at one end or perhaps tipped with horn and weighted by a perforated stone which was wedged in place about 12 inches from the bottom. Each woman collected her own food, packing it into skin bags, and returning home, together with the other women, when she had gathered sufficient (Moffat 1842: 54; Barrow, *op. cit.*, Vol 1, 271ff; D.F. Bleek 1923: vi).

Judging by other hunter-gatherer groups, it is likely that the women contributed much more *veldkos* to the group than men contributed meat (Lee & DeVore 1968: 92ff). They were also responsible for fetching water. A woman would set out for a water-hole with as many ostrich egg-shells as she could carry in her nets of leather thongs. Each egg-shell had a small hole drilled at the top plugged with a stopper. She would fill the shells in turn with a perforated half-shell, plug each shell firmly, and return to the encampment. Most of the shells were then stored near the huts or buried to keep them cool and lifted out when required.

Some types of gathering were also performed by the men. Honey was exclusively the province of men. The |Xam were extremely fond of honey and any nest that was discovered would be marked by a small pile of stones or other sign to make ownership explicit. A nest was the property of the man who discovered it and the responsibility for distributing the honey was initially his. Another form of gathering in which the men engaged was the digging-out and sifting of ants' chrysalids, also a favourite and common food for the |Xam. The men used digging sticks for this job but the sticks they used were unweighted (Moffat, *op. cit.*, 172; Bleek & Lloyd 1911: 353ff; Lloyd, *op. cit.*, 17).

Industries and trade

The main goods manufactured by the group were hunting implements, digging-sticks, cooking and eating utensils, clothing, bags, nets, small containers for buchu[6] or various medicines, body ornaments, musical instruments and pipes for smoking. The only division of labour was between the sexes. Anything to do with hunting, arrows, bows, poisons, etc. was made by the men as were clothes and some small eating utensils. Women made clay cooking pots, egg-shell beads, drums and dancing rattles. From what is known of the division of labour, it appears that the manufacturing tasks falling to women tended to be for items only infrequently in need of manufacture, while those of the men would be likely to occur more frequently. Without a complete inventory, however, it is difficult to tell what this indicates in terms of relative hours spent in hunting and gathering. In any case it is known that both sexes enjoyed a great deal of leisure time except in periods of scarcity when the women would have greater difficulty in collecting sufficient *veldkos* (Bleek & Lloyd 1911: 11, 343ff, 351, 359; Bleek & Stow, *op. cit.*, xxiiif).

Most of the manufactured tools were of flint, bone or reed, except where iron had been obtained through trade. These included blades, scrapers, awls and borers. On the manufacture of clothing and bags Dorothea Bleek writes:

> Every hunter owns the skin of the animal he shoots and dresses it himself. After being scraped with a stone it will be squeezed, rolled and unrolled, wetted, buried in sand, and rubbed with fat. Then he will make it up into a bag or garment for his family or for barter (Bleek & Duggin-Cronin 1942: vii).

Nets, bowstrings, the strings of musical instruments, harpoon cords, etc., were made by rubbing strands of sinew together between the palms. Spoons were made either from springbok horn, from a shaped rib bone or from a small piece of wood to which animal hair was attached by binding. Pipes were of many kinds but were usually made from a short section of an antelope's leg bone (Bleek & Lloyd 1911: 251, 293; Stow, *op. cit.*, 52).

Trade was carried on both with other groups and with other races. Between |Xam groups exchange was sometimes for articles of value which could not be obtained within the territory of the group. Colouring, for example, used as a body decoration, might be acquired from a group living in an area where pigments were found and these would be purchased in exchange for arrows, skin bags, or other manufactured articles (Bleek & Lloyd 1911: 377). Such exchange, however, is difficult to distinguish from reciprocal gift-giving. Trade with other races is more recognisably barter. Dorothea Bleek writes:

> Barter with Hottentot or Bantu tribes has long been carried on by the Bushmen. Besides utensils and iron for knives and arrowheads, tobacco has been the object of greatest demand. In exchange Bushmen give game or skins, but they adore smoking, and as they grow no tobacco, must obtain that from others. Everyone smokes, even the children (Bleek & Duggin-Cronin, *op. cit.*, 5).

Food-sharing

The division and sharing of food was a complex matter governed by a number of rules, obligations and avoidances. It appears that *veldkos* was gathered for each nuclear family independently but all meat was shared by the whole group. Springbok seem to have been the game most commonly eaten by the |Xam of the northern Cape and something is known of its division.

Assuming that three hunters tracked and killed a springbok, the division into parts was made by the two whose arrows did not secure the kill. The viscera were divided between the three families, and the killer received the upper bones of the forelegs and the neck. Of the other two hunters, one received the back, the tail and the skin, and the other the stomach and the blood. It is not recorded who had the remaining parts, but the shoulder-blades were not given to the hunter who made the kill. This division was made prior to the cooking, the meat being then given by the men to the women of each of their households to prepare and cook. When the meat was ready to be eaten, a second distribution was made, the men cutting for their male children, the women cutting for the girls. The children were especially given the leg bones which were broken open for the marrow (Bleek & Lloyd 1911: 275ff).

Lorna Marshall (1961: 236ff) has recorded how, in the !Kung-speaking bands of the Nyae Nyae region of the Kalahari, a third wave of sharing takes place throughout the group, this being governed by a network of obligations of various kinds. One such obligation exists where the user of an arrow which has been received as a gift gives meat which has been shot with that arrow to the person who made the gift. The arrow-giver might then share that meat with another from whom they had initially received the same arrow and so on. The |Xam also practiced the exchange of arrows (D.F. Bleek 1931–36, Part VIII, 149; Bleek & Lloyd 1911: 281ff) and it is, therefore, likely that some similar system of obligation also operated amongst them. Lorna Marshall also observed that the hunter who secured the kill often ended up with less meat than those further down the line of distribution. The missionary Robert Moffat (*op. cit.*, 59) noticed that in the division of food-gifts from Dutch farmers to the |Xam, 'Generally it is observed the one who first received the boon retained least for himself'. Lorna Marshall believed that amongst the !Kung-speakers, this custom might be designed to avoid tensions and jealousies that could arise if the hunter was consistently given preference.

However complex the initial system of meat distribution, another principle influenced the sharing at a different level and this consisted in a variety of avoidances and preferences based on certain beliefs and superstitions. Certain kinds of food were not eaten by adults at all, only by children. The flesh of the lynx was not eaten by women and it was regarded as unlucky for women with young children to eat hartebeest (an animal thought to resemble the mantis, which, in turn, was associated with the supernatural being |Kaggen). Children were not given the tips of springbok tongues, and certain portions of the ostrich were also forbidden them. Some children were not given jackals' hearts for fear of promoting cowardice, but given leopards' hearts, where possible, to encourage bravery. Baboon were not eaten at all by the San inhabiting the north-western plains because of their resemblance to humans. The variety and range of these preferences and avoidances was very great and possibly varied from one area to another and from one time to another (D.F. Bleek 1931–36, Part I, 175f; W.H.I. Bleek, *op. cit.*, 16f; Lloyd, *op. cit.*, 23; Bleek & Lloyd 1911: 373).

Social life

As was noted above, the |Xam had a great amount of leisure time at their disposal. The men only hunted for a few hours of the day, and only a few days in any week, and the women's work of gathering food and wood or collecting water took little time out of each day. Even on days when the men did hunt they would return to their encampment before noon and sleep for a few hours or sit in the shade making arrows or simply talking or smoking together. Often members of the group would visit relatives in other groups and sit exchanging news and anecdotes. The whole group were in more or less continual contact with each other, secrets were practically impossible and most grievances would be endlessly discussed by the members.

The |Xam were particularly fond of music and dancing. Their musical instruments were simply constructed, mainly being variations on the musical bow. One of the most popular of these was the '*goura*' which consisted of an ordinary bow in which one end of the string, instead of being attached directly to the stave, was fastened onto a small piece of quill which was tied on to the end of the stave. This quill was held to the lips and made to vibrate by strong expirations and inspirations of breath. Drums, made by stretching the skin of a springbok thigh tight across a clay pot, were played by women at dances. Dancing rattles of springbok ears filled with small stones or dried berries were worn by the men which added to the percussion (Bleek & Stow, *op. cit.*, xxiiif; Lichtenstein, *op. cit.*, 292; Balfour 1902; Bleek & Lloyd 1911: 325, 351ff).

Dancing was an extremely popular activity amongst the |Xam. Most dances only involved the men, who moved rhythmically in a circle, while the women clapped their hands. One or two women might also play the drums. One dance, known as the |Ku, which consisted of the men nodding their heads as they moved in a circle while the women clapped, seems to have been some kind of expression of criticism of one member of the band, but details are sparse on this matter. Another dance known as the ‡Gebbi-gu was said to have been taught them by the baboons and had also been known by the Lion and the Ostrich, characters in a story, who fought and in consequence became animals. In the story the Lion is jealous of the voice of the Ostrich who gains the admiration of the women by his singing while doing this dance. The Lion, furious with jealousy, kills the Ostrich. The dance seems to have been performed by |Xam women who were led in song by one of their number. The songs were simply imitations of various animals, springbok ewes, partridges, ostriches, etc., the lead singer calling out a line of song which was then repeated by the others. The men stood around and called out in response.

Dances took place after a big kill by the hunters but some dances were reserved for special occasions, e.g., following the first thunder after the dry season, and the !giten, 'shamans' (sing. !gi: xa) had an initiation dance of their own called the ‖Keng performed by both men and women. In this dance the initiator held a stick of office known as the 'dancing stick' and performed a sequence of movements which was followed by the initiates. All participants wore caps made from the heads of young gemsbok and special bangles known as the '‖Keng's rings'. Often dances, whether purely social or ritualistic, would last the entire night and well into the following morning (D.F. Bleek 1923: ix; 1931–36, Part I, 177f; Part VII, 11ff; and Stow, *op. cit.*, pls. 13–14; Lloyd, *op. cit.*, 18; Bleek & Lloyd 1911: 91ff, 129, 353; Barrow, *op. cit.*, Vol 1, 283f; Sparrman, *op. cit.*, Vol 1, 356).

Belief and ritual

There is no evidence in the writings of the early travellers and missionaries, or in the many thousands of pages of |Xam texts collected by Bleek and Lloyd, of a belief in a deity resembling those deities, such as |Gaua, ‡Gao n!a, Hishe, Thora, Huwe, etc., of the central and northern San. Two important supernatural beings, |Kaggen and !Khwa, were believed in by the |Xam. |Kaggen was credited with the creation of certain things in the natural world (see Chapter 7) although his main activities lay in the protection of the antelopes. The beliefs about him can only properly be situated within the complex of beliefs concerning hunting and the relationship between hunters and game animals.[7] |Kaggen was the central character of a large number of narratives and these narratives together with the beliefs concerning him are discussed at length in Chapters 6–10.

!Khwa, whose name means 'water' or 'rain' – the |Xam used the same word for both – was principally related to girls' puberty rituals. He was a threatening force and was believed to cause death by lightning or transformation into non-human forms to girls who did not observe the correct ritual practices during and immediately following menstruation, and to other members of the group as a consequence of this. The beliefs concerning !Khwa and menstruation rituals are discussed in Chapters 4, 7, and 10. !Khwa was never requested to cause rain but was requested by certain men to stop thundering and lightening during particularly heavy storms (D.F. Bleek 1931–36, Part V, 304; 1929a: 307).

The powers of |Kaggen and !Khwa were discrete and concerned only with specific areas of activity. This is typical of all |Xam beliefs in the supernatural. What the texts collected by Bleek and Lloyd display is a complex of beliefs in which different things are credited with various powers which might be tapped or avoided depending on their nature. The new moon and Canopus were addressed at certain times in the belief that they could influence favourably both the gathering of ants' chrysalids and the abundance of game (D.F. Bleek 1929a: 305ff). The spirits of dead !giten were prayed to for rain on some occasions (D.F. Bleek 1931–36, Part V, 383; Part VII, 37ff). On the other hand a large number of beliefs concerned the sympathetic bond which was thought to obtain between hunters and game animals, and many ritualistic strategies were employed to maintain, exploit, or avoid undesirable consequences of that relationship (*ibid.*, Part VIII, 146ff; Bleek & Lloyd 1911: 67ff, 271ff, 353ff).

The concept known amongst the Zu|wasi as n!ow was also held by the |Xam, although many details collected by Lorna Marshall (1957a) on this subject are absent from the |Xam accounts, and no |Xam word was recorded which referred to it. The belief as held by the |Xam may be summarised as follows. Each male[8] had a wind associated with him, cold and harsh or warm and pleasant, easterly, westerly, etc. This wind was said to blow when a hunter had killed an animal. 'The wind is one with the man', one informant expressed it (D.F. Bleek 1931–36, Part IV, 338). Certain game animals and certain stars also had winds associated with them and these were believed to interact with a hunter who had killed an animal. The nature of this interaction is unclear but in some way the man's wind was affected by the animals wind, and the star's by his. Different kinds of rain, mild or hard, were also believed to be linked to individuals in the same manner. A man's wind and rain was a permanent attribute. When a person died his wind blew, removing his footprints from the ground. What kind of wind and rain a man had might influence his deployment in the hunt or whether or not he could address !Khwa. There is no textual evidence to suggest that the |Xam regarded this force as supernatural or magical. Indeed it appears to have been thought of more as a physical attribute than a spiritual one (*ibid.*, 328f, 336; Part V, 303f; Bleek & Lloyd 1911: 397).

The most commonly invoked supernatural power was known as !gi, the power possessed by !giten who were responsible for curing illness, making rain and, in some cases, influencing the movements of specific animals. The !giten who were curers could be either men or women, as could game !giten but rain-makers seem to have been exclusively men. These three offices frequently overlapped. !Giten often went into a state of trance during curing and, hidden under a *kaross* made a heavy snoring noise close to the patient's body. By this means the illness was taken into the !gi:xa's nose and was then expelled by repeated sneezing.

Malignant !giten were believed to be able to cause illness and death to those who displeased them in some way, and to take the form of various animals. !Gi was transmitted to !giten at the special initiation dance during which an initiator would snore each of the initiates in turn. This power was capable of diminishing over a period of many years and it was possible for a !gi:xa to lose his or her power completely. !Giten were greatly respected and feared by the |Xam and represented one of the most dominant aspects of |Xam belief in the supernatural.[9]

Two distinct beliefs about the after-life were collected. One informant described how the spirit of a dead person travelled along an underground path leading from the grave to a vast hole where it then lived. The spirits of all San went to this place, so did the spirits of animals and the spirits of Afrikaners (B. VI, 699 rev.; see also Stow, *op. cit.*, 129). Another belief concerning the dead was that the cavity in any new moon which had the appearance of horns was the 'catching place' for people who had recently died. As the moon grew full by this means, the corpses inside were revived by the 'moon-water'. When no more room was left, the people were tipped out onto the earth and lived again until they died again when the whole process was repeated. These two apparently conflicting accounts are all that is known of beliefs about the after-life, although it was also believed that a spirit might haunt the area of the grave briefly following death because the dead person was reluctant to leave his friends and still thought about them (Bleek & Lloyd 1911: 399; von Wielligh, *op. cit.*, Vol 3, 43f).

The extermination of the |Xam

The gradual extermination of the San by European settlers and others is well documented.[10] By the early 20th century only a small remnant remained alive. Commando raids, first by the military and, soon after, by civilian farmers, were made upon the San, initially as reprisals for cattle stealing and with increasing frequency. This activity soon assumed the character of a sport, farmers going out to shoot San in large numbers 'for the fun of the thing' (Anthing 1563:11).

The area from which Bleek and Lloyd's informants came became subjected to an intensification of such events after about 1850. In a lengthy official report of 1863, horrific details of the atrocities committed against the San of the northwestern Cape, L. Anthing (*ibid.*, 4f) states that

> The evidence I had obtained respecting the past and existing state of things was, that the colonists had intruded into that part of the country which borders on the Hartebeest and Orange [Gariep] rivers some years before, and that they had from time to time killed numbers of Bushmen resident there; that in some cases the latter had stolen cattle from the intruders, but that the killing of the Bushmen was not confined to the avenging or punishing of such thefts, but that, with or without provocation, Bushmen were killed, – sometimes by hunting parties, at other times by commandos going out for the express purpose. That in consequence of the colonists having guns and horses, and their being expert hunters (the pursuit of game being their daily occupation), the wild game of the country had become scarce, and almost inaccessible to the Bushmen, whose weapon is the bow and arrow, having a comparatively short range. That ostrich eggs, honey, grass-seed, and roots had all become exceedingly scarce, the ostriches being destroyed by hunters, the seed and roots in consequence of the intrusion of the colonists' flocks. From these various causes, the Bushman's subsistence failed him, and, in many cases they died from hunger. Those who went into the service of the newcomers did not find their condition thereby improved. Harsh treatment, an insufficient allowance of food, and continued injuries inflicted on their kinsmen are alleged as having driven them back into the bush, from whence hunger again led them to invade the flocks and herds of the intruders, regardless of the consequences, and resigning themselves, as they say to the thought of being shot in preference to death from starvation.

Such is the immediate historical background to the texts collected by Bleek and Lloyd, although as Dorothea Bleek (1923: vi) points out:

> Their narrators were all Colonial Bushmen, who lived on the rolling plains south of the Orange [Gariep] river in the Prieska, Kenhardt and northern Calvinia districts. They had themselves seen their country invaded by white

men for permanent settlement, but not so the parents from whom they heard the stories.

The dreadful conditions under which the |Xam lived at the time of collection impinges only infrequently on the collected texts, and in only one narrative are the settlers even mentioned (Bleek & Lloyd 1911: 254ff). Within a few years, however, the |Xam were to vanish completely.

Notes

1 Accounts of the distribution of San languages may be found in D.F. Bleek (1927, 1929b, 1956) and Westphal (1971).

2 This convenient Afrikaans word meaning 'field food' will be used throughout.

3 The following account is based on Bleek (1927: 57ff).

4 'Kaross' is the common Afrikaans word for the skin cloak worn by San men and women.

5 A sympathetic bond was believed to exist between a hunter and his quarry. Because of this, his activities, including his eating, were ordered by the need to prevent undesirable attributes, such as speed, from being transmitted to the game. See D.F. Bleek (1931–36, Part III: 233ff; Bleek & Lloyd 1911: 271ff).

6 A commonly used powder made from the leaves of aromatic shrubs.

7 This relationship is also discussed in Chapter 7.

8 There is no evidence that the same attributes could be possessed by women.

9 See Appendix B for a more detailed account of !Giten and their role in |Xam society.

10 Details of these events are given throughout Stow, op. cit., and, more recently in Ellenberger (1953), and in Laurens van der Post (1958).

2

Introduction to the narratives: their context, performance and scope

Like many other San groups, the |Xam had a highly verbal culture. Indeed, speech was almost a continual social activity. In Dorothea Bleek's words:

Men hunted for a few hours or a few days then had nothing to do as long as the game lasted. A woman's daily task of gathering roots and wood and fetching water was soon finished except in times of scarcity. Half or more than half of each day was spent lounging about watching bird and beast, and talking – always talking. Every event of a hunt was told and re-told. Every phase of a meeting with other people, the action of each person and animal being described and acted, the voice and gesture admirably imitated (Bleek & Stow, *op. cit.*, xxiiif).

It is easy to see how such a culture should be rich in narrative, how narrative would be part of daily living to an extent unknown in literate societies where leisure time is limited.

It is difficult for us to realise how large a part talking, and hence storytelling, makes in primitive man's life. Where a man's only labour is hunting which occupies only a few hours of a day, and probably not every day, there is an amount of leisure unparalleled among civilised people … There are many hours at midday under a bush and in the evening round a fire, when all sit and talk and listen. Stories mingled with songs accompanied by mimicry are the chief daily recreations (D.F. Bleek 1929a: 311).[1]

Such is the verbal context of the one hundred or so narratives collected by Bleek and Lloyd and indeed they show the impress of that context very clearly – particularly in their heavy use of dialogue, exploring narrative events now from one character's perspective, now from another. Even in the difficult conditions under which they were recorded, these narratives are alive with speech.

The |Xam employed only one term for narrative, kum, (plural kukummi). There is no record of their making distinctions between kinds of narrative such as myth, legend or fable. All narratives were kukummi whether they related the activities of supernatural beings, humans or animals. The word also appears in the titles of narratives, for example: ‖khā:ka kum – 'the lion's story', or !gā ka kum – 'the frog's story'. The same word, however, was also occasionally used simply to mean conversation and news, although there is no doubt from the texts that narratives were formally structured and constituted a distinct mode of expression. Verbal formulae are often encountered as is the stylised treatment of certain familiar episodes in some of the narratives, and the use of song. By contrast, conversation amongst the |Xam does not appear to have been formal in any respect and not one example of a proverb or similarly structured discourse was recorded by either Bleek or Lloyd.

The great majority of kukummi are concerned with animal characters, although set in a time when the animals were human. These narratives may be simple fables or very complex and semantically dense – more suggestive of myth than fable. The characters in these narratives were the !Xwe-‖na-s'o !kʔe,[2] 'people of the first or early race' – a term similar to that used by the Zu|wa of today who refer to their stories of people long ago as N‡wasi o n!osimasi, 'stories of the old people' (Biesele, *op. cit.*, 96). The term was not exclusively applied to animal characters however: some kukummi which we might classify as legends – featuring human beings and often appearing to be set in an immediate historical past – were also said to refer to the !Xwe-‖na-s'o !kʔe, as were those portraying the stars, the sun and the moon as people. These !Xwe-‖na-s'o !kʔe were not regarded with any special reverence. Indeed they were said to be often stupid and lacking in understanding – hence their actions in the narratives are generally extraordinary and rarely correspond to what the |Xam would have regarded as normal or proper behaviour. This fictive early period seems to have been thought of as a formative one for the San race, where the raw materials of life – both cosmological and social – were constantly interacting, rearranging themselves, revealing social truths and the natural order of things. How the sun, moon and stars came into being; how death came into the world; how correct marriages were to be made; how the sharing of food resources was to be conducted; how young people should behave; where the sources of danger lay in social life, these and many other things are laid bare by the activities of the !Xwe-‖na-s'o !k?e.

Perhaps for this reason there is often a strong educational strain in many of the narratives. Lessons were drawn from them and explanations for customs and beliefs were to be found there too. The instruction of the young was very important to the |Xam and many narratives involving disasters, particularly to young people, conclude with the assertion that the characters who acted foolishly, and thus brought about disaster, had not received proper instruction from their parents. The importance of the education of young children is also frequently to be seen in the texts outside of the narratives or in the occasional asides of the narrators. Apart from their function as entertainments, therefore, kukummi were also regarded as the residuum of the social and practical knowledge which constituted an essential code of |Xam life – something to be learned by all. Through the naiveté and foolishness, as well, on very rare occasions, as the bravery and competence of the !Xwe-‖na-s'o !k?e, this knowledge was revealed.

There is no record of any specialised or socially recognised group of story-tellers in |Xam society, professional or otherwise. Story-telling seems to have been something which anyone might do, although Bleek wrote of |Ak!ungta, the youngest of his |Xam informants, that he could 'relate hardly any of the numerous tales and fables which are met with in the traditionary literature of this nation' (Bleek & Lloyd 1911: 443), and it may have been the case that younger people lacked the knowledge of their elders and did not engage in narration very often.

The informants frequently attributed their knowledge of narratives to members of their family. Thus, for example, |Hang‡kass'o would tell a story that he said he had heard from his mother, |Xabbi-ang, perhaps adding that she in turn had heard it from her mother or some other relative. Informants attributed the great majority of their narratives to their mothers, although, as one would expect, no original authorship was ever indicated by this. However, several of Bleek's male informants were not only familiar with a large number of kukummi but were clearly themselves also very used to performing. It cannot be construed from the predominance of mothers in the attributing of sources, therefore, that story-telling was primarily the province of women. While it was undoubtedly the women who usually told stories to children, when kukummi were performed to adult audiences the evidence is that this might be by any mature man or woman. No doubt some narrators were more skilled than others – although no mention is made in the texts of any narrator well known for his excellence – but it would seem that most people could perform if called upon to do so.

There is very little evidence relating to when kukummi were performed. |Hang‡kass'o speaks only of two separate occasions on which his mother comforted him as a child by telling him stories (*ibid.*, 317ff; L. VIII, (17) 7519). The only account of story-telling by and to adults comes from ‖Kabbo. In a well-known passage in *Specimens of Bushman Folklore*, ‖Kabbo, speaking of his release from captivity, has this to say:

> You know I sit waiting for the moon to change for me so that I can go back to my own place. I will listen to everyone's stories when I visit them. I will listen to the stories that they tell. They listen to the stories of the Flat people[3] from the other side of the place and re-tell the stories with their own – when the sun gets a little warm. I will sit listening to the stories that come from far away. And I will have their story when the sun feels a little bit warm and I feel that I must go on visiting. I must be talking with my men friends, for I work here at women's work. My men friends listen to stories which travel from a long way away. They listen to stories from other places. But I am here. I don't get stories because I don't do any visiting to let me get the stories which come along … The Flat people go to each other's huts to sit smoking in front of them. So they get stories because they often visit. They are smoking people (Bleek & Lloyd 1911: 298ff).

Story-telling appears from this to have been part of sociability. As well as spending their leisure time in their own camps, |Xam frequently visited friends and relatives and so an occasion for story-telling was never far away.

Amongst !Kung speakers today the same kind of emphasis on story-telling as an adult pastime is also found. Megan Biesele (*op. cit.*, 97) writes:

> It has been my pleasure to discover not only that the number of (non-farm) Bushmen who tell stories competently is quite large but that virtually every old person (among the ju|wasi every man or woman who carries the appellation 'n!a' after his or her name – perhaps 45 and older) is able and

usually willing to tell stories. In fact of the many old people from whom I requested stories there were only a scant handful who could not tell stories of the old time with confidence and vigor.

So much is this the case that the telling of stories specifically to children is of little concern to the Zu|wasi.

> The story-telling groups I observed consisted much more frequently of a small group of old people getting together for some real grown-up enjoyment. The telling of stories among Bushmen is no watered-down pastime but the substantial adult pleasure of old cronies over a bawdy or horrific or ridiculous tale (*ibid.*, 97f).

This seems to be very much the sort of thing which ‖Kabbo has in mind when he speaks of sitting during the day, talking and telling stories with his friends.

It is, inevitably, very difficult to discover much about story-telling as live performance. Because the narratives were collected outside of their native context everything is lost to us in the way of dramatic presentation, gesture, facial expression, narrator/audience interaction – indeed most of what characterises narrative in performance. However, a little is known of the |Xam which can give an indication of how narratives were performed. It may be seen from many of the texts – both narrative and non-narrative – what keen powers of observation the |Xam had for their natural environment. Not only are the habits and physical characteristics of animals observed in great detail but many pages of close description of plants and insects were collected, which bear witness to an attention to detail far beyond that needed for daily survival. Furthermore some |Xam at least also felt an attunement to their environment which reached almost mystical proportions. ‖Kabbo, for example, speaks of powerful premonitions which he had while out hunting and which created in him actual physical sensations connected with his quarry. He reports that such sensations were common for people who understood them. A man may feel

> a tapping at his ribs; he says to his children, the Springbok seem to be coming for I feel the black hair (on the sides of the Springbok). Climb the Brinkkop over there and look around because I feel the Springbok sensation (Bleek & Lloyd 1911: 332).

Or again he reports that

> We have a sensation in our feet as the Springbok come rustling the bushes.
> In the same way we have a sensation in our heads when we are about to
> chop the Springbok's horns. We have a sensation in our face because of the
> blackness of the stripe on the face of the Springbok (*ibid.*, 334).

Such close identification with animals must find its way into narrative
presentation, and indeed the |Xam, like other San groups were well known
for their great capacity for imitation (Currlé 1913: 114). Dorothea Bleek
(1929a: 310f) writes:

> Most stories are long drawn out, an evening's entertainment interspersed
> with scraps of poetry or songs. All are told with great imitation of animal
> voices and the tones of anger, disappointment, triumph and so on.

The fact that the characters in most of the narratives are animals presented
story-tellers with a special challenge to their powers of observation and
imitation. It was a challenge to which they responded in one very unusual
way. As W.H.I. Bleek (1875: 6) observed after a short period of collection:

> A most curious feature in Bushman folklore is formed by the speeches of
> various animals, recited in modes of pronouncing Bushman, said to be
> peculiar to the animals in whose mouths they are placed. It is a remarkable
> attempt to imitate the shape and position of the mouth of the animal to
> be represented. Among the Bushman sounds which are hereby affected,
> and often entirely commuted, are principally the clicks. These are either
> converted into other consonants, as into labials (in the language of the
> Tortoise), or into palatals and compound dentals and sibilants (as in the
> language of the Ichneumon) or into clicks unheard in Bushmen (as far
> as our present experience goes), – as in the language of the Jackal, who
> is introduced as making use of a strange labial click, which bears to the
> ordinary labial click ⊙, a relation in sound similar to that which the palatal
> click ǂ bears to the cerebral click !. Again, the moon – and it seems also the
> Hare and Anteater – substitute a most unpronounceable click in place of all
> others, excepting the lip click … Another animal, the Blue Crane, differs in
> its speech from ordinary Bushmen, mainly by the insertion of a tt at the end
> of the first syllable of almost every word.

A number of examples of this special mode of speech have been published by Dorothea Bleek (1936), and a small sample will, therefore, suffice here. In the phrases which follow the conventional |Xam form is given on the top line, the altered speech is given on the line below and a translation below that.

Blue Crane:

    Ng kang ka ng se ‖na hi u,u se ‖a twaja ke

    Ng katten katt ng sett ‖natt hi ut,ut sett ‖at twatatt kett

    (I wish I could be with you so that you could louse me

    ta ☉mwing doa tsi: |ki ng |na.

    tat ☉mwoatten doatt tsitt |kott ng |natt.

    because the lice hurt my head with their biting.)

The Tortoise:

    A se !kenn |na hi, ha !kwi a: !kwi:ja.ha ko:a ‖kuwa,

    A se penn mha hi, ha pi a: pi:ja. ha ko:a puwa,

    (You shall take out that big man for us. He will be fat,

    I se !kung ha.

    I se punn a.

    we will go behind him.)

The Ichneumon:

    !Khe, !khe, ng !koing !arruxu, kwa: ka |ne di ts-a de

    'Tse, 'tse, ng tshuing tsarruxu, kwa: kan dje djit ts-a de

    (Oh, oh, what has my grandfather !arruxu done

    hing e !e e: hi k"auki se ‖khwai?

    hing e tse e: hi k"auki tse tswai?

    so that these people will not chew (meat) ?)

    (B. XXIV, 2266f; B. XIV,

    1365; B. XXIV, 2251).

These distortions of ordinary speech represent, as Bleek says, observations on the shape and position of the mouths of various animals.[4]

Here the texts provide one of the few insights into the nature of live performances, where the vitality and imitative powers of the |Xam narrators had consequences in the language itself. Other indications of the style of performance, such as the use of song and chant are, perhaps, more predictable, although not without interest.

Songs in narrative, like most of the songs collected by Bleek and Lloyd, tend to be brief, unelaborated statements repeated several times. Thus in the story of the young woman who disobeyed her mother, and later trapped her breast in a cleft rock, the woman in question returned home singing:

> Ng !khwai-tu si tauna-taunu,
> Ng !khwai-tu si tauna-taunu,
> Ng !khwai tu si tauna-taunu.
> (My nipple will grow into shape again.) (*ibid.*, L. VIII, (32) 8821–42)

Very occasionally songs will tell more of the story, as in this song from an old woman whose family had been forced by drought and hunger to abandon her and who had escaped from the hyena which came to kill her:

> !Gwãi tara,
> !gwãi tara,
> |kammang |kammang ho |nu tara au ‖kau:.
> |Nu tara i kykui,
> hang‡ko: shing sha;
> hang koang |hing
> hang !kuarre !gwãi,
> !gwãi ‖e
> !gwãing |ki !gwãi.
> (The old she-hyena, the old she-hyena, was carrying off the old woman from the old hut. In this way the old woman sprang aside: she got up, she beat the hyena. The hyena killed herself.) (Bleek &Lloyd 1911: 228)

There is no record of musical instruments of any kind being used to accompany kukummi so it must be assumed that songs such as these arose naturally in the course of narration with no special break or other circumstance introducing them.

Often in the texts, short chants and reiterated phrases are used. These, like the songs quoted above, are put into the mouths of the characters and are part of the dramatic materials used by the narrator to maintain the energy of the performance and keep the attention of his audience.

The extensive use of dialogue mentioned above is a distinctive feature of many of the narratives in the collection. Some narratives employ dialogue much more than others, but all use it a great deal. It occurs naturally during the action of narratives, but, when the action is over, events may be endlessly discussed by the characters, argued about, seen from different points of view and told from the perspectives of even quite peripheral characters. Often narratives will not return to the narrator's own voice but conclude in mid-discussion in the voice of one of the characters. A very strong sense of the actors as a community, rather than a collection of inter-acting individuals, is conveyed by this emphasis on discussion. Its presence in the narratives seems to be a reflection of real |Xam life where, as Dorothea Bleek said in the passage quoted above, people were 'talking – always talking' and 'every event … was told and retold'.

Occasionally, whole stories are recounted from the point of view of one character, whose special view of things colours our comprehension of events. Long discourses by certain animals also conclude or form a substantial part of kukummi. In the narratives about the trickster, |Kaggen, |Kaggen's grandson, the Ichneumon, is the one who characteristically engages in this kind of thing. In another small group of narratives, the Anteater and the Lynx lay down at great length the rules by which the animals should make appropriate marriages. Again, elsewhere, the 'Dawn's Heart star' (Jupiter), personified, is given a speech, lasting several hundred columns of text, which discusses not only his own family and history, but also deals with the sun, moon and stars and the habits of various animals. A few narratives were also collected which consist almost entirely of dialogue. Speech was, as it were, the formal protagonist of narrative; an extension into fiction of that ever-present surface of |Xam life.

While it is true that many kukummi do have a strong educational flavour, it is very rarely the case that a moral is overtly drawn from a narrative by a narrator himself and when it is done it is not presented in any way which might suggest a formal mode of conclusion. Characters in the narratives are often given to making explicitly didactic statements and it is here, embedded in a drama of socially situated characters, that the narrators tended to place such lessons as their audiences were expected to draw. Here again, just as speech of a community provides one of the primary surfaces of |Xam narrative, so social education is continuous with the lives of people living together, seen in fictional constructs and separate from any directly asserted view of the narrator himself.

This is not to say that a narrator's guiding voice is absent. There are certainly cases where irony is employed, plainly intended to influence the audience's perception of characters. In several of |Hang‡kass'o's |Kaggen narratives there is also a visible attempt on the part of the narrator to interpret the protagonist in a special light (see Chapter 7). Such acts of interpretation, however, are only engaged in tentatively and always with reference to well-established and communally owned values. As is so often true in oral literature, the individual narrator puts his own stamp on what is communally held, just as any individual speaker of a language draws on that language in his own characteristic way expressing simultaneously both his distinctiveness and his membership of the community.[5]

Turning to the subject matter of the narratives, a number of distinctions can be made for purposes of description on the basis of content even though, as was pointed out above, the |Xam themselves did not distinguish between kinds of narrative. Besides a substantial amount of material concerning the beliefs and customs of the informants, a few accounts of the personal experiences of the informants were also collected. These represent a simple form of narrative and provide a useful source of contrast to the purely fictional narratives in the collection. These accounts relate both ordinary and extraordinary events in the lives of the informants and are often of great ethnographic interest. Of more concern as oral literature are a few accounts, some quite extensive, of events which had occurred apparently during the lifetime of the narrators but which were not personally witnessed by them. Such narratives were not said to be about the !Xwe-‖na-s'o !k?e and involve no magical happenings. They are, however, quite similar in theme to other narratives which do purport to be about this early race and it must be said that the distinction between these narratives and what might be termed 'historical legends' possibly only resides in the embellishment of the latter.

The historical legends, which the narrators did claim recounted events in the lives of the !Xwe-‖na-s'o !k?e, do not involve animals in human form, or even humans with animal names but simply human beings in a context which could be that of |Xam life contemporary with the time of collection. These narratives often involve mysterious or magical events but this was by no means a necessary condition for a narrative being said to be concerned with the !Xwe-‖na-s'o !k?e. Such a narrative is the simple tale of the man who ordered his wife to cut off his ears because his wife had shaved his brother's hair so closely that he believed his brother had been skinned; wishing himself to have a similarly unusual appearance, he told his wife, against her protestations, to perform the operation and naturally ended up screaming with pain. This short narrative contains nothing magical, but the man's foolishness may have been the aspect which marked him out as one of the !Xwe-‖na-s'o !k?e as far as the narrator was concerned. Other narratives of this kind concern dangerous encounters with lions and even conflicts with the !Korana which may well have had some foundation in actual events in recent history (see Chapter 3).

The majority of |Xam kukummi concern the !Xwe-‖na-s'o !k?e as animals – or rather people who were said to have later become the animals whose names they bear and who often also have at least some of the attributes of those animals. Apparently any living creature, from an elephant to the lava of a caterpillar, could be regarded as having once been one of the !Xwe-‖na-s'o !k?e. Many varieties of birds feature in these narratives, as do insects, burrowing animals, reptiles, large and small antelopes and beasts of prey. All are described as the !Xwe-‖na-s'o !k?e who preceded the |Xam in their country and, apparently, no special distinction was made between these characters and those, not identified with animals, who were the subject of historical legends. Nor were either of these groups of narratives regarded as more true than the other. Like the !Kung tales of today both seem to have been regarded as equally true or untrue with no clear distinction being made either way.

The themes of these animal narratives are various but often involve inter-family relations, the consequences of bad marriages and the conflicting interests of in-laws. Many of the problems which form their subject are caused by the fact that although the characters are in human form they are essentially animals. As such, difficulties inevitably arise if marriages take place between people who in their animal form would be incompatible. Such is the case of the Jackal who married a Quagga and was persuaded by his family that his wife was food and therefore should be killed. The Anteater and the Lynx are also both involved in the problems of making inappropriate alliances although here both creatures come to realise the order of things and articulate the need for proper marriages between animals and proper (i.e. animal-like) life-styles. The Lynx marries another lynx and lives as a lynx lives, while the Anteater becomes an actual anteater and lives in a hole.

All collections of San oral literature contain the notion that the animals were once people and were later changed into the animals we know. In the Bleek and Lloyd collection, narrators credited this change to the Anteater and the Lynx who commanded the animals to take their real form and henceforth live as animals – which they did (see Chapter 5).

Beside the animals, the sun, moon and stars were also said to have once been numbered amongst the !Xwe-‖na-s'o !kʔe and the narratives concerning their lives on earth at that time often account for the existence and movements of celestial bodies. Such a narrative is the well-known account of the man whose armpit glowed with light while everywhere else was in gloom. While he slept a group of children, on the instructions of their mother, threw him up into the sky where he became the sun. The moon was also said to have once been a man, as was the 'Dawn's Heart Star' Jupiter, while several stories describe two lions, !Haue ta ǂhou and !Gu, who, according to one narrative, are now the two pointers on the Southern Cross. Some narratives speak of whole families becoming groups of stars. In some instances such transformations were said to be caused by the disobedient actions of girls subjected to puberty observances, while some fragmentary narratives given by ‖Kabbo simply describe the appearance of certain constellations as families of people moving across the sky, the children being the smaller stars, the parents the larger ones.

Many of the stars were given animal names. W.H.I. Bleek (1874: 102) comments:

> With regard to the constellations, – it is especially worthy of remark that their names in Bushman seem, generally speaking, to be unconnected with their shapes in the sky, – and that many of them seem only to be named from the fact of their being seen at certain times when the animals, or other objects, whose names they bear, come into season, or are more abundant.

This led Bleek (*loc. cit.*) under the influence of Max Müller's theory of myth,[6] to the following speculation:

> Of course, when such names as steinbok, hartebeest, eland, anteater, lion, tortoise, etc., had once become attached to certain stars or constellations, fancy might step in, and try to discover the shapes of those animals (or other objects) in the configuration of the stars; whilst at the same time, mythological personification would begin its work, and make the heavens the theatre of numberless poetically conceived histories.

While there is some evidence for this being the case in certain minor instances, there are only a few narratives where animals named are actually associated with those stars possessing animal names. However, there is no doubt that explanations for the presence of the sun, moon and stars were taken up into narrative form.

Apart from these narratives of animals and celestial bodies there are, finally, those concerning the supernatural beings who were part of |Xam religious belief. These narratives relate the activities of !Khwa (the Rain) and |Kaggen, the trickster associated with the mantis. The narratives involving !Khwa are mainly to do with the consequences of failure to observe the rules relating to girls during puberty. !Khwa is not credited with a human personality and never appears in the narratives in human form. In one instance he appears as an eland but most often he is a bull. He also takes the form of actual water and is described as appearing on the ground as a long shallow pool in the shape of a bull. In other narratives he does not actually appear but transforms people into frogs, snakes, and porcupines. He is always represented as threatening and the narratives concerning him appear to have been an important support for the beliefs and practices concerning menstruation.

The largest single group of narratives in the collection, and no doubt the best known, is that concerned with the trickster |Kaggen whom Dorothea Bleek (1929a: 305) describes as 'the favourite hero of all |kham folklore'. Like !Khwa he was also part of religious belief, and stories and beliefs about him have been recorded from many parts of the Republic of South Africa although, in some instances, with marked differences in his nature in both narrative and belief. The further east he is found, the more his religious nature resembles that of a deity credited with having created everything in the world and prayed to for food (Orpen, *op. cit.*; Stow, *op. cit.*, 119f, 134; Arbousset & Daumas 1846: 253ff; Potgieter 1955: 29). Amongst the |Xam, however, this aspect of him was undeveloped and instead he is presented as primarily working against their interests. The stories about him for the most part situate him in a family context where his impish personality frequently brings him into conflict with others. Unlike !Khwa, he does have a distinctively human personality and in the majority of the narratives the action centres on what he does. !Khwa's presence in narratives, however, is only ever consequential upon the actions of others.

These groupings of |Xam kukummi are too broad to do full justice to the richness of the collection, but they do provide a general framework within which particular narratives or clusters of narratives can be discussed. Unsurprisingly, the narratives which come closest to them in terms of themes, motifs and plots are those of other San groups but there are many points at which they overlap with and show the influence of the narrative tradition of the Khoe-khoen. Indeed, it has been argued that in narrative as in many other cultural aspects, the distinction between what is San and what is Khoe-khoe can be at best only vague (Wilson & Thompson, *op. cit.*, ix, 41ff ; Tobias 1957; Schmidt 1975). The famous story of the Moon and Hare, describing the origin of death, has been found widely distributed throughout both San and Khoe-khoe groups. Seven versions of this narrative were collected by Bleek and Lloyd, three of them from ǂKasing, whose father was a !Kora. Also in this collection is a version of the story of the woman who transformed herself into a lion, given by |A!kungta, which Bleek had acquired earlier from another source and published in his anthology of Khoe-khoen lore, *Reynard the Fox in South Africa* (1864). Similarly, a few narratives featuring the Khoe-khoe trickster, the Jackal, were collected from Bleek and Lloyd's informants – three from ǂKasing and one each from ‖Kabbo and Dia!kwain.

There are almost no signs of Bantu influence on |Xam kukummi. In only one case is it possible to discern the presence of Bantu oral tradition, and in that instance much modification has taken place in order to accommodate the narrative to the |Xam socio-cultural setting (see Chapter 10). Contact between the |Xam and the Bantu-speaking peoples was late and intermittent, whereas trading was carried out between the |Xam and the Khoe-khoen, inter-marriage was common and, as Shula Marks (1972) has pointed out, in situations where San acquired cattle the Khoe-khoen became devoid of them, cultural distinctions became blurred.

The long process of extermination to which the |Xam were subjected continued late into the 19th century. The few remaining San lived in fear of random attacks by 'commandos'. Cultural extinction was also threatened 'as the |Xam took to menial farm work for the white farmers. In 1929 Dorothea Bleek (1929a: 311f) wrote:

Fifty years ago every adult Bushman knew all his people's lore. A tale begun by a person from one place could be finished by someone from another place at a later date.[7] In 1910 I visited the northern parts of the Cape Colony and found the children, nephews and nieces of some of the former informants among the few Bushmen still living there. Not one of them knew a single story. On my reading some of the old texts a couple of old men recognised a few customs and said, 'I once heard my people tell that'. But the folklore was dead, killed by a life of service among strangers and the breaking up of families.

The collection made by Bleek and Lloyd indeed represents an opportunity taken which was soon to disappear. In the chapters which follow, these narratives are discussed in several groupings: the legends and the narratives involving !Khwa are discussed together, these being the only narratives in which, with the exception of !Khwa himself, the characters are not associated either with animals or with celestial bodies. The sidereal and animal narratives are then discussed, and these chapters are followed by a detailed examination of the complex of beliefs and narratives concerning |Kaggen.

Notes

1 This perhaps idealised version of hunter-gatherer life does have some support from recent studies. See Lee (1968b, 1969b) and Sahlins (1972: 1–39).

2 Literally, 'first-at-sitting-people'.

3 The |Xam made distinctions between the San living in various areas. Those living on the plains were the 'Flat People', others were the 'Grass People', the 'Mountain People' and so on.

4 Such observation also marks |Hang‡kass'o's statement that 'Bushmen talk with the body of their tongue, while Europeans are those who talk with the tip of their tongue' (L. VIII, (20) 8528 rev.).

5 This same aspect in another oral literature is discussed in Lord (1958: 14–29).

6 In the same paper, p. 98, Bleek makes it clear that he had read Müller's *Comparative Mythology* and his *Introduction to the Science of Religion*.

7 Miss Bleek may have been thinking here of a particular version of the story of the Moon and the Hare (L. IV, (4), 3882–89) which was begun by ‡Kasing and concluded later by Dia!kwain.

3

Legends and the stories of !Khwa

Contained in the Bleek and Lloyd collection are many narratives which are clearly fictional, and a few which are clearly factual. Between these categories there are a number of narratives which appear to be grounded in fact but which contain fictional elements which are elaborated to varying degrees in different narratives. It is evident from such narratives that factual accounts of real events were subjected to a fictionalising process taking place over a long period of time which could ultimately convert the account into pure fiction.

These remarks particularly apply to a small group of narratives which shall be here termed legends. These narratives frequently relate events which could, and probably did, have some foundation in historical fact. They recount the activities of human beings, and these humans, like the animals prior to their transformation into animal form, were said to be !Xwe ‖na s'o !kʔe. In spite of the characters in these narratives being thus called the temporal setting of the stories cannot be regarded as mythological time for they are clearly set in a recent past which was not significantly different from the world of the |Xam in the 19th century. Furthermore, magic and other non-naturalistic elements are, if not totally absent, usually inessential features of the plot. Thus, as a group, they conform precisely to William Bascom's classification of legends (Bascom 1965: 4f) while some evince those characteristics which Bascom further attributes to narrative material which has moved in the course of time from a factual base towards the fictive. He writes (*ibid.*):

> Reminiscences or anecdotes concern human characters who are known to the narrator or his audience, but apparently they may be retold frequently enough to acquire the style of verbal art and some may be retold after the

characters are no longer known at firsthand. They are accepted as truth and can be considered as a sub-type of the legend, or a proto-legend.

It would seem that at some stage during this process the characters described came to be regarded as !Xwe ∥na s'o !k?e and this designation may itself have legitimated further fictional elaborations.

These legends number only about a dozen although a few of them are amongst the longest and most carefully told in the collection. They tend to be concerned with the responses of individuals to dangerous situations involving either beasts of prey – notably lions – or !Korana war parties. A few, such as the story of the man who ordered his wife to cut off his ears, are certainly apocryphal and are to do with the deeds of notably stupid people. Of those dealing with people in danger some warn against carelessness and describe what befell those who were insufficiently cautious; others describe resourceful or intelligent responses to dangerous events.

Dorothea Bleek (1929a: 310) has pointed out that the |Xam do not seem to have had legendary human heroes.

> I think that their life in small family groups scattered over very wide spaces has tended to make the surrounding animal world and the heavenly bodies loom large in their sight, the human hero small.

Certainly this is the impression given by the Bleek and Lloyd collection. However, while individual human heroes are not celebrated, bravery, independent thinking and social responsibility often are. Indeed the value of these qualities is implicit throughout the entire range of |Xam narratives and it is possible that some of the narratives which had a foundation in historical fact were elaborated from news which specifically demonstrated the value of these qualities. In all cases what happened is of more importance than who performed the action.

What narrators made of their central core of fact illuminates much about the principles of |Xam oral composition. As soon as news became distanced from its immediate source it was open to special emphases, the introduction of motifs from existing stories, the recasting of *dramatis personae*, the employment of songs and, indeed, a host of traditional elements as well as the individual narrator's personal shaping of his material. In the course of this process both the factual core and the human hero could become obscured and action *qua* action rise to predominance. In this way the social value of say, intelligence and bravery were displayed while attributable heroics were played down.

The narratives concerned with encounters with !Korana war parties are amongst those most likely to have been elaborated from real events[1] and provide a useful insight into this fictionalising process. Of these only one contains a strongly stressed non-naturalistic element and this may well have been an extraneous introduction; the narrative also contains a number of stereotypical features which are worthy of note. The story is as follows.

!Kotta koë a young boy, goes out to collect ostrich eggs together with his younger brother. While the younger brother packs and carries his eggs in the customary manner, i.e. in a net on his back, !Kotta koë swallows his whole and in such numbers that his stomach sticks out in many places. The collection of eggs continues for several days, each day the boys returning home in the evening, the younger brother eating his eggs in the traditional manner, with a small brush of gemsbok tail hair. While collecting eggs one day, the younger brother notices a number of !Koranas and, it is implied, the !Koranas notice the boys. !Kotta koë and his brother take flight although !Kotta koë is impeded by his over-laden stomach. The boys come to a stream which the younger brother jumps with ease. !Kotta koë attempts the same feat but falls into the water where his stomach breaks open and the eggs pour out. A !Kora warrior then comes into view brandishing an assegai but !Kotta koë persuades him that, as he is already almost dead, the !Korana would do better to chase the younger brother. This the gullible !Kora does, whereupon !Kotta koë replaces the eggs in his stomach, stitches himself up with thorns, takes a short cut to where he knows his brother to be waiting and together they return home safely (L. VIII, (28) 8486–8506).

This narrative shows signs of being a naturalistic account of an escape from hostile !Koranas which has been merged with a more fanciful narrative about a foolish person who swallows eggs whole. The younger brother is typical of many younger siblings in |Xam narrative tradition in that he is more acute and able than his brother. It is he who first notices the !Koranas; he is fleet while his brother is slow, and he conforms to normal behaviour in everything which we see him do. In many |Xam narratives such bright, able and conformist young siblings are responsible for interventions in dangerous or otherwise abnormal situations, especially on behalf of their parents. In this narrative the younger brother has these attributes but they are not exploited in any way which fundamentally affects the plot. At the same time the ostrich eggs which weigh down !Kotta koë, while being the cause of his fall, do not constitute a necessary condition for his slowness. In naturalistic terms no cause as such need have been given, and as !Kotta koë appears to have been known outside of the context of this narrative (Bleek & Lloyd 1911: 309) it is possible that in other or earlier versions some other factual or fictional element may have been employed at this point in the plot if the central figure had indeed been added to a fundamentally factual account.

The full text of the narrative also contains a motif found in another narrative in the collection; reference is made to the !Kora leaving his assegai on the ground near to !Kotta koë while he goes to chase the younger brother. This he does on the advice of !Kotta koë who then uses it in his escape. The same motif occurs in the story of the girl whose breast is caught in a rock (L. VIII, (32) 8821–42). She is captured by two lions and is quite helpless. Like !Kotta koë and the assegai she persuades them to leave their arrows behind while they go away to drink before devouring her. She then makes use of the arrows to effect her escape. Both this narrative and the story about the boys were given by |Hang ‡kass'o and the motif is likely to have been part of a common stock of narrative materials available to him.

Here, where we find a narrative displaying several strands and motifs common to other narratives, the imprint of, no doubt, a line of narrators becomes visible and any actual event which may have formed the basis of the story is lost from view. It must also be borne in mind that once stories of bravery and cleverness in the face of hostile !Koranas had been established as traditional elaborated narratives, rather than simply as anecdotes or news, they too would be capable of contributing plot frameworks or motifs to the tradition.

Another, less fanciful, narrative of interest concerning the !Korana has been well summarised by Dorothea Bleek (1929a: 309) as follows:

> A youth of the early race was sent to fetch water. Coming over a hill he saw a Korana war party at the water, and they saw him. He made himself small and went down to the water swaying about like a little child, so that the Korana called out: 'Pity! Look! Why do the people send him to the water and not a grown-up person?' The boy behaved so stupidly that the Koranas helped him fill his egg-shells and let him go, though one old man told them to kill the child lest he warn his parents. As soon as the youth was over the hill he resumed his normal size and went home to tell of the Koranas. The women went away to hide, the men made fires at the huts with large

stumps which would burn long, then followed the women. The Koranas were deceived and surrounded the huts, only to find them empty.

Commenting on the possible veracity of this narrative Miss Bleek (*ibid.*) writes:

> This sounds to me like the recital of a real event, in which a boy deceived the enemy by pretending to be more stupid than he really was; but in the course of time the boy's identity had been lost and his clever acting been changed into magic transformation, whereupon the story has been ascribed to a youth of the Early Race.

Apart from the 'magic transformation' mentioned by Miss Bleek the obviously fictional elaborations are few. In the original text (L. VIII, (25) 8251–68) the boy returns home singing that the !Koranas had tied on their feathered head-dresses for war. This kind of unextended song often occurs when individuals are described returning home alone, and, like the detailed dialogue, is clearly a narrator's own contribution. The old man who, alone out of the !Korana party, thinks that the boy should be killed also returns at the end of the story to berate his fellows for not having listened to him. Again this kind of vindication motif is common to many |Xam narratives. Here, where a factual core seems more obvious[2] than it was in the case of the !Kotta koë story, the undeniably fictive materials stand out plainly. This is not simply because the non-naturalistic elements are fewer but because the stereotypical features are less and there is no reliance on such narrative techniques as the repetition of figures – something which the !Kotta koë story employs in its opening phases where several egg-collecting excursions are described prior to the one on which they meet the !Koranas.

The only totally naturalistic narrative in this !Korana set may have been apocryphal for it implicitly warns against obstinacy and over-confidence when communal safety is concerned and commends the protagonist for speaking her mind forcefully in the face of the complacency of her fellow band members. The heroine, |Kamang, spies a !Korana war party while she is out collecting *veldkos*. She returns to her people and warns them but they do not heed her warning. One man insists that the place where she saw the !Koranas is a feeding-ground for young ostriches and that it was these that she had probably seen. They argue but the man is adamant and patronising. 'My, my, why is the old woman so obstinate?' he says. When the sun sets the

!Koranas surround the camp and slaughter everyone. Only |Kamang escapes (she was also a fast runner) but not before she had exchanged words with the man who had rejected her warning. She says, 'Now you can see that I was speaking the truth', and he admits that he ought to have listened to her (L. VIII, (26) 8269–85).

Here the virtues of independent judgement and social responsibility are counterposed to an over-confidence in 'what everybody knows', and linked to physical prowess in the form of |Kamang's ability to run fast.

One indication that the narrator believed the story to be literally true is his comment that he did not actually know the place where these events took place – although he names it – because he did not have first-hand knowledge of the case. The fact that both protagonist's name and the place name is preserved might be taken as some evidence of the truthfulness of the story but |Kamang's independence of mind and fleetness of foot are stereotypical of a certain kind of |Xam fictional character and again the vindication motif is employed. However, she may well have been a real person who was attributed with recognisable qualities by successive narrators.

It is apparent from these !Korana stories that to some extent the social resonance and value of certain types of behaviour and attitudes may be traced in the manner of oral composition, where what is of significance in a story was emphasised by the employment of traditional elements that had long been established as conveyors of fundamental values. On the other hand purely imaginative traditional elements – such as Kotta koë's egg-eating – can completely dominate the basic tale in the hands of a narrator disposed to make them do so. The traditional elements which provide the narrator with the materials for his embellishments or, indeed, frameworks for new plots do not, therefore, owe their survival exclusively to their place in the matrix of social value though this may often be an important factor. The purely imaginative or – in case of the lion stories described below – the purely exciting, also have a resilience and attraction of their own which can guarantee perpetuation without help from elements of more clear-cut social relevance. However, the very subject matter of these legends is frequently didactic and recurring motifs, such as the vindication scenes, do generally function to recommend types of behaviour.

Another kind of didacticism may be seen in those narratives which describe the extremely foolish actions of people who fail to make the fundamental connections which form the basis of common sense. The story of the man who commanded his wife to cut off his ears is of this kind;

another is the story of a man who cut open his wife's stomach to see what she had been eating and found that she was pregnant. He tried to sew her up again when he realised his mistake, thinking that she would come alive again. Finally he was told that women do look as if they are full of food when pregnant and asked if his own people had not educated him to understand such things. This kind of stupidity was often attributed to the !Xwe ǁna s'o !kʔe, although it appears only infrequently in quite this unmitigated form. Such stories, like many of the animal stories and the |Kaggen trickster narratives, seem to show a world where even the most basic truths of social life remain unlearned by many, even though there are also often sensible and well-socialised people around to point out the true nature and order of things. It is a world not unlike that of a child where parents loom out of the mists of incomprehension to admonish and point the way towards maturity.

There remain, however, several legends where the didactic element is almost completely absent. They can be purely adventure stories and where they do attribute foolishness to their protagonists it is never as blatant as it is in the narratives referred to immediately above. Two such narratives were published in *Specimens of Bushman Folklore* (pp. 174ff, 260ff) while von Wielligh gives an entire volume to narratives of this kind (*op. cit.*, Vol 4).

Two lion stories were collected which show some traces of purposeful didacticism, one concerning a man who brought home a lion cub and insisted that it was a hunting dog (L. II, (26) 2320–2504, 2597–2873) and another describing the fate of two men who hunted lions with clubs made from bone (L. VIII, (18) 7551–88). Neither narrative contains any non-naturalistic elements and both are told very vividly. ǁKabbo, who gave the story of the lion cub, took several months to complete his narration, yet the story is very coherent and its plot sections well balanced. It describes the reaction of the man's wife to her obstinate husband's insistence that the cub was a dog given to him by his brother; her warnings to her children; the man's increasingly dangerous hunting expeditions as the cub grows bigger; and the man's eventual death. The narrative concludes with the eldest son taking his uncles to the scene of the accident and showing them where he had stood watching when his father was attacked. There they see the man's bow and arrows lying on the ground and the clump of bushes to which the lion dragged him. Finally the whole family move to another mountain where they can live in safety from the lion and its parents, which it has rejoined.

Certain parts of the narrative lend themselves to repetition – especially in the early part of the story where the father is described hunting with his son and his 'dog' on successive occasions. In each repetition the same phrases tend to recur and the same details are given. After the death of the man, however, the reiterations of descriptive passages give way to a more free-flowing style. It is very expansively told with many small, but telling details. There is a lengthy vindication passage in which the wife recalls her repeated warnings and her observations on the physical appearance of the cub, and the eldest son is commended by his uncles for his bravery and wisdom but the centres of interest in the narrative are uncharacteristically greatly enriched by careful description.

The story itself appears to have been well known, for Dia!kwain (who came from the Katkop area) on having it read to him some three years after its collection commented that he had heard the story both from his mother and his paternal grandfather. W.H.I. Bleek (1875: 14) describes this version as a 'legend told with great epic breadth', as indeed it is. Much of this is due to ‖Kabbo's facility with creating dialogue which simultaneously promotes the action of the narrative while reflecting the specific viewpoint and character of the speaker.

Another narrative, given by |Hang‡kass'o, concerning two brothers who hunted lions, opens with a brief description of how the men went out together, followed the lions' spoor, waited until charged and threw heavy bones, thus killing the lion which they cut up and carried home. The description is given four times in succession with only minor changes in the phrasing. Then the younger brother goes hunting alone; the assegais he uses are not made of sufficiently heavy bone and he, failing to kill the lion, is himself killed. The story then focuses on the man's children and his elder brother waiting for his return. The children believe their father to be dead but the elder brother does not. While the children and their mother move away from the place where they have been living, the elder brother remains, waiting for his brother's return and singing alone in his hut. The lion which had killed his brother eventually retraces the dead man's spoor to his home. There in the darkness the man sings:

Ng ‖ka-☉pwawe
Ng ‖ka-☉pwa ka !khwe
ta |kwẽi:da
Au ng ‖ka-☉pwa s'o
|khā: ‖kwamma.

(My little brother! My little brother's wind [see Chapter 1] feels like this wind when he has killed a lion.)

but his singing is interspersed with questions directed to his absent brother about the little lights which he is seeing in the darkness outside his hut. He asks, 'Brother, brother can these be stars?' In reality they are the eyes of the approaching lion. He sings his song again and calls out to his brother about the stars but within moments he is dragged from the hut and bitten to death.

By way of a coda, apparently for the benefit of the collector, |Hang‡kass'o explains that the !Xwe ‖na s'o !kʔe called lions ‖kwamma[3] and frequently hunted them for food. The men in the story, therefore, were not doing anything unusual as such (although this may have been another example of the stupidity of this early race) but the younger brother had acted foolishly, firstly in hunting alone, and secondly by only using ostrich bones which were too light to kill a lion. According to |Hang ‡kass'o he should have used either an elephant's thigh bone or the bone of a giraffe. There is no record of such bones being used by the |Xam in any way connected with lions[4] (for example as defensive weapons) although they were commonly used for hunting and to this extent some educational value might be attached to the story. It remains, however, primarily a probably fairly hair-raising adventure story told for entertainment rather than instruction.

The range of socially motivated fictional accretions which narratives (both with and without factual foundations) may have is no doubt very large but one final example of the role which legends about human characters can perform is the story of the old woman whose family was forced to abandon her when their food and water supply could not support them all. Her success in killing the hyena which came to attack her, and in eating it and thereby gaining the strength to follow after her family, possibly represented a narrative expression of the fears connected with institutionalised geriatricide while offering an albeit far-fetched possibility for hope. A narrative which gives expression to the necessarily internalised feelings aroused by such practices obviously has a role to play in making them acceptable.

These narratives exclusively involving human characters comprise only a small fraction of the total collection, but they are singular in being capable of pointing out both the formal differences between themselves and accounts of personal experience, as well as indicating the ways in which traditional narrative materials could be used to emphasise the social content of what was originally news. Once we enter the realm of stories concerning animals or supernatural beings this basic contrast recedes from view; the purely imaginative world begins to obscure the seams of fictional composition and the heterogeneous elements, which together form a narrative dislodged from any factual basis, become much harder to separate from each other.

The stories of !Khwa

A further group of narratives in which the !Xwe ‖na s'o !k?e are represented as human beings are those dealing with the fate of people who violated the various taboos and rituals relating to menstruation and to !Khwa, the supernatural being associated with those observances. Unlike the legends discussed above, these narratives have no counterpart in accounts of personal experience although they were believed to accurately describe the consequences of ritual violations. They all involve supernatural events, particularly transformations of people into frogs.

By way of ethnographic background it should be explained that at the onset of her menses a young girl was segregated from the band and placed in a small hut built by her mother some distance from the camp.[5] There she would remain in isolation until a new moon appeared. The hut was so small that she was forced to lie prone. Her food and water supply was restricted and she was forbidden to leave the hut for anything except defecation. When she did leave the hut for this purpose she was instructed to look at nothing but to keep her eyes downcast as she walked to and from the hut. On the appearance of a new moon she was released by her mother and her mother's close friends. This group of older women were her xoakengu, mothers, and were responsible for the instruction of the girl in those rites which she had to perform to protect the band from !Khwa, who might strike people down with lightning or show his displeasure in other ways. These duties included daubing members of the band with red paint, treating her father's hands with buchu to counteract the pollution entailed by contact with his daughter, and a large number of taboos relating to the preparation and eating of food and to any contact which she may have had with hunters.

The girl's parents would request the xoakengu to instruct the girl in all of these matters. Indeed this group of women was largely responsible both for the articulation and dissemination of the beliefs and practices relating to menstruation and with the management of the rites themselves. This task included the recounting of the narratives specifically dealing with these matters and there is no doubt that these narratives primarily functioned to support the practices outlined above.

The occasions on which the narratives were told were informal. When it rained young girls were taken into a hut by one of the older women in case !Khwa should notice them and claim their lives. Here the old woman would speak of !Khwa and tell of her own observance of the rites as a girl, but the narratives might be performed on even quite casual occasions – just as might any other story. The stories were not only for the ears of girls and young women. Many of the narratives concerning these matters were collected from male informants and |Hang ‡kass'o describes how his own xoakengu had told him the story of the girl who killed !Khwa's children, purely as a distraction when, as a child, he had been crying about the small amount of food he had been given to eat (L. VIII, (17) 7519).

It is clear from informants' attempts to describe the observances to the collectors that the narratives were used to explain beliefs and practices. Dia!kwain, for example, explains why young women should avoid eating certain foods, or leaving their isolation hut entirely by referring to cautionary narratives, and in this he is typical of most of the informants who dealt with these matters.

Something should also be said here about the beliefs concerning !Khwa. His name is usually translated as 'Rain' although the word also simply meant water. The |Xam made a distinction between male rain and female rain. Male rain was violent and usually accompanied by thunder and lightning; female rain was gentle and regarded as very welcome. Female rain is not mentioned at all in the lore relating to puberty. !Khwa, when conceived of as a supernatural being, was exclusively a male figure who could not only mobilise the harmful effects of male rain but who might also effect various transformations on disobedient girls and those which whom she came into contact. There is no question of prayers being addressed to !Khwa, although during particularly threatening storms, certain old men might address him in the form of short reiterated requests to stop storming. He was, as it were, a personification of all water but particularly rain-water.

The punishments administered by !Khwa were mainly death by lightning or transformations into non-human forms – especially frogs, creatures which were not eaten by anyone of any age because they were believed to have once been disobedient girls. The girl, her xoakengu and her parents could be taken up by a whirlwind and deposited in a pool where they would live as frogs. According to several of the narratives, which seem to have accurately mirrored belief, their possessions would revert to their original forms, skin bags becoming animals again, arrows and mats becoming reeds once more, and bows becoming trees. These formal reversions wrought by !Khwa were exclusively related to girls' menstruation rules. It was frequently emphasised by the informants that it was the odour of the girls which attracted the attention of !Khwa hence the heavy use of buchu which was believed to counteract this odour.

A number of animals, particularly reptiles, were associated with !Khwa: these included the cobra, the puffadder, the tortoise and the water tortoise. They were regarded as set aside for his food and highly taboo for young girls. Certain kinds of *veldkos* were also symbolically connected with !Khwa and strenuously avoided.

!Khwa was capable of taking many forms. Strictly speaking, however, his body was water even though his shape was most frequently said to resemble that of a bull ox – the animal with which he was predominantly associated. Unlike |Kaggen, the other primary supernatural being believed in by the |Xam, !Khwa was very much an impersonal force, greatly feared for his powers, with no anthropomorphic traits. His appearance in both belief and narrative, as having a distinct animal form, did nothing to reduce his impersonality.

The narratives which relate to !Khwa and to menstruation, range from sketchily rendered fragments offered in support of beliefs, to fully elaborated stories told with much care and attention to presentation and narrative technique. Approximately 16 narratives with this subject matter were collected, but, for the purposes of this discussion, fragments and unelaborated story-outlines will be ignored except where they have some bearing on the fuller texts.

Thematically, these narratives are all rather similar. In most cases a girl violates her ritual separation from the band by leaving or looking out of her hut. The consequences of her behaviour might include any or all of the following: the appearance of a thick mist said to be !Khwa's breath when he leaves the waterhole where he lives; the arrival of a whirlwind which first carries away the girl and then her parents and her xoakengu and deposits them in a muddy pool where they become frogs; and the transformation of their belongings into their natural constituents. On the other hand, a glance from the eye of a girl might simply transfix those she had looked at and turn them into stars. In one story a young man takes his goura out to a hill where he can play in solitude. A girl lying in her hut nearby finds the music so sweet that she determines to see who is playing. She looks out of her hut and sees the young man but, as she looks, he is turned to stone (L. V, (20) 5581–91). The ending of this story is atypical – transformations following fixity are usually into stars – and the narrative as a whole seems to have been aetiological, for the place where these events took place is named, and the group of stones said by the narrator still to have been there in 1875.[6]

The message which is driven home in all of these narratives is that menstruating girls are an extreme source of danger to society and need to behave in strict accordance with the rules laid down for their behaviour if disaster is to be averted. The imagery which is employed to underline this message frequently draws on the distinction between culture, represented by food and artefacts, and nature represented by !Khwa, the mists of his breath, whirlwinds and reptilian imagery. The motif, encountered in several narratives, of artefacts reverting to their natural forms crystallises this contrast into a single vivid image. Here the logical structure of belief declares itself in the juxtaposition of opposing concepts with the girl – of the cultural world but differentiated from it by her condition – clearly regarded as standing between these alternatives. Only by the application of ritual practices can she hope to return herself fully to society and if she fails in this she is bound to move in the other direction and become absorbed into pure nature. It is interesting to note that in but a few of the narratives is it not only the girl who suffers from her violations: everyone who is immediately involved with her is liable to suffer, especially her parents and her xaokengu – significantly the very people most directly concerned with the articulation and propagation of these beliefs. It is as though the xoakengu were saying to a young girl, 'If you act in this way not only you but all of us will suffer'.

While the content of these narratives is distinctive, there are no formal traits which are exclusively observable in the narratives relating to menstruation rules, although in this small sample, with the exception of the vindication motif, there is a notable lack of motifs found outside the group. No special introductions, codas or other structuring devices are employed which set these narratives apart from the other thematic groupings found in the collection, and the stories themselves were formally open to any mode of presentation and structuring chosen by the narrator. No clearer example of this formal flexibility could be desired than that which emerges from a comparison of the story told by !Kweiten ta ‖ken as !Kui|a ga kum; !Gã ka kum ('the young woman's story'; 'the frog's story') and by |Hang‡Kass'o as

'The girl who killed the children of !Khwa' (Bleek & Lloyd 1911: 198ff; L. VIII, (17) 7473–7519).[7]

The basic story is as follows: a young woman who is submitted to ritual seclusion leaves her hut each day when all the people have gone out to collect food. She goes to a waterhole and catches a Waterchild ('!Khwa ʘpwaken') which she kills, takes back to the camp and eats. She then returns to her hut. When the people return from the hunting ground the girl's mother brings her food, but, because the girl is already full, her appetite is small. Her mother suspects that she is getting food from elsewhere and takes steps to discover what is happening. However, before the mother confronts her daughter !Khwa is so angered by the girl's behaviour that he carries her, her xoakengu, and her mother and father off in a whirlwind, depositing them in a pool where they become frogs. Their possessions also fly to the same pool and return to their natural forms.

The differences between !Kweiten ta ‖ken's plot and that of |Hang‡kass'o are few. In !Kweiten ta ‖ken's plot the girl's poor appetite makes her xoakengu suspicious and they order the girl's younger sister to conceal herself in her mother's hut to spy on the girl and report to them on what she eats. This she does and the girl's mother realises that it is a Waterchild (a striped creature the size of a calf). This discovery, however, prompts no immediate response from the mother. She does not speak to her daughter about the matter but on the following day leaves the camp in the usual way. It is on this day that !Khwa takes his revenge on the girl and all of the other people.

In |Hang ‡kass'o's version the same emphasis is placed on the girl's reduced appetite but this is not what makes her mother suspicious. Instead it is an unextinguished fire which the mother knew herself to have put out. She, too, says nothing to her daughter but next day leaves a large log on the fire, presumably to determine if the fire was being touched while she and the others are away. On this day, however, the girl, instead of catching a Waterchild, catches, with great difficulty, a mature creature with horns.[8] This she takes home and cuts up but !Khwa is so angered that water pours from the ground beneath the fire and extinguishes it. Then, as in the other version, the whirlwind disposes of the girl, her parents and her xoakengu in the usual fashion. In this version the Waterchildren are again said to resemble calves.

While these are the only differences in plot detail between the two versions, the differences in how the stories are told are radical. !Kweiten ta ‖ken opens her version with three simple statements: a girl lay ill;[9] she did not eat the food which her xoakengu gave her: she killed !Khwa's children and this was the food which she ate. The narrative then relates how the xoakengu ordered the girl's younger sister to remain behind and spy. Only at this point is any dramatic patterning introduced, for, once the people have been described leaving the camp on the following day, the statements concerning the young girl's actions – leaving her hut, going to the water, killing the Waterchild, carrying it home, boiling its flesh and eating it – are interleaved with statements about the child who is secretly watching. This interleaving of statements linguistically enacts the drama and is an important departure from the circumstantial statements which open the narrative.

The narrative then proceeds directly to the mother's return. The child reports innocently that her sister had killed a 'Tcha a aken o !khwa' – 'a beautiful thing at the water' – and it is the mother who identifies it as a Waterchild. Only two statements separate the story so far from the description of the disaster which follows: 'he ha xoa k"auki ǂkakken, ī:; hang ‖xa ha |kua ta:ī o ‖xe' ('and her mother did not speak about it; she went out again to seek ants' chrysalids'). From this point until the end – more than half of the total narrative – !Kweiten ta //ken describes the gathering clouds, the mother's forebodings of trouble, the coming of the whirlwind taking first the young woman, then her xoakengu, then her father who is lifted from the hunting ground together with his arrows, and eventually the mother. All become frogs and are dropped into the pool. The narrative concludes with the words: '‖Kagen |hin xhwarra, ‖ke‖keja !nwa; he ta tchuenjan |ne |kagen |hin xhwarra, ī:'. ('The mats grew out of the spring like the arrows; their things grew from the spring.').

Only in the second half of the narrative does the language take on that repetitive density which is so characteristic of all |Xam kukummi – both fictional and non-fictional:

!Kui |a a mai-i ha|e: xhwarra he e |ku-g |ne
di -!ga i:. Ha xoakengu hing ! hou |e xhwarra.
‖Go ‖go |ku-g |ne |ki sa he,ī: au hang
|kweiten |ku |e: ta xhwarra. Hang |ku-g |ne
e ⁻!ga. Ha xoakengu sang ‖xam a: ke di ⁻!ga,
i: o ‖go‖go |ku-g |ne e: |ki sa he au hing
‖na !kau:xu. ‖Go ‖go |ku-g |ne |ki sa he
o xhwarra, au ha ☉pwaxai |kweiten |ku |ne |e:
ta xhwarra. Hang |ku-g |ne e ⁻!ga (Bleek & Lloyd 1911: 292).

(The girl went first into the spring, and she became a frog. Afterwards her xoakengu went into the spring. The whirlwind brought them to it when she was already in the spring. She was a frog. Her xoakengu also became frogs because the whirlwind had brought them when they were on the hunting ground. The whirlwind brought them to the spring when her daughter was already in the spring. She was a frog.)

It is this aspect of the story which mainly captures !Kweiten ta ‖ken's interest – the awesome results of the girl's wrongdoing – and, apart from the scene involving the watchful younger sister, she brings the narrative rapidly to that point.

In strong contrast to this approach, |Hang ǂkass'o handles his version in quite a different fashion. His narrative is highly patterned throughout and is structured by a series of repeated segments with alternating conclusions. He opens his version well before the events described at the outset of !Kweiten ta ‖ken's. Indeed, what is only there by implication in !Kweiten ta ‖ken's version – the repeated killing of the Waterchildren prior to any suspicion on the part of her xoakengu – takes up the bulk of |Hang ǂkass'o's narrative. The first statement tells us that a girl peeped out of her hut to make sure that her xoakengu had left the camp. Having assured herself of this she then went to a waterhole and, stroking the surface of the water with her hand, says: '!gu swi-swiriten !khwa' ('ripples twirl the water'). At this a Waterchild leapt like a fish from the water and the girl caught it and killed it by striking its head. She put it over her shoulder, walked home and laid it down. Once home she looked about her to make sure that her xoakengu were not returning, and all that she did from this point on was done in haste because she was fearful of being caught. Here nearly every sentence contains the adverb arruko, 'quickly'. She quickly lit the fire; quickly cut up the Waterchild; quickly roasted it; looked about her again then took the meat from the fire, brushed the ashes off and ate it. She then made the fire tidy, swept away her footprints and returned to her hut to lie down. Her xoakengu later returned and her mother brought her food of which she ate a little but was naturally soon satisfied and left most of what she had been given. We are then told that the sun set and the people slept. When the sun rose the people woke up and left the camp to search for food again.

The foregoing description is repeated four times, each repetition containing almost exactly the same details rendered in the same words. '!Ku swi-swiriten !khwa' is followed by the creature's leap from the water and, 'ha |ne ku:i xupp.i' ('she hit it, thud!') and so on. All that changes is the girl's response to being offered food. The first segment concludes with her eating a little; the second with her refusing it all and the mother promising to put some aside for her. The third segment concludes as does the first; the fourth concludes as does the second, thus forming an AB, AB pattern. Between each segment the sun is described setting and rising again – a common piece of structural punctuation in |Xam narrative – and, following segments two and four, the mother is described taking food to the young woman in the morning prior to leaving the camp with the other women.

The same description is now repeated a fifth time but apparently the girl's haste has made her careless and her mother notices that the fire is smouldering. No mention is made of food being taken to the young woman and we are only told that the mother puts a large log on the fire before she departs the next morning. From here on everything begins to go wrong for the girl and the narrative concludes in the fashion described above with everyone becoming frogs and their possessions reverting to their natural form.

In contrast to !Kweiten ta ‖ken's version, the space given here to the episode – after the girl had cut up the mature creature – is very small indeed. |Hang ǂkass'o's version is much more concerned with dramatising the events which lead up to this conclusion, vivifying them through the natural centres of dramatic interest – the girl's cautious peeping from the hut, her chanting by the pool, her watchful nervousness when cutting up and cooking the meat, her reaction to the food offered by her mother, and so on. It is such things as these which mark him out as an experienced and fluent narrator, and the careful patterning of his description with its precise alternations, indicate that this version was unlikely to have been the spontaneous recollection of a story heard only in childhood, but one which |Hang ǂkass'o was well used to performing.

In the two versions of this narrative, the girl's violation of the taboo coincides with a neglect of her duty to remain confined within the hut. Other narratives were collected where the misbehaviour is less extreme but nevertheless provokes the same punishments. One narrative given by Dia!kwain describes how a young woman left her hut and merely washed herself in the spring. !Khwa was angered and changed her into a frog.[10] In another narrative given by ‖Kabbo, !Khwa scented a young woman while she was out seeking food. In the form of an ox he cantered after her and surrounded her with a mist. A small whirlwind carried her up high into the air with her *kaross* flying open. After a while the *kaross* closed and she came down into a pond where she became a frog. Her *kaross* became a springbok and her digging stick became a tree. Her people were also deposited in the same pool and became frogs. Their bows became trees, jackal tail swats became jackal tails and their *karosses* became springbok.

The pattern of these narratives – an offence to !Khwa followed by a standardised punishment – remains fairly constant, and the theme is capable of countless variations based on this template. !Khwa is most frequently seen in the form of a bull in all of these narratives but not in all cases. One of !Khwa's most interesting manifestations occurs in another narrative given by !Kweiten ta ‖ken. The narrative opens with an abstract of the plot – a feature occasionally encountered throughout the collection – which simply states that three girls, one of whom should have been in confinement, were out digging for !haggen (a variety of ants' chrysalids) when clouds appeared and they were caught in a rain-storm. A great waterhole engulfed the girl who should have been in her hut and she became a frog. !Kweiten ta ‖ken then elaborates on this abstract and recounts how, as the rain fell it formed a pool in the shape of a bull. The two older girls sprinkled buchu between the horns of this creature, passed through the horns, walked along the back and landed safely on dry ground beyond the water. The remaining girl attempted to do the same but !Khwa drew her into the waterhole and there she became a frog. Nothing befell her companions or anyone else, and the narrative concludes with the two surviving girls returning home and telling their mothers about what had happened.

In only one narrative does !Khwa feature unconnected with menstruation observances, yet the punishments which he administers are of the familiar kind. |Hang ǂkass'o tells the story of a man who unwittingly hunted and shot !Khwa when !Khwa had taken the form of an eland. The hunter is described creeping up to the grazing animal, shooting it, retrieving his arrow and returning to the camp. No mention is made of the elaborate ritual used by the |Xam when eland was shot (see Chapter 6). The man simply sleeps the night in his hut and together with several other men goes out the next morning to follow the spoor of the dying 'eland'. The 'eland' is found, cut up and roasted on the spot. However, the meat keeps vanishing from the fire which itself slowly becomes extinguished. The men decide that the meat must have been something strange and to be avoided and so they prepare to leave. Before they can do this, however, !Khwa forms a ring of water around them shutting them into the temporary shelter which they have erected. They try to escape but !Khwa's navel (!Khwa !uhai:n) encircles them completely. A pond develops where they stand and they all become frogs. They hop out of the hut and away past the people who have followed after the hunters along the 'eland' spoor (L. VIII, (16) 7461–72).

Apart from the cause of the disaster, the general shape of the story is not unlike some of the others described above. The motif of the meat which seems to melt in the gradually dying fire is similar to that which |Hang ǂkass'o also used in version of the story about the young woman who killed the children of !Khwa – and in comparable circumstances. It is difficult, however, to discover any overtly didactic impulse behind this narrative unless it resides in the generation of awe surrounding !Khwa and perhaps too in the respect which the |Xam felt for eland – those antelope so dear to |Kaggen the trickster. One might hazard a guess that this narrative is the product of a male imagination working away from the central concerns of xoakengu.

There are hardly any narratives told with much care concerning transformations into stars, although a few recount the deliberate creation of stars by young girls – not by glancing at people but by throwing certain things into the sky. These are discussed, together with other sidereal narratives, in Chapter 4. Only one narrative was recounted in any detail and even that does not really come under the heading of narratives about human beings because the people who were transfixed by the glance of a girl peeping from her hut were said to be hares. Neither was the punishment administered by !Khwa for it was the girl who proclaimed that the people should become the Corona Australis. ‖Kabbo is at pains to show the exact seating arrangements when this transfixing occurred and even drew a plan of the scene with the fire, the hut, a dish of food, and positions of three people sitting around (L. II, (37) 3333–43). As an example of oral composition, however, it is very weak.

With few exceptions, the social message of these narratives is clear. They were used to support the numerous observances relating to menstruation, although it is unlikely that they were taken very seriously by their audiences. Indeed they may even have appeared in response to the natural impulses of young women confined for long periods who might well have been lenient with themselves during those times when the band were out searching for food. The gap between rule and practice is often wider than ideologues care to admit, as is that between beliefs which can be rationally acted upon and those employed to make the world more intelligible and ordered. There is no evidence that the |Xam were any less aware of these distinctions than any other group of people. The experience of the Marshall expedition in witnessing a Zu|wa rain dance which was rapidly overtaken by rain is always worth recalling. The anthropologists were amazed by the downpour but an informant declared that it would, of course, have rained whether they had danced or not (L. Marshall 1957a: 238). Whatever the status in belief of these narratives, their intention is at least clear. So too is the basic opposition of elemental nature and |Xam culture, creating that conceptual no-man's-land to which menstruating young women were consigned. It was from these materials that |Xam narrators created their stories and elaborated them into often highly structured performances.

Notes

1   An historical account of the conflict between the San and the !Korana is given in J.A. Engelbrecht (1936: 17ff). The book also contains descriptions, given by !Kora informants, of some of these conflicts. The !Korana accounts emphasise how the San response to their physically superior enemies characteristically involved cunning and trickery. The |Xam narratives not only describe events which are very similar to those in the !Korana accounts, but also place a high value on intelligence and trickery in encounters with enemies. The !Korana factual accounts, therefore, support both the factual basis of the |Xam fictions and confirm that the San did not only value intelligence and cunning but succeeded in putting them into practice in real life (see *op. cit.*, 66ff, 203ff).

2   Engelbrecht (*op. cit.*, 71) reports the experience of those involved in the expeditions against the San in the following way: 'Where possible they would surround the Bushmen and often kill them to a man. This, however, was not easily done, for these wild people were as agile and fleet-footed as many of their animal friends. There was, indeed, something almost uncanny about the way they disappeared behind some bush only to reappear a few moments later at some place a few hundred yards ahead'.

3   According to the informant this word was used only by the !Xwe ‖na s'o k?e. Certainly there are no instances of its use in normal |Xam speech.

4   The |Xam had no rule against eating beasts of prey, but it is unknown if lion-hunting was practised.

5   For a fuller account of these rites see Appendix A.

6   A similar narrative given sketchily by ‖Kabbo, in which men were turned into trees by a girl's glance (L. II, (2) 295–305).

7   The title of |Hang ǂkass'o's version was given in English only.

8   It is unclear from the texts if this was simply a mature form of the creatures previously caught, or if it was !Khwa himself. The expression used is !Khwa a ¯kija, '!Khwa who is grown'.

9   That is, she is confined to her hut during a menstrual period.

10   B. XXXII, 2609–18, L. V, (2) 3864–81. Dia!kwain also gave sketches of two similar narratives in which a girl is transformed into a snake and the girl's brother into a porcupine (L. V, (13) 4981–5054).

4

Sidereal narratives: the story of the Dawn's Heart and his wife the Lynx

Both in Bleek's report of 1875 and Lloyd's of 1889 much prominence was given to collected materials which related to the sun, the moon and the stars, and it is indeed true that their informants had much to say concerning celestial bodies. However, the number of actual narratives collected – as opposed to beliefs and superstitions – is extremely small indeed. A story of the creation of the sun was collected (two versions); a narrative accounting for the waxing and waning of the moon (three versions); another relating to Jupiter (three versions); the Moon and the Hare (seven versions); one very brief sketch of a story about a disobedient girl who made stars; a note about the two lions who became the pointers of the Southern Cross; and an allusion to a family who were stars. If the story mentioned in the last chapter concerning the girl who changed a family into the Corona Australis by glancing at them, and the narrative relating to |Kaggen's creation of the moon are added to this number, it is clear that, at the very most, only nine distinct stories, out of the total collection of over a hundred, were concerned with celestial phenomena. The long-standing belief that 'the heavenly bodies figured largely in Bushman mythology' (Dornan 1922: 432) – based mainly on the emphasis Bleek gave to this material – is clearly not a reflection of the actual incidence of such narratives in the collection. Furthermore, only four or five of these narratives were told with sufficient expansiveness or care to warrant much attention as examples of verbal art.

Almost all of the sidereal narratives are well known from published sources and there is little need to describe their content here. However, something should be said briefly about the beliefs concerning the sun, moon and stars since Bleek (1875: 9) claimed that 'the Bushmen are clearly to be included among the nations who have attained to sidereal worship' and were this statement true it would plainly have consequences for how these narratives should be regarded.

The sun, moon, Canopus and possibly other stars, were all addressed at certain times. According to ‖Kabbo, the sun could be asked for nothing except warmth and light (L. II, (1) 218 rev.). None of the 'prayers' recorded by Bleek (L. II, (1) 251; B. I, 315), go further than requests for these things. Von Wielligh's (op. cit., Vol 1, 188) informants, however, while still placing the emphasis on the sun's physical attributes, also elaborate on these in an address which includes the idea of the sun as a hunter who is well fed and who can afford to leave to others his surplus game. Requests to the sun to steady the hunter's arm when aiming at game were also made in the same address. This type of prayer was made in the early morning before the day's hunting took place. Again according to von Wielligh (ibid.), another 'prayer' was uttered in the early evening which said in effect, 'we would like you to stay with us because beasts of prey attack us at night and it is bitterly cold, but if you must go please do not stay away too long'.

Two addresses to the new moon were collected by Bleek and Lloyd (D.F. Bleek 1929a: 306). From these it is evident that the new moon was regarded as capable of favourably influencing hunting and the gathering of ants' chrysalids. These 'prayers' were only made on the appearance of a new moon. Once the moon began to grow large it became more a figure of ridicule than of respect. Its growth was conceived of as an enlarging stomach and children would call to it in a derisive manner (L. II, (35) 3158 rev.).

Two 'prayers' to a star, both of them to Canopus, were collected by Bleek and Lloyd and these clearly involved a belief in the ability of that star to influence favourably both the gathering of ants' chrysalids and the abundance of game (L. II, (1) 216f). A ceremony was also performed on the appearance of Canopus (Bleek & Lloyd 1911: 338ff) which was followed by a search for ants' chrysalids. Except in this single case, the manuscripts do not bear out Dorothea Bleek's (1929a: 307) statement that 'certain stars are asked for certain foods' but perhaps this was something which she had personally observed.

While the moon and Canopus were believed to possess the power to benefit the |Xam with respect to food supplies, no celestial body was held to relate in any way to illness or to rain. No information was collected which told how often or by whom such 'prayers' were made. It is likely that the beliefs about the sun, moon and stars, rather than being of primary religious importance, were simply an aspect of a more general attitude to nature which credited various phenomena including the rain, the wind, the larger game animals etc. with nonphysical attributes affecting the lives of humans. To use the term 'worship' in this context is to greatly exaggerate the case.

The narratives which deal with the sun, moon and stars are, with few exceptions, entirely aetiological constructions but none of them has anything to say about the influence which celestial phenomena were believed to have over food resources, although some do celebrate the fact that hunting at night is facilitated by the light of the moon. The sun, moon and some of the stars were regarded as having once been !Xwe ‖na s'o !k?e, living on earth and having the power of speech. The stories concerning them explain, (a) how the sun was thrown into the sky; (b) how the sun (a male being) chases the moon (also a male being) cutting off a little of the moon each day until the moon, left with only his back-bone, begs the sun to spare him this much, which the sun does; the moon then grows back to his full size and the whole process begins again; (c) how the Milky Way was created by a girl throwing ashes and roots into the sky because she was angry about her restricted food rations given to her during her isolation at menarche; (d) the origin of death through the Hare's disbelief of the Moon's message of resurrection; (e) the origin of the moon;[1] (f) the origin of Corona Australis; (g) the origin of the pointers on the Southern Cross.

With the exception of the origin of death and the creation of the moon, all of the aetiological narratives in this group are very undeveloped as narratives. They consist mainly in the description of a single figure, e.g. the sun chasing the moon, or the girl throwing up the roots and ashes, with little or no attempt to build up the narrative in any way, and no plotting of events. As such they must be regarded more as static figurative conceptions than as narratives.

Of the few developed narratives, the story of the Moon and the Hare is too well known to require discussion here, but the story concerning Jupiter, known as Gaue ‖ẽ, Dawn's Heart, and his wife the Lynx, displays several features which permit a glimpse of conceptual elements already partially touched upon in the discussion of the narratives relating to !Khwa and which will also be seen again in the chapters concerning ǀKaggen.

An examination of narratives collected from an extinct society must, when possible, deal with texts at several levels, if a plausible reconstruction of the meaning and resonance which those narratives may have had for their original audiences is to be made. Below the formal level of a text there is the simple level of ethnographic detail which may or may not have been preserved in materials outside of the narrative. Beyond this there is the social function and weight of motifs or whole narratives, and occasionally shaping not only narratives but also rituals, beliefs and superstition – basic ways of conceiving of the world which declare themselves in narrative form.

Where groups of similarly structured narratives are found – as in the case of the narratives relating to puberty – conceptual frameworks reveal themselves more readily and these in turn may provide insights into other narratives outside of these groups. The story of the Dawn's Heart and his wife does not fall within any thematically or structurally definable group yet it can be analysed with reference both to other narratives and to certain beliefs and practices in such a way that some of the concepts which provide its parameters may be seen more clearly. As such it is unique in this small collection of sidereal narratives. This narrative also provides an opportunity for illustrating the relationship between narrative materials and the conceptual frameworks and ethnography which inform and, to varying degrees, influence their content. For these reasons the rest of this chapter will be given over to its discussion.

The three versions of this story, one by |Hang ǂkass'o, the other two by ‖Kabbo, differ in the style of their telling and in a few content details but in terms of plot they are almost identical. The full text of |Hang ǂkass'o's version may be found in *Specimens of Bushman Folklore* (Bleek & Lloyd 1911: 84ff). The following summary includes details from all versions:

Dawn's Heart hides his daughter, Dawn's Heart Child, in a pile of roots where his wife, the Lynx, may find her. He instructs her to come out only when the Lynx approaches, saying 'You will know your mother by the beautiful ornaments which she wears and by her two *karosses*. She will come with her younger sister. Both of them have white faces and red bodies.'

Several animals approach the child including the Jackal and Hyena but the child will not go with any of them. However, when she hears the sound of her mother's ornaments, she leaps out, climbs on the Lynx's back and together they go to collect !kuise (an edible root). They return home and roast the roots but the Hyena offers her some ants' chrysalids which she too is toasting. However, the Hyena and the Jackal (in |Hang ǂkass'o's version just the Hyena) have first put their own breast milk (in |Hang ǂkass'o's version the Hyena's underarm perspiration) into the food, and, as soon as the Lynx eats the food, she leaps up, her ornaments falling from her, and runs off into some reeds where she begins to be transformed into a beast of prey.

The Hyena's original intention in approaching the Dawn's Heart Child was apparently to gain access to the Dawn's Heart himself and oust the Lynx from his affections. Now she puts on the Lynx's ornaments, goes to the hut of the Dawn's Heart and lies waiting for him. Meanwhile the Lynx's younger sister, carrying the child, follows the Lynx to the reeds and calls to her to feed the child. The Lynx, well aware that she is becoming a beast, and little by little losing all sense of her former self, comes out of the reeds and does manage to feed the child. She tells her sister to return on successive days until her transformation is so complete that she is a danger both to her child and her sister. This the sister does, until, after a few days, the Lynx, now almost completely transformed, tells her that she should not come again because her reason is all but gone.

That evening, after Dawn's Heart has returned home from hunting, a dance is held. The Hyena, not wishing to draw attention to herself, sits quietly in the hut having laid aside the noisy ornaments. She has spent all of her time since joining the Dawn's Heart, in attempting to pose as the Lynx. Outside at the dance the Dawn's Heart approaches his wife's younger sister in a friendly manner but is subjected to a stream of abuse about the fact that he had had sexual intercourse with the Hyena. The Dawn's Heart had been genuinely fooled by the Hyena's deception and is now very angry both with the Hyena and with his sister-in-law for not having told him sooner. He picks up his assegai, goes to the Hyena and stabs at her. She leaps aside, landing with her foot in the fire, but manages to scamper off and escape.

When it is light, a party of people, headed by the Lynx's sister carrying the child and the Dawn's Heart himself, go to the reeds where the Lynx is hiding. The sister calls to the Lynx who rushes ferociously from the reeds. However, the people have brought a number of goats with them to distract the Lynx and, as they predicted, the Lynx catches hold of one of these. As she does so her husband and sister catch hold of her with the help of the other people. The animal hair which has grown on her is rubbed and plucked off and the goats' stomachs are cut open, gutted, and she is anointed with the blood. Only the tufts of hair on her ears are left on because she claims that she would not be able to hear properly if they were removed. Apart from this, she becomes her normal self once more.

In ‖Kabbo's versions (L. II, (15) 1432–1710; B. V, 645–997) the Lynx is transformed into a lion and the goats and anointing are omitted. Instead she is pacified only by the hair being plucked away and by her male relatives forcing her to smell their body odour. In |Hang ǂkass'o's version the Lynx is transformed into an actual lynx and his narrative omits the opening sequence relating the hiding of the child and starts from the point at which the Hyena deliberately gives the Lynx contaminated food. Both narrators conclude with references to the brightness and fearful aspect of the Dawn's Heart star, and ‖Kabbo also adds that because the Lynx had been given polluted ants' chrysalids, she no longer ate that food but became a real lynx, while the Dawn's Heart and his daughter went to live in the sky.

There are a number of simple observations which can be made to clarify this narrative a little. It can be readily seen that the story contains three aetiological elements: the Hyena's 'burnt foot'; the Lynx's ear tufts; and Jupiter's brightness. In |Hang ǂkass'o's version we are told that since the Hyena had angered him the Dawn's Heart's eyes burn fierce and large when he returns home from hunting. Of these three aetiological elements the last is the most emphasised by |Hang ǂkass'o while ‖Kabbo, who often displays great interest in how the animals came to assume their present characteristics, emphasises equally the burning of the Hyena's foot and the Lynx's ear tufts, and pays less attention to the brightness of the Dawn's Heart.

With the exception of the Dawn's Heart himself, all of the central characters are female and foods mentioned in the story were either exclusively or primarily collected by women. In |Hang ǂkass'o's version, the women gather !haken, a variety of ants' chrysalids, and it is this which Hyena contaminates and gives to the Lynx. In ‖Kabbo's versions the Lynx has been collecting !kuisi; this she roasts and intends to eat. The Hyena, however, has been gathering ‖xe, a kind of ants's chrysalid different from and, for the |Xam, more tasty than !haken; it is this which she contaminates and gives to the Lynx. There is, therefore, little conformity between the two narrators regarding what had been gathered although both of them agree that some kind of ants' chrysalids was given to the Lynx. This may be because ants' chrysalids would be more absorbent than other foods.

The narrators also differ on the kind of roots used by the Dawn's Heart to bury his child. ‖Kabbo claims that it was the same plant which the Lynx subsequently collected – !kuise. |Hang ǂkass'o however, says that it was !huing, a plant with a scented white root which turns red when old, and which possibly (Bleek & Lloyd 1911: 84ff) had a red flower. The colour of the roots, their flowers and foliage, may have been important factors in camouflaging the child who, like her father, was said to be red. The colour of the !kuise, mentioned by ‖Kabbo in this connection, was not recorded.

The fact that kinds of food are specified in these narratives is not, in itself, significant. Very many |Xam narratives are specific about foods gathered and eaten. Given the variations in the versions of this story, the foods themselves may have been of little significance beside their place in women's work.

In looking for the significant features of this narrative, there is no better starting point than the narrator's own observations. Both ‖Kabbo and |Hang ǂkass'o provide some useful insights into the basic co-ordinates of the story by consciously drawing attention to two sets of contrast. ‖Kabbo points out the fact that the Dawn's Heart and his child were really of the sky while his wife, the Lynx was of the earth. In one version the Dawn's Heart explains to his daughter: 'Your mother, the Lynx, must walk on the ground. We two walk in the sky. I came out of the sky and married your mother. My name is Dawn's Heart and you and I are red, but mother's flesh is different. Mother walks the earth; I walk the sky.' This aspect is frequently alluded to in ‖Kabbo's versions although it remains unstated by |Hang ǂkass'o. ‖Kabbo's emphasis clearly expresses what is perhaps one of the most obvious features of this narrative, i.e. that the marriage with which it deals forms a link between earth and sky.

The other contrast, explicitly indicated by both narrators, is that of day and night. The |Xam divided all stars into night stars and day stars. Jupiter was a day star *par excellence* and his brightness in the early morning was said to frighten those animals which hunted mainly at night – which included jackals (which feature peripherally in all versions) and, pre-eminently, hyenas, creatures notorious for their nocturnal activities. Lynxes, which also hunt at night, were not mentioned in this connection.

When these two oppositions, Earth/Sky, Day/Night, are taken for granted, as the narrators apparently intended them to be, other co-ordinates of the narrative can be examined.

In all versions much is made of the Lynx's ornaments and clothing. They are carefully described by both ‖Kabbo and |Hang ǂkass'o and distinguish the Lynx from other people. They also act as symbols of culture for they fall from her as soon as she eats the contaminated food which transforms her from a human into a beast of prey. They suggest, indeed, that their wearer was more cultured than the other creatures featured in the story. This symbolic expression of cultural differentiation also makes her singularly suitable as a marriage partner for the authoritatively masculine hunter, Dawn's Heart.

The Lynx is at once more beautiful than the other women and more capable of maintaining the marriage which balanced the opposing elements of Sky and Earth, and, perhaps also, as the lynx is a creature of the night, of Night and Day. Regarded by the |Xam in any case as a beautiful creature (L. II, (3) 420ff), the ornamented Lynx was – to cull an epithet from well outside of San culture – a queen among women.

Just as the ornaments are symbols of culture, their fall from the Lynx is a symbolic representation of her defection to raw and menacing nature. The symbolism is quite blatant in all versions and requires no special knowledge to uncover it. It is further underlined by the Hyena's own insecure relationship with the ornaments, which she cannot wear for fear of drawing attention to herself and which she leaves behind when escaping from the angry Dawn's Heart.

The central character is the Lynx herself. What happens to her is, in essence, that she is transformed from an emphatic cultural condition to an emphatic natural condition, losing first her ornaments and gradually all sense of her human self. This, in quite a different form, is another example of the opposition observed in the narratives concerning !Khwa and menstruating women, that of culture and nature. Here it operates together with the other co-ordinates noted above. However, the fact that most of the characters in this story are associated with different wild animals is liable to make the culture/nature opposition highly influential at the behavioural level and this is indeed the case.

The true animal nature of these characters is masked by their human form but is liable to become exposed under certain conditions.[2] The Lynx's nature as a beast of prey is forced into the open by the Hyena's action. The Hyena's very malevolence and desire to destroy the marriage of the Dawn's Heart and the Lynx, already mark her out as opposed to the balanced order for which that marriage stands. The Lynx's transformation from a placid gatherer of ground foods, which we have seen her to be, into a ferocious predator who threatens human life, is also the realisation of the Hyena's destructiveness, which is itself reflective of her animal nature as characterised by the |Xam.[3]

The nature of the Lynx's transformation is, in itself, important, and it can be usefully examined with reference to certain aspects of shamanism amongst the |Xam which appear to be strongly echoed in this section of the narrative.

!Giten (shamans) performed cures for illness whilst in a state of trance and it was sometimes the case that a !gi:xa would become violently possessed, beating the air and biting those attempting to restrain him.[4] His jugular vein stood out rigid and the tiny hairs on his back became erect. These hairs were known as 'lion's hair', and, while the entranced !gi:xa was held down, fat was rubbed onto his neck to remove them. It was believed that if these measures were not taken to pacify him and return him to his senses he would turn into a lion and attack people. His powers were highly valued but extreme states of trance were regarded as highly dangerous and threatening to the community. This association of !giten with beasts of prey was both common and dominant. Furthermore, !giten were distinguished by the bracelets which they wore at special dances and by the fact that they wore their *karosses* at all times because, it was said, their blood was colder than that of ordinary people.

These beliefs connected with shamanism do bear a strong resemblance to what happens in the narrative under discussion. Dangers to society were often represented through animal imagery (see Chapter 6) and, although the !gi:xa's ornamental bracelets may only be a coincidental parallel with the Lynx's ornaments, the Lynx's sudden growth of hair – actually called 'lion's hair' in ‖Kabbo's versions – her loss of reason, and her return to normality through the efforts of her family and friends, indicate that at least the same conceptual process is being expressed in both cases. In the narrative, as in real life, a highly valued member of the community becomes transformed into a threat to the community which is represented as a transformation into a beast of prey. It seems highly unlikely that a |Xam audience would have been unaware of the similarities here, indeed the continuity may well have been quite obvious to them.

The agents of transformation in the narrative may also be elucidated by reference to |Xam custom and belief. In all versions the central action of the story is precipitated by an act of food contamination perpetrated by a character associated with a much despised animal. In ‖Kabbo's version the contaminating agent is the Hyena's breast-milk and in |Hang ‡kass'o's it is the blackened perspiration of her armpits. Physically secreted matter such as the breast-milk or perspiration used here, or saliva and blood from the nose, was regarded as highly potent in certain contexts, and capable of affecting in various ways anyone who came into contact with it. Such secretions could be active in transferring essential characteristics from one person to another (D.F. Bleek 1923: 50) and, for this reason, the disparity between ‖Kabbo's versions and that of |Hang ‡kass'o in the kind of secretion employed, is not significant. What is significant is that an essential characteristic of malevolent wildness, submerged but nevertheless strongly present in the Hyena, is transferred to the Lynx and exposes the Lynx's own dangerous nature. It is worth noting, however, that even when she is transformed, the Lynx's breast-milk does not have a similar effect on the child. Perhaps it can be construed from this that her nature is essentially less dangerous than that of the Hyena. This view would be consonant with |Xam attitudes to the two animals.

The same kind of transforming agent (physical secretion) could also be used for good, and this is what occurs at the end of the story where, in ‖Kabbo's version, the Lynx is pacified partly by being forced to smell the body-odour of the male members of her family, and, in |Hang ǂkass'o's version, by being anointed with blood from the viscera of domestic, i.e. cultured, animals; both acts, together with the plucking and rubbing away of the hair, being an important part of her return to normality.

If the central actors can, in various ways, be seen in terms of the binary co-ordinates of this narrative, then the two other main characters, the Lynx's sister and the Dawn's Heart Child, are still in need of explication. The only answer as to why the Dawn's Heart buries his daughter is given by ‖Kabbo in terms far removed from narrative coherence as it is usually understood in literate societies; the same can be said for plausibility and internal coherence for the most part in |Xam narratives. In the speech of the Dawn's Heart to his daughter quoted above, the Dawn's Heart says: 'You are the Dawn's Heart Child, a star. I am your father, a star. And so I bury you as a star. You are my heart. I made a child with my heart and so swallow you. I walk with you. When you grow I spit you out from my mouth. You go from me and I walk behind.' The child was identified with a small star standing close to Jupiter in the sky. Bleek (1875: 11) writes: 'At the time when we asked it was Regulus or Alpha Leonis.' What ‖Kabbo is saying is that the Dawn's Heart buries his daughter in the narrative because this is how he behaves in the sky. Whatever the sidereal reference of this observation might be,[5] it is at least evident that, for the narration, the child was, in a very real sense, of the same flesh as the Dawn's Heart himself.

The Lynx's relationship to her sister is comparable in this sense. Furthermore the sister accompanies the Lynx wherever she goes and acts for her – by bringing the child regularly to suckle – as long as the Lynx has any capacity for human responsibility. Perhaps her reticence in not revealing the truth sooner to the Dawn's Heart is due to uncertainty about how he will act.

What is certain is that she clearly sees her primary obligation to be to her sister and the child. Her involvement with the child is at least a shadow of the unity expressed in the marriage of the Lynx and the Dawn's Heart.

While it is apparent that there are binary oppositions present in this narrative, the primary pair, Earth and Sky, are not strictly mediated in the way Claude Lévi-Strauss (1972b: 206ff) suggests occurs in myth, but linked by a social institution, namely marriage. This link is temporarily destroyed by the Hyena; an unsuccessful substitution is made, and, ultimately, the original state is restored. The temporary destruction of the effective social institution is represented both by the socially unsanctioned sexual intercourse of the Dawn's Heart and the Hyena, and by the Lynx's transformation to a natural state – a state which is itself opposed to the culture which enshrines the institution of marriage. There are, therefore, two movements to the establishment of the problem which, as it were, the narrative solves: marriage (Culture) linking Sky and Earth (and possibly also Day and Night), is superseded by socially unsanctioned sexual intercourse (Nature) and this substitutional movement from Culture to Nature is reflected in the transformation of the Lynx herself.

The solution to the problem is provided during what should be an expression of social cohesion – a dance (from which the Hyena excludes herself). The sister's argument with the Dawn's Heart at the dance again declares the cultural collapse but now in such a way as to make it known to Dawn's Heart, whose decisive action resolves the situation.

If this may be said to be the categorical structure of the narrative (i.e., the structure displayed be the manipulation of the categories involved, Earth/Sky, Day/Night, Culture/Nature) the means by which that manipulation is achieved – especially the use of physical secretions and the images associated with shamanism – can be seen to be firmly set within |Xam culture, and would be unlikely to survive were the narrative to be transposed to a different culture.[6] Furthermore, it can be seen that the categorical distinctions themselves, particularly the Nature/Culture distinction, seen before in the narratives dealing with menstruation, were conceptual apparatus with strong meaning for the |Xam.

This narrative has been dealt with at some length – although far from exhaustively – to indicate the relationship between the various levels at which a narrative may have meaning. A number of other features also make this narrative a particularly useful introduction to the narratives which will be discussed below. It is, of course, both a sidereal and an animal narrative and as such inevitably has some things in common with the narratives only concerning animals. The importance of food; relationships between in-laws; the family characteristics of certain animals; and problems in married life, are all things which can be seen repeatedly in the animal stories, as, indeed is the tension between the ostensible human form of the characters and their fundamental animal nature.

Notes

1   This narrative which features the trickster |Kaggen is dealt with at length in Chapter 10.
2   Further examples of this situation are described in Chapter 5.
3   Hyenas were regarded by the |Xam as ugly, evil-smelling and vicious.
4   Both men and women could be !giten. Their practices and social roles are described at length in Appendix B.
5   A.R. Willcox (1963: 31f) asserts that this narrative 'can hardly be other than their explanation of the disappearance of one of Jupiter's moons as it passes behind the planet in temporary occlusion and then reappears, but even the brightest moon can be seen by very few, if any, people of other races without optical aid.'
6   Stories of a substituted wife are found amongst other San and Khoe-khoe groups, and Megan Biesele has recently collected a !Kung narrative which bears a very strong resemblance to the story of the Dawn's Heart and his wife (Biesele, *op. cit.*, 110ff). However, none of these versions share the specific ethnographic features of the /Xam narrative described here.

5

Animal narratives

The majority of |Xam narratives are about the !Xwe ‖na s'o !kʔe who were associated with certain animals. Many of the narratives describe communities of different groups, each having a common name like 'the Jackals' or 'the Striped Mice', living in close contact with each other, and all having human form although often with some of the attributes of the animals they will in time become. Where they live may be affected by their animal association – the Anteater lives in the ground, the Black Crow lives in a tree – but not how they live. They are all hunters and gatherers like the San.[1]

Nearly 50 different creatures are represented in these stories, from insects to the larger animals such as the elephant and the rhinoceros. Antelope, much prized as game, are poorly represented; rhebok, springbok and wildebeest feature rarely as actors, other antelope not at all. Of the larger game animals only the quagga is given any prominence. Birds and the smaller animals such as the ratel, mouse, polecat etc., form the largest group but are distributed in such a way that single species tend to recur infrequently. The ostrich, blue crane, black crow, lizard and baboon all appear in several narratives but the animals which occur with most frequency are the lion, the jackal and the hyena.

Because the characters in these narratives are only ambiguously human, there is a tension between the apparent human society and the dispositions of the characters as animals. The stories therefore explore both natural history and, perhaps unconsciously, areas of stress in real life. If the characters in the stories are not really human at all, then, as was seen in the case of the story of Dawn's Heart and his wife, there may be times when their needs and propensities as animals will come to the fore in such a way as to shape their interaction with each other.

Not only will there be stress between husband and wife but also between in-laws out to protect the interests of their kin. Because of this, food, marriage and inter-family relationships are at the heart of this narrative tradition and seem to echo the concerns which were of special importance to the |Xam.

This chapter will examine the themes of this group of narratives and indicate some of the social values which are stressed through them. In these stories lions, jackals and hyenas are most frequently involved in the basest forms of dispute concerning food, while baboons are seen as the least desirable of neighbours and quite unsuitable as in-laws. The narratives concerning these animals will be discussed first to give some idea of the parameters of the social world described in these narratives.

Lions, Jackals and Hyenas

In the legends discussed in Chapter 3, where lions are lions and humans are humans, there is no doubt about the fear with which lions were regarded. But when we come to the narratives in which the lion is a social being, one of the !Xwe ǁna s'o !kʔe, the awe surrounding him is considerably diminished and he is 'everywhere … the vanquished party' (D.F. Bleek 1929a: 304). Caged in a world of pure fiction he can be placed on a more equal footing with the other creatures and even made to look foolish.

A few stories were collected about two lions called !Haue ta ǂhou and !Gu. These stories seem to have been part of a series relating the encounters of various characters with this pair of malevolent but foolish, wandering lions. The lions are outwitted almost everywhere they go, although they are not victims, and, like many other popular fictional characters, provided narrators with an opportunity for inventions on the basis of a pre-established familiarity. They are social outsiders, having no fixed home and moving from the promise of one meal to the promise of another. Because of this wandering they can turn up anywhere, endangering those who are unwise or unlucky enough to be caught unprotected. Their often highly comical stupidity renders them unsuccessful in most of their exploits and in the end they die: according to one version they are turned into the pointers on the Southern Cross; in other versions they are killed by their own victims.

Although they obviously could have been used in narratives in the way in which !Khwa was used, i.e. as a sanction against misbehaviour, there is only one narrative in which someone misbehaves himself and a result meets up with the two lions (L. VIII, (32) 8821–42). In every other case the characters whom they threaten are innocent of any wrong-doing or even social deviance. It would seem that !Haue ta ǂhou and !Gu were butts for a lot of anti-lion feeling which was taken up into narrative in much the same way as certain national groups become the subjects of numerous anecdotes and jokes in our own society. Certainly the differences between |Hang ǂkass'o and ‖Kabbo's handling of the episodes in the lives of these two lions shows what great scope there was for endlessly inserting various humiliating adventures for these hapless creatures.

In other narratives lions are seen in equally unflattering lights. They are characterised as essentially greedy and selfish with regard to food and always end up as victims as a result of this. In two narratives a lioness steals children and forces them to live with her (L. VIII, (24) 8084–8197). This theme of forced adoption is the only one in which any relationship to shamanism can be traced in these lion stories for there is some evidence that a !gi:xa would force parents to give them their children to live with them and perform small tasks such as fetching water and firewood. There is no overt connection made between the lionesses and !giten in the narratives but some suggestion of this practice may have been implicitly present.

Hyenas and Jackals also feature in several stories, sometimes together with Lions, sometimes not. The Jackal is the cleverer of the three and behaves with the same nimble cunning as he does in real life. The disputes between these creatures always centre on food. In one narrative the Hyena has just killed a quagga and asks the Jackal to fetch his wife for him so that she too can eat. The Jackal points out that the Hyena's wife will not believe anything told to her by a Jackal and suggests instead that the Hyena goes to fetch her himself: meanwhile he, the Jackal, will light a fire and build a house of sticks where the Hyena and all his family can come to eat. To this the gullible Hyena agrees and sets off for his home. The Jackal builds the fire at the foot of a low cliff and the hut on the cliff above. He places stones in the fire to heat and then sits above with his own wife.

He instructs his wife to make a long rope out of mice entrails and, when the Hyena arrives with his family at the foot of the cliff, asking how he is to get up to the food, the Jackal lowers the fragile rope down to him. Even with great effort the Hyena only succeeds in falling into the fire because the Jackal and his wife cut through the entrails whenever he looks like succeeding. The Jackal and his wife and children then consume the quagga meat themselves (L. V, (4) 4231–65).

This narrative combines a number of very simple features. It rests on the fact that jackals do habitually rob lone hyenas of their food by being both crafty and quick. It also gives another explanation for why hyenas' hind quarters and legs appear burnt and withered; and it gets the Hyena into the fire by using a motif found elsewhere in this collection – the motif of the mice entrails suspended above a fire. !Gu and !Haue ta ǂhou are also the victims of the same trick in one episode in the saga of the their humiliation. Characteristically this narrative concludes with a conversation between the Jackal and another Hyena, who thinks he recognises in the Jackal the person who had tricked his relative. As is so often the case, the narrative ends in mid-dispute.

A Jackal is also successful in defeating a Lion with the help of a !gi:xa who magically elevates the Jackal's camp so that it is again situated on a cliff. The Lion, who has been repeatedly stealing food killed by the Jackal, stands below begging for food, and the Jackal heats stones in the fire and tells the Lion that if he opens his mouth and shuts his eyes food will be dropped down to him. The Lion stupidly does as he told; a burning hot stone is dropped into his mouth and he dies horribly. This narrative, which shows some relation to the other described above, closes with a discussion with the Jackal about how one apparently so small and weak could defeat someone as big and strong as the lion (L. IV, (1) 3486–3515).

When the Lion meets the Hyena, in the well-known story in which the Hyena, taking revenge on the Lion for an act of meanness, inverts a pot of boiling soup upon the Lion's head, it is again the Lion who is the loser. Nevertheless the narrators clearly felt that there was little to choose between the two animals for the Hyena is also described as a k"waken ǁkūng (decayed arm), i.e. one who is ungenerous about food (Bleek & Lloyd 1911: 122ff).

Baboons

If the Lion, the Jackal and the Hyena consistently represent the basest form of dispute about food, the Baboons represent the stereotype of undesirable in-laws. They are seen repeatedly as strange and hostile neighbours whom one would certainly not want one's daughter to marry. According to one narrative, they once lived with other people but they killed a girl and served her up as gemsbok meat. A child revealed the truth to the people who punished the Baboons by tricking them into sitting on hot stones. Hence baboons have raw and hairless buttocks and are cursed forever to eat |gua (a very bitter plant) (L. V, (24) 5974–97). In other stories they are decidedly vicious, living separately from the other people. One narrative which describes a young girl being seduced into marrying a Baboon, concludes with a description of the gradual transformation of the girl's face into that of a baboon, and the conversation of the members of the band as they castigate the girl's parents for their failure to educate the girl sufficiently about the undesirability of mixing with Baboons (L. VIII, (18) 7608–25). While this narrative may be an unspecific expression of the desirability of marrying within one's own racial group, the living proximity of the Baboons and their hostility might be seen as a narrative formulation of conscious or subconscious attitudes to the Khoe-khoen who greatly prized San women and frequently stole them as wives.

It is inevitable that stereotypical characters, such as those described above, should consistently generate thematic material which is repetitive, but disputes about food, baldly displayed by the Hyenas, Jackals and Lions, and the problems of actual or potential affinal kinship ties – for which the Baboons stand as almost an ultimate in undesirability – not only form the basis of a great many narratives but are also capable of a wide variety of expressions.

Consanguinity presents no problems; the story of the Kori Bustard who had sexual intercourse with his elder sister and was severely punished by his elder brother, is the only narrative where blood relatives are in conflict with one another (L. V (5) 4292–4320; L. II, (3) 406–16). Conflicts between husband and wife or between in-laws, however, are numerous and often involve problems relating to food.

The stories which deal directly with couples getting married do reveal something about the notion of suitability. The story of the Rhinoceros and her daughter is perhaps typical of suitor stories everywhere. The Rhinoceros terrifies each of her daughter's suitors – the Jackal, the Hyena and the Lynx – by charging at them until at last a brave man, the Leopard, is found who does not run away. The mother then admits that she had been testing the suitors for their courage and is at last satisfied that the Leopard is the right man for her daughter (L. VIII, (5) 6456–6504). A less common notion of suitability may be seen in the story of the ǂKangara (a small yellow bird) who is abducted by the Ostrich and taken to the Ostrich's daughter whose name is ǂKariten (yolk). As both ǂKangara and ǂKariten are associated with the colour yellow, the Ostrich knows this to be a good match (D.F. Bleek

1936: 165ff). The same notion of suitability through colour-matching also provided one justification offered by the Dawn's Heart for his marriage to the Lynx who was said to be red. It is worth noting that in the case of the Ostrich and the Hyena it is the mother who decides on the match.

Neither of these narratives follows the marriage any further, so there is no way of knowing how successful they are. It is left to other narratives to explore the various problems which can befall a marriage, and this is where the differences between the animals really begin to have consequences. Differences in habit can, apparently, be just as destructive as anything else, as the story of the ǂNerru (a small bird) and her husband illustrates. The husband's name was not recorded but he is certainly not a ǂNerru for he attempts to use his wife's short *kaross* to carry unwashed ‖xe (ants' chrysalids). According to the ǂNerru putting dirty ‖xe into a short *kaross* is not done by anyone from a ǂNerru household. The husband, angered by his wife's refusal to use her *kaross* in this way, snatches at her clothing and badly injures her. He is horrified at having hurt his wife but she returns home to her mother who declares that her daughters' husbands do stupid things and seem to lack all understanding. 'Hing|hang|hang| e: i: u hi ‖kuakka', (they marry into us as if they understand) the mother complains, and in the end orders her son-in-law to return to his own people (Bleek & Lloyd 1911: 206ff).

Physical differences between people can also cause trouble. The woman, married to the Mason Wasp, who noticed for the first time her husband's slender waist, mocked him for it and was shot on the spot by him (*ibid.*, 170ff).

Yet another area of conflict is revealed in the story of the man who is unfortunate enough to marry a woman whose sisters are vultures (*ibid.*, 154ff). The sisters eat everything which the poor man attempts to provide. The situation is never really resolved although in the end the sisters do fly off but for how long we are not told. Other narratives show how even petty grievances against in-laws can assume such importance that they can lead to violence, as in the story of the young man who was so upset by the scolding he got from his brother's wife that he became transformed into a lion and killed her. He is treated with every appearance of sympathy by the rest of his band (L. VIII, (17) 7527–41).

Such divisions between in-laws seem almost arbitrary compared to the great gulf that separates the Quagga from her husband the Jackal. It is a gulf concealed by human form but once it becomes revealed the consequences are dire. Two versions of this story were collected, one from |Hang ǂkass'o (L. VIII

(29) 8603–27) and another from !Kweiten ta ‖ken (D.F. Bleek 1936: 181ff) and the differences between them are slight. The story is as follows:

The Quagga, who is married to a Jackal, gives one of her children some of her own liver (i.e. her own flesh) to eat. A tortoise steals the piece of liver and takes it to the old Jackals who eat it with relish and declare that their relative had married meat. When the Quagga's husband joins them they tell him that he has married a Quagga and should kill his wife. So the Jackal poisons some sharp bones, hides them in his hut and encourages his wife to lie down on them. She is pierced by the bones and the poison soon begins to work. The Quagga, followed by her children, then goes to the water and attempts to drink before she dies. Having drunk, she collapses at the water's edge and is soon tracked-down by the Jackals who skin her, cut her up and begin to boil her in a large pot. The Quagga's daughter, however, climbs an overhanging tree and, as she watches the horrible scene beneath, her tears fall onto the pot and split it open. Although surprised at the apparently inexplicable breakage, the Jackals still manage to consume all of the meat. The daughter then runs off to tell her mother's family about what has happened, and these old Quaggas, with the pretence of making a social visit, wait for an opportune moment and then trample the husband to death.

In a long passage from quite another narrative ‖Kabbo is at pains to describe how, when the animals at last assumed their present form, such creatures as the Quagga and the Jackal mated only with their own kind and ate only the foods appropriate to them. Quaggas now marry quaggas who eat grass and are handsome; jackals marry jackals who eat meat and are ugly. This marriage, however, is between people who, as animals, should have totally different eating habits for one is herbivorous, the other carnivorous.

Although this narrative is the only example of animals actually 'marrying meat',[2] several other narratives were collected in which 'human' flesh is used as food. In one instance the Lizard repeatedly feeds his family on his own flesh, which he pretends is quagga meat. In consequence his wife and child – again it is the child who discovers the deception – leave the Lizard and return to the wife's parents who kill real animals and do not serve up their own flesh. In another instance the Striped Polecat hungrily eats his own flesh instead of hunting for mice as he should. The narrative consists only in the repeated description of the Polecat's actions and is given no conclusion except that he seems to get smaller every time.[3] In the story discussed above, in which the Baboons kill a girl and serve her up as gemsbok meat, the girl is again said to have been a Quagga. The two lions also trick the Blue Crane into eating her own husband, and in another adventure !Gu roasts his own flesh. Little significance is given to these instances of apparent cannibalism except as curious and sometimes brutal absurdities. The occurrence of quagga in three of the narratives may be related to the fact that they were said to smell like humans. Quaggas were eaten by the |Xam, and, relevantly for the story of the Quagga and the Jackal, their livers were often eaten raw.

What is revealed in the narrative of the Quagga and the Jackal is again how the categories of things in the world were once obscured. The revelation of the differences between these categories was a necessary part of the establishment and maintenance of order in the world as seen through the eyes of |Xam narrative tradition. The high incidence of conflict in interfamily relations in the narratives might suggest that the various kinship rules which operated amongst the |Xam, formed not only a strong basis for social structure and organisation but also entered deeply into their understanding of the integrated orders of existence. It is to be regretted that more details concerning |Xam kinship and marriage were not collected, although a precise reflection of such institutions might well not be found in the narratives. Nevertheless the very fact that the disorder in the animal kingdom so often relates to these issues does suggest that the orderliness of nature was essentially bound up with the orderliness of society.

The story of the Quagga and the Jackal poses the opposition of an unnatural consanguinal bond (Quagga feeds her child from her own flesh) and an extreme affinal disjuncture (Jackals kill Quagga). One side of the family kills the wife, the other side kills the husband. There is no way in which this situation is rectified or mediated for only a complete disengagement of the two families can secure peace. The categories obscured by the marriage are established by its dissolution. The fact that the argument should centre on food is also significant coming from a society in which social relationships dictated patterns of food distribution. Lack of kinship implies lack of formal obligation to share. In all of the other narratives which contain cannibalistic elements, the characters offering 'human' flesh are, or become, isolated as individuals. In this narrative the Quagga offers a small part of her flesh to her children and by this act inadvertently offers the rest of her body for consumption by her affinal relatives. In terms of food distribution this much is a logical extension of a process which she herself initiated. The two contradictions involved in this narrative – the Quagga offering her own flesh to her daughter, and the Quagga (a herbivore) being married to a Jackal (a predator) – leads to a distribution of food which itself blatantly declares the logical contradictions in this particular kinship grouping.

The intervention of in-laws is again the theme of the story of ǂKagara (a small bird) and !Haūnū (who was not identified with any animal) (Bleek & Lloyd 1911: 112ff). ǂKagara goes to fetch his younger sister and take her away from !Haūnū, her husband. The reason for this intervention is not stated but it results in a fight between the two men. ǂKagara successfully manages to take his sister home, although both men are badly hurt. The fight itself provided the |Xam with a figurative conception of the elements, for old |Xam women, on hearing thunder and lightning, would say: 'ǂKagara e: hing koa !Haūnū' (it is ǂKagara with !Haūnū) – ǂKagara being identified with lightning and !Haūnū with thunder. Perhaps this conception suggests that conflicts between in-laws are as eternal as the elements.

This is not the only example of violence between brothers-in-law. |Hang ǂkass'o also gave a version of a story concerning the Hyena who had killed his sister-in-law (L. VIII, (25) 8198–8211). No reason is given for this killing but her brother attempts to revenge this death by killing the Hyena. Although he lays an elaborate trap for the Hyena, he is unsuccessful and the narrative ends inconclusively.

Throughout these recurrent themes of marriage, the relationship between in-laws, and the sharing of food, certain basic values are continually evident. The distribution of food was the cornerstone of |Xam life just as it is for the San living today in the traditional manner. The tension surrounding food sharing amongst the !Kung speakers studied by Lorna Marshall, was very great indeed but such fastidiousness in distribution may eliminate the development of economic elites at this and progressively higher levels (Marshall 1961). The significance of sharing, therefore, is inevitably greater than it is in clearly stratified societies. The stories about selfishness with regard to food – especially those concerning the Lion, the Jackal and the Hyena – are bound to have had a different social resonance for the |Xam than similar stories have for more complex societies.

As has been seen, stressful affinal relationships are expressed in a number of forms: between a man and his brother's wife; between a man and his wife's sisters; between a man and his sister's husband, and so on. There is a notable lack of narratives featuring fathers intervening in their married children's affairs but mothers are often influential. How far these features reflect actual patterns of behaviour in |Xam life is, unfortunately, now impossible to determine, and the ethnographies of existing San groups provide no certain guides.

As far as narratives about relationships between married couples are concerned, the majority of problems arise out of differences of custom – usually expressed through differences between types of animals – not out of domestic or personality conflicts. What problems there are tend, in any case, to move quickly into the arena of interfamily affairs with blood relatives taking steps to protect the interests of their own kind.

The two bold messages enshrined in the values expressed through these narratives are: marry your own kind, and share the resources available to you. Other values are sometimes also apparent; the need for children to be obedient, and the responsibility which adults have teaching their young, are among the most frequently expressed. The sense of community, so obvious to an outsider from a society which encourages individualism, is not stressed as an imperative in the narratives but is totally implicit in the lives described and, as was observed in Chapter 2, taken up into the form of the narratives in terminal dialogue.

There are, in this collection, a number of narratives which are not covered by the major themes described above. What all of the narratives have in common, however, is the fact that a world of human beings acting according to animal natures is highly problematic and often dangerous. It is a world clearly in need of ordering and this ordering is achieved in part through piecemeal adjustments such as the +Nerru returning to the stability of her own family, or the Baboons being forced to live away from other people. The ultimate solution, however, can only be found in a radical change involving the animals in recognizing their natures as animals and living henceforth according to these natures. This state is achieved in a single narrative, collected in several versions, in which the Anteater, with the help of the Lynx, lays down the rules by which animals shall live in future. These rules are expressed in a long sequence of sayings, given by the Anteater, called in the text |kukente ta kukummi (the Anteater's 'laws'), the word kukummi standing here not simply for 'stories' but for discourse containing important knowledge. It was translated by Bleek in this context alternatively as 'stories', 'laws' and' sayings'.

The Anteater's laws

The story which gives rise to the Anteater's 'laws' was collected in four versions – two from ‖Kabbo and one each from !Kweiten ta ‖ken and |Hang ǂkass'o (L. II, (2) 323–56; (3) 383–475; L. VI, (1) 3916–29; L. VIII, (29) 8561–8602). The versions given by ‖Kabbo and |Hang ǂkass'o are essentially the same and may be summarised as follows:

> The Anteater, a spinster, called out to a group of Springbok mothers who were passing by with their children. From each she demanded to know the sex of child, and all replied that their children were male. One mother, however, admitted that her child was a girl, and the Anteater, by offering food and appearing friendly, soon tricked the mother into handing her the child. The Anteater then quickly disappeared into her hole with the child, and called out to the distraught mother to go away. The Anteater kept the child to live with her, and in time the girl reached menarche. The Lynx, intending to marry the young Springbok, crept into the hole while the Anteater was out collecting food, and told her that the Anteater was not her real mother and that she had no need to stay with her. With the girl's consent, he carried her off, but the Partridge flew and told the Anteater of the abduction.
>
> The Anteater followed the escaping couple by burrowing underground after them. The Lynx, seeing the earth bulging and trembling behind them, set a trap for the Anteater with his bowstring. The Anteater was caught in the string but called out denouncing the Lynx and saying that he should marry a she-Lynx, and eat springbok as food. The Lynx also denounced the Anteater and told her to become a real Anteater and return to her hole. The Lynx went to the girl's parents and told them what the Anteater had said. The Springboks asked what they should do and the Lynx advised them that they should eat only bushes in future. 'We beasts of prey must kill you and eat your flesh' said the Lynx, and the Springbok agreed. The Lynx then called the other animals together and they listened to his account of the Anteater's command. All of the animals then agreed to eat the foods appropriate to them and to marry their own kind. The Anteater then articulated the new order at great length. From that day on the animals truly became the animals they are today.

In ‖Kabbo's versions the Lynx is seen as acting on behalf of the Springbok's parents as well as for his own sake, and !Kweiten ta ‖ken gives a version in which the Anteater dies in the trap: in this version the 'laws' are not given at all. Elsewhere, however, |Hang ǂkass'o mentions this narrative in passing and explains that

> The beasts of prey were once people. They became beasts of prey because of the Lynx and the Anteater. They were the ones who made this happen: they cursed each other about the little Springbok. They cursed each other (L. VIII, (18) 7593 rev.).

The story giving rise to the Anteater's 'laws' does not contain a conflict of interests as disastrous as many of these contained in other narratives. Unlike the story of the Quagga and the Jackal, the immediate need for differentiation between the animals is not forced into prominence by any extremity of violence,[4] but rather by the creation of a situation in which the Anteater and the Lynx, both of whom wish to live with the young Springbok find that neither of them can argue the justice of their case. The Lynx tells the Springbok that the Anteater is not her real mother and that she is not obliged to stay with her. But the Anteater can rebuke the Lynx on the same grounds, saying that the Lynx should not marry the Springbok because Springbok are, in reality, food to the Lynx. Through the mutual accusations entailed at this point, the laws of life which animals should henceforth obey become articulated.

In this narrative a structural balance is achieved by the fact that the Springbok child is stolen twice: once, as a very young child, by the Anteater wishing to 'make her child of the girl', and later, after she has reached puberty, by the Lynx wishing to make her his wife. Both the Lynx and the Anteater are concerned to maintain a relationship which is fundamentally flawed by the differences between themselves and the Springbok. Thus when they curse each other, they each discover that the logic of their accusations applies equally to both of them. The logical insight informing this story is extraordinarily subtle: the contradiction of human characters acting under the influence of basic animal natures, seen in so many of the narratives, is brought to a point of focus in the form of an actual argument between characters who are, with regard to this contradiction, equally in the wrong.

The list of 'laws' which are hereby articulated is enormous. It contains very specific details about who should marry whom and what food each animal should eat. The ostrich should marry a female ostrich because the Anteater says so; the gemsbok marries a female gemsbok; the eland marries a female eland; the springbok marries a female springbok which eats bushes; the quagga marries a female quagga which eats grass; the hartebeest marries a female hartebeest and they eat grass. The list goes on for pages of manuscript, and the detailed diets of all the animals is also given: the hyena shall eat ostrich egg yolks at night; the lynx shall eat springbok and hare; the leopard will eat raw meat; jackals will eat locusts, long-nosed mice, striped mice, shrews and gerbils, and so on. All, we are told, henceforth eat only the foods appropriate to them and marry their 'equals' (‖kagen).

‖Kabbo seems to have been particularly aware of the fact that as the animals are expected to marry their own kind and, until that point, their own kind are blood relatives, incest is inevitable. He appears to find this unproblematic, however, and insists that the lynx marries his elder sister, gemsbok marries his elder sister, the hartebeest marries his elder sister, indeed they all marry their elder sisters (‖kaxuken).

Those who retain human form, however, are also given instructions on how they will live: they will eat food cooked at a fire; they shall boil food in pots; drink water from ostrich egg-shells and make clothes from animal skins. They shall make shoes from gemsbok, quagga, eland and wildebeest skin and shall eat all kinds of animals excluding wild dog because these are like hunting dogs, and they shall eat *veldkos*. The list of animals to be eaten by these people is again very long and detailed.

These references to people who maintained human form seems to be a curious insertion in a narrative which deals with problems between animals but, in several of the narratives in the collection, there are characters who, although living together with people having animal names, are not, themselves, associated with animals. They do not live in any way which fundamentally differs from the others, except, of course, that their behaviour is not influenced by animal traits. Such characters are few but they appear to have been regarded as the forerunners of the San.

From the time of the Anteater's 'laws' onwards, the world was a less difficult and more ordered place to live in. From here on the !Xwe ‖na s'o !k?e were real humans with exclusively human problems such as those described in Chapter 3. The world had at last achieved some measure of order.

The narratives discussed in this Chapter do not formally differ from other narratives in the collection, except from the structurally distinct groups relating to !Khwa, described in Chapter 3, and to |Kaggen, discussed in greater detail in Chapters 6–10. Motifs often appear in several narratives, and devices for the promotion of the plot through the revelations of a mediator are consistently applied. The child-informant, featuring in many of the narratives, and mediating figures such as the Partridge in the story of the Anteater and the Lynx, or the Tortoise who appears in the story the Quagga and the Jackal and elsewhere, are ciphers functioning as part of the mechanics of the plot. Such particles of plot construction were, like the stereotypical animal characters, the common property of narrators. Other formal features such as the extensive use of dialogue and the insertion of songs and chants are also neither restricted to this group of narratives nor to any particular narrators. In terms of plot structure there is great variety, even though certain motifs can be said to function in the same way *vis-à-vis* plot in many narratives. The only large group of narratives which shows a structural uniformity at the level of plot and is also set in the period in which the animals were people, is that concerning |Kaggen, the trickster, discussed in the following chapters.

Notes

1   The keeping of domestic animals is referred to in a handful of narratives, however, and in one of the |Kaggen narratives the Ticks are said to be black people who keep sheep (see Chapter 10).

2   The same notion of 'marrying meat' is found in a |Gwi narrative collected by Lorna Marshall in 1955.

3   A confusion in the text renders it possible, however, that the narrator had forgotten the conclusion of the story (L. VIII, (13) 7158–7205).

4   This is, of course, not true of !Kweiten ta ‖ken's version, but this version is anomalous in several ways, and in any case does not conclude with an enumeration of 'laws'.

6

|Kaggen in belief and ritual

The largest group of narratives which deals with a single character or group of characters, is that concerned with |Kaggen, the trickster, and his family. Twenty-one distinct narratives concerning |Kaggen were collected, many of these in several versions. In addition to the narratives, a large number of statements concerning |Kaggen were also recorded which show that his reality for the |Xam was more than fictive, that, in fact, as a supernatural being, |Kaggen was believed to participate actively in their lives.

The narratives themselves give an account of |Kaggen's life set in the time when he and the other animals were people. He lived amongst men but was set apart notably by his marked anti-social behaviour. At the point at which, with the exception of the San, the inhabitants of this world were transformed into the animals they are today, |Kaggen continued to live on as a supernatural being who could take many forms. Thus, for the |Xam, there were two phases to |Kaggen's life: one in the distant past, recorded in the narratives; the other in the present, as a supernatural being.

While it is now impossible to discover the extent to which the narratives were believed to be true accounts of |Kaggen's life before the world became changed, the statements of belief about him do offer some indication of the relationship between his supernatural and his fictional natures. Indeed his early exploits were occasionally referred to by the informants as explanations for his actions in the present. Furthermore, the beliefs about him evince several implicit characteristics which were directly transformed into fictional terms in the narratives. Both aspects – fictional and supernatural – may, therefore, be seen to be, in some respects, different projections of a single conception.

As a supernatural being, |Kaggen related principally to hunting and game, and the beliefs about him were situated in a context of beliefs about the relationship thought to exist between humans and animals. In Dorothea Bleek's (1929a: 309) words:

> The whole world is very much alive to the Bushmen; the borderline between the powers of nature and animals is vague, that between animals and men more so.

A few examples of this relationship will serve as an introduction to the beliefs concerning |Kaggen.

Sympathy and hunting

Expressions of belief in the sympathy of nature are frequently to be encountered in the texts collected by Bleek and Lloyd and the process of sympathy is often described. This process is made particularly clear by an account of presentiments given by ‖Kabbo. A presentiment could give a hunter foreknowledge of danger and of such things as which direction he should take, or which arrow he should not use. It could also tell him of the approach of game. It was felt as a tapping either inside of the hunter's body or on an old wound, and could be of a very specific kind as the following extract demonstrates:

> When an ostrich is coming and is scratching the back of its neck with its foot, the Bushman feels the tapping in the back of his own neck at the same place where the ostrich is scratching (Bleek & Lloyd 1911: 333).

The informant described this process in terms of the reception of messages:

> The Bushman's letters are in their bodies. They (the letters) speak, they move, they make their (the Bushmen's) bodies move (*ibid.*, 331).

As will be seen below this concept of sympathetic causality recurred frequently in the beliefs of the |Xam.

With regard to the pursuit of game many sympathetic observances were thought necessary for success. Most of these observances related to the special relationship that was believed to obtain between a hunter and his wounded quarry. A hunter, having shot a large animal, would return to the camp and wait overnight for the poison to take effect. He would then return to the vicinity of the shooting and follow the spoor of the wounded animal. During the period in which the animal was dying, he strenuously avoided any contact with animals whose attributes, such as speed or night travel, he did not wish to reproduce in the dying animal (*ibid.*, 270ff). These avoidances extended to smell, touch and taste, and were responsible for many complex eating rules.

Retrospective explanations of the failure of a hunter to secure a kill over a long period were of various kinds but frequently involved the notion of sympathy. A death in the band was said to be foreknown by the game and this caused the animals to act in unpredictable ways. Illness in the band was also believed to cause the game to behave in a manner that put them beyond the reach of the hunter's skills. Other reasons given for unsuccessful hunting were unruly behaviour by wives and children (D.F. Bleek 1931–36: Part III, 240, 247; W.H.I. Bleek 1875: 19).

In the case of taste, smell, touch, sight and, as will be seen below, noise avoidances, the emphasis was always on the hunter as a medium through which messages might be transmitted to the game. Sympathy was a force which had to be controlled by a careful ordering and limiting of the hunter's activities if the transmission of undesirable messages was to be prevented. Disjunctions in the sympathetic bond could also occur and these manifested themselves mainly in the hunter repeatedly missing his aim. Both cases resulted in the game being placed beyond the powers of men to control. Disjunctions in particular seem to have been caused by deviations from stable social life, and a disruption of a man's relationship with game animals inevitably found its social corollary in a disruptive social event – particularly those events, such as illness and death, involving economic loss to the band. Stable social life would be reflected in stable relations with the game and, if it was not, other sympathetic explanations would be employed (D.F. Bleek 1931–36: Part IV, 325).

|Kaggen

The ritualistic acts which related to |Kaggen were mainly concerned with hunting observances: the accounts of these observances relate to procedures adopted when gemsbok and eland had been shot.

Gemsbok

In addition to the usual observances which took place when a gemsbok had been shot, hares were not killed by the hunter during the period of waiting because it was believed that |Kaggen took the form of a hare and deliberately made himself apparent to the hunter so that the hunter would kill it and thereby permit the gemsbok to recover because of the contamination of the sympathetic relationship between hunter and gemsbok. |Kaggen was regarded as acting in the interests of the gemsbok and against the hunter (L. VIII, (23) 8036 rev.–38 rev.). This same feature was also dominant in the elaborate procedures adopted when an eland was shot.

Eland

Upon shooting an eland a hunter would attempt to recover the arrow shaft from the ground where it had fallen after striking the animal. He would not cross the spoor but would walk to one side and, having found the shaft, lifted it with the use of a leaf and another arrow. This was done to shelter the arrow-shaft from the wind. Having put the shaft into the quiver, he returned home. He would move very slowly, limping, not looking about him, and gazing only passively at what he saw. It was believed that if he did not do this the eland would look actively at things, feel unafraid and thus the poison would be weakened.

When the hunter neared the encampment he would sit down at a distance and wait until he was approached by the older men. When asked why he did not enter the encampment he would give an evasive answer to avoid saying that he had shot an eland. The men then carefully examined the contents of his quiver to discover from the hair on the arrow shaft what animal he had shot. When they discovered that he had shot an eland, one of the men then rolled up the hunter's front apron and tucked it into the belt. The hunter then urinated affecting great difficulty and much pain in imitation of the eland because the poison was said to have this effect on the wounded animal.

A special hut was then made for the hunter well away from the other huts where the children could not disturb him. It was believed that the sudden noise of children's voices could, through the medium of the hunter, startle the eland into activity. The older men performed the task of hut-building and one old man was appointed to stay with the hunter, taking care of him and making a fire just outside the hut. Throughout this period the hunter would act as though he were in pain and the old man's duty was to keep him warm and comfortable as though he were ill. The hunter would lie down and attempt to sleep. If a louse bit him he did not scratch but gently wriggled his body because it was believed that |Kaggen came at this time, sometimes in the form of a louse, to keep the man awake and make him move about so that the eland would also move. It was stated by one informant that |Kaggen was 'trying to cheat him' by getting him to kill the louse so that the louse's blood would be on the hands which had grasped the arrow which had shot the eland. This blood would then enter the arrow and cool the poison.

> |Kaggen is biting our eyes to make us look about. He bites all parts of us, for he wants us to take hold of that part. He knows that if we do then the eland will live (D.F. Bleek 1931–36: Part III, 236).

Another informant gave more details about his belief:

> |Kaggen does not love us if we kill eland, for he comes to pinch our ear because he wishes us to exclaim, 'Fff, |i, |i, |i' and he goes to the eland. He goes to strike the eland's horn and the eland arises. The eland eats for it feels alive because of |Kaggen … And this is why |Kaggen goes to the man who shot the eland. People say that he goes to feel the man's bowstring to see if it is tight. Then he goes and stands pinching the inside of the man's ear. He is not visible there for the people do not perceive him (L. VIII, (23) 8033–39).

It was also stated that |Kaggen might take the form of a puffadder and attempt to startle the hunter into jumping up, thus also energising the eland. If the old man saw that |Kaggen was troubling the hunter he would make up the fire, attempting to drive him away.

At daybreak the old man would tell another old man to take a brand and light a fire at a little distance from the hut so that he could cook a small quantity of food for the hunter. The second old man then walked as if he too were ill, limping, 'for he wants the eland to limp too, not to trot far off but to stumble along' (D.F. Bleek 1931–36: Part III, 237). Also at daybreak, the other hunters would go to find the eland. The hunter who had shot it was not allowed to follow the spoor but would take the others to the place where he had found the arrow. He would return to the old man at the encampment and could not join the men cutting up the eland until it's heart was cut out, for it was believed that his scent could render the eland lean and that

|Kaggen had the power to effect this change because, '|Kaggen is with the eland as it lies dying' (*ibid.*, 238).

Hartebeest

The eland and the hartebeest were regarded as 'things of |Kaggen' and said to have (unspecified) magical powers. The identification of |Kaggen with the hartebeest seems to have been the result of the resemblance between the shape of the head and the horns of the hartebeest, and the shape of the head and the antennae of the mantis – the insect with which |Kaggen was predominantly associated.[1] This association gave rise to a custom concerning |Kaggen and the mothers of young children. Any woman who had a young child would not eat hartebeest meat for fear that her child would be endangered by |Kaggen. Neither would she step over a hartebeest head because it was believed that |Kaggen would press in the child's fontanelle. A protective charm was made from a small piece of a hartebeest foot which was then threaded on sinew and placed around the neck of the child so that |Kaggen would smell the charm and not harm the child (L. V, 4414 rev.–18 rev.). While the currency of this custom is undeterminable it does indicate that again |Kaggen was a being to be feared and not one regarded as acting in the interests of men.

The |Kaggen dance

One further area of behaviour which demonstrates the reality of |Kaggen for the |Xam is the song to him recorded by von Wielligh. It was sung as part of a dance during which, as is usual with San dances, clapping provided the rhythmic background. Rock-paintings of dances featuring men dressed up in angular mantis-like head-masks and holding long sticks in their hands, appearing to represent mantis legs, show the women clapping while the men danced (Willcox, *op. cit.*, 16). The positive identification of the subject of rock-paintings must always remain uncertain but von Wielligh's collection contains the first and only textual confirmation that a dance with |Kaggen as its theme actually existed. The song is as follows:

> You, |Kaggen, keep your head held high.
> You hold fast what you catch.
> Teach us your ability to kill
> And we won't have to fast.

You eat greedily but you eat well.
'Full-up-with-food' is your name (*op. cit.*, Vol 1, 191).

Here |Kaggen appears to have been regarded as a successful hunter in his own right, but also greedy – a quality which he also evidences in the stories about him. While he is seen as set apart from men, going his own way in the wild, the San's envy and admiration for his success is obvious. It is impossible to know how seriously the request was made to him to teach the San his skills, but the context in which it was made differed radically from the context of 'prayers' to the new moon and Canopus, and the tone seems to be more one of distanced admiration than of supplication. The inspiration for this song might have come more from the stories about him than from the beliefs supporting the observances outlined above, but his association with hunting and his privileged position with regard to animals is also apparent.

Several beliefs respecting |Kaggen which did not have behavioural consequences were also expressed outside of the narratives by some of the informants. |Kaggen was specifically said to have created the eland and the hartebeest and to have given gemsbok, hartebeest, eland, quagga and springbok their colours by feeding them on different kinds of honey (D.F. Bleek 1923: 10). He was also commonly believed to have created the moon. Perhaps significantly, evening dew was said to emanate from the moon and to resemble liquid honey. It was believed that it could revive animals which had been shot by hunters. Honey also appears in the narratives in which |Kaggen creates an eland. |Kaggen rubs the eland with honey thus causing it to grow. Besides his creative powers |Kaggen was also said to have given places their names (L. VIII, (12) 7033 rev.–34 rev.).

The only indication that |Kaggen showed any concern for the San was a single statement expressing the belief that the San had once been springbok and had cried when |Kaggen had shot at them. In consequence of this, |Kaggen mercifully turned them into people (L. V, (4) 6365 rev.). This belief seems to contradict the commonly held view that all the animals were once people and, with the exception of the San, later became animals. It may, however, have been an explanation of why the San alone retained human form.

Another informant expressed the view that |Kaggen was responsible for putting wicked thoughts into the minds of the San, tempting them to do such things as steal sheep or cattle (L. II, (4) 500–03). However, W.H.I. Bleek (1875: 9) felt that this belief might have been influenced by the association of |Kaggen with the Devil, caused by contact with European farmers.

The belief that a being described as 'the chaser of game' was responsible for making the game wild may also have been referring to |Kaggen. It was believed that the game was once tame and could be handled like oxen. The 'chaser of game' made the animals fear men by beating them with a stick because he did not wish the people to kill them. It was also believed that he still continued to chase and beat them from time to time to perpetuate this fear (L. V, (19) 5457–77).

George Stow (*op. cit.*, 129f) gives the following account of a belief held by an unspecified San group about a being who also made the game wild:

> They imagined that in the beginning of time all the animals as well as the Bushmen themselves, were endowed with the attributes of men and the faculty of speech, and that at that time there existed a vicious and quarrelsome being named 'Hoc-'higan, who was always quarrelling with every animal he came near, and trying on that account to injure it. He at length disappeared but they state that none of their race was ever able to discover what became of him, nor is there any tradition to tell where he went. But upon his disappearance he committed, as a parting gift, a deed of vengeance; for immediately afterwards all the animals forsook the abodes of men, and were changed into their present condition, while the Bushmen alone retained the faculties of human beings and the power of speech.

The description of this being so closely resembles |Kaggen as he appears in the narratives collected from the |Xam that an identification of the 'chaser of game' with |Kaggen becomes a possibility.

In summary of the above beliefs it may be said that |Kaggen was regarded as the creator and protector of game, with a special affection for the larger animals. He stood for the world of animals and against the world of men but he did have a creative capacity with which he unintentionally benefited men. As the creator of game and the moon, and the namer of places he can be seen as a transformer of the world. References to him in the narratives as 'Tinderbox' lend support to the suggestion that he was also a fire-bringer. In these respects he appears to come close to one of Paul Radin's two classes of deity in primitive societies. This type of being Radin calls the 'Transformer' and describes in the following terms:

> The Transformer (is) the establisher of the present order of things, utterly non-ethical, only incidentally and inconsistently beneficent; approachable

KAGGEN IN BELIEF AND RITUAL ■ 105

and directly intervening in a very human way in the affairs of the world (Radin 1924: 22f).

The context

|Kaggen was not regarded by the |Xam as the only supernatural being but shared his position with !Khwa and with the spirits of dead shamans. Of these only |Kaggen had creative powers. All of these beings represented threats of various kinds to the |Xam, !Khwa relating primarily to women, |Kaggen to men, and the spirits of dead shamans to all. !Khwa and |Kaggen had a direct bearing on rites of isolation and avoidance. A comparison of these rites usefully serves to illuminate |Kaggen's role.

The hunter's observances with regard to eland and the observances which applied to girls at menarche very closely resembled each other. Indeed, with the exception of a number of elaborations in each case, the eland observances were formally a male counterpart to the girls' rites. In each rite an isolation-hut was built where the subject was expected to lie excluded from the band; both were treated as if they were ill; neither girl nor hunter was allowed to look about them; certain foods were avoided; both were guarded and taken care of by a group of elderly people of their own sex; both were believed to invite danger by their scent, and both were assimilated into the group only gradually. The timespans involved differed greatly but the sequencing and nature of the events was identical.

The beliefs which supported these rites were also very similar. The hunter, by being the medium through which messages could pass to the eland, was no longer simply a person who had brought a benefit to the band but was now regarded as the source of possible loss. He was therefore encouraged to mimic the dying animal in an attempt to exclude undesirable influences upon it. In the same way a girl was regarded as the potential cause of numerous disasters to herself and the band. Both the hunter and the girl had the capacity to harm the band by causing nature to follow its own course beyond the influence of men and against the interests of the band. The isolation of hunters and girls was, therefore, not only analogous in form but also analogous in this aspect of its meaning.

The relationship of |Kaggen and !Khwa to these beliefs was again very similar. Where !Khwa was the agent of danger to menstruating girls and to the band as a whole, |Kaggen was agent of danger (loss of food) to the hunter and his band: !Khwa endangered the humans' capacity to manage the world by threatening death by lightning, transformation into non-human forms, and the conversion of cultural artifacts into their natural constituents. He was, therefore, a counterpart to |Kaggen whose role was to exploit the sympathetic bond between hunter and eland, and thus place the eland beyond the control of the hunters. In this way |Kaggen behaved in accordance with the beliefs about him which equated him with the world of animals which stood apart from, and in opposition to, that of the |Xam and their needs. Thus both |Kaggen and !Khwa may crudely be seen as representing much that was beyond human order – the wild and the natural, the animal and the elemental.

The main differences between the beliefs in these rites lay in those concerning the subject and his or her relationship to danger. Whereas it was said that a girl was excluded from society because, amongst other things, she might become one of !Khwa's creatures, a hunter was encouraged to take on the attributes of the animal. Furthermore the dangers which !Khwa represented were far more serious than the single danger of temporary loss of food which |Kaggen might cause.

Socially the girls' puberty observances and the hunters' observances were also dissimilar. The former related to a specific point of transition in the life of a girl, and her subsequent move from one social category to another. The latter related at most only to temporary subsistence factors. As ceremonial ways of dealing with the relationship between nature and society, however, the affinities between these observances are very striking. The position of |Kaggen within this framework of activity may be seen more clearly when the area of discussion is extended to include other regions of continuity.

Danger, nature and society

Dangers to the band were frequently conceived of through an imagery which employed animals or beings which were only ambiguously human. !Khwa was thought of as a bull; shamans could take the form of beasts of prey and, in the extremities of trance, might become lions who would attack and kill people; menstruating girls were on the point of transformation into frogs, and, it might be added, strangers were thought to approach in the form of lions (see Appendices).

For whatever reasons shamans and menstruating girls were regarded as perpetually verging on the animal world, always capable of the movement from human society to the natural world beyond the social order.

This movement is significantly paralleled both by the reversions which !Khwa could effect on cultural artifacts, and by the variously caused transformations of game from the familiar and predictable into the purely 'wild' state beyond the hunter's skills. It might also be noted that transformations of these kinds were frequently thought to occur through the agency of body fluids such as saliva, perspiration, menstrual blood, the blood of shamans or the blood of animals. This concept of potential transformation from the social, ordered world of humans to the purely natural was one of the most common features of |Xam magico-religious thought. The more social life was threatened, the more the natural world tended to be seen as beyond the powers of men to control.

For survival the band depended upon social stability and a consistent relationship with nature. In both cases between order and disorder there existed a borderland inhabited, in the imagination of the |Xam, by various ambiguous creatures and powers which symbolised all kinds of natural danger: !Khwa, the reptiles of puberty avoidances, the water-side plants which were !Khwa's children (Bleek & Lloyd 1911: 199), beasts of prey causing illness and death, and |Kaggen himself.

This borderland is very close to that conceptual margin described by Edmund Leach (1964: 39) as the gap between 'this world' and 'a hypothetical "other world" which is the antithesis of "this world"'. According to Leach this is the product of a binary antithesis of God and man which religions everywhere attempt to mediate:

> The gap between the two logically distinct categories, this world – other world, is filled with tabooed ambiguity. The gap is bridged by supernatural beings of a highly ambiguous kind – incarnate deities, virgin mothers, supernatural monsters are half man – half beast. These marginal ambiguous creatures are specifically credited with the power of mediating between gods and men. They are the object of the most intense taboos, more sacred than the gods themselves.

For the |Xam, however, the 'other world' contained no deities in Leach's sense, only the hostile forces of nature which threatened the |Xam's attempt to etch order from the natural world. 'This world' on the other hand not only consisted in the order of social life itself but also the order of the |Xam's daily interaction with amenable nature.

The social aspect of order was, to some extent, shaped by its own dangerous elements. As Mary Douglas (1966: 137) has argued:

> The idea of society is a powerful image. It is potent in its own right to control or to stir men to action. This image has form; it has external boundaries, margins, internal structure. Its outlines contain power to reward conformity and repulse attack. There is energy in its margins and unstructured areas. For symbols of society any human experience of structures, margins of boundaries is ready to hand.

The margin to which shamans, menstruating girls, and, predictably, strangers were consigned, was symbolically represented through animal imagery, but the precise social mechanisms which necessitated the separating off of these groups are not always clear. Any attempt, therefore, to fit the often complex symbolism into a purely causal relationship with social factors would be both fruitless and reductionistic. It may be observed, however, that symbols drawn from nature were frequently employed in connection with social elements which were regarded as dangerous, and that the margin between society and nature to which their resultant ambiguity consigned them was also paralleled by the potent symbolism of various exudations of the human body which are 'universally the object of intense taboo' (Leach, *op. cit.*, 38). In this area !Khwa was powerfully operative.

|Kaggen's role as supernatural agent of the world beyond the human world was clearly not unique to him. What was unique to him, however, was that whereas !Khwa operated exclusively at a point of transition within society, |Kaggen, as a supernatural being, did not relate directly to the social structure in any respect. The social genesis of !Khwa's activities was quite absent from |Kaggen's, for it was to the other area of order that |Kaggen predominantly related – the order of the |Xam's interaction with nature.

The |Xam's relationship with nature was patterned and familiar. It had rules of separation as intricate as those that applied to society. Meats had to be separated and distinct from each other or grouped together (Bleek & Lloyd 1911: 271ff), just as groups within society related to each other on the basis of joking or avoidance, male and female, kin or not kin. Both of these areas represented ordered frameworks and both were regarded as particularly vulnerable at certain points. |Kaggen threatened the relationship between men and game – which took the form of sympathy – and !Khwa represented a specific threat which came from within society. As has been seen, there were many rules relating to the sympathetic bond between men and animals beside those in which |Kaggen intervened, just as there were other social rules beside those laid down for menstruating girls but, for whatever reasons, these areas were singled out by the |Xam as ones of singular import.

Two basic points emerge from these facts. Firstly, given the equation of socially dangerous boundaries and symbolic ambiguities (such as the water-bull !Khwa, lion-shamans and frog-girls) |Kaggen's position within the social setting provided for him in the narratives was but a translation of his religious nature into social terms. As a trickster who habitually violated social norms, his narrative persona can be seen to be a corollary of his sacred position on the borderline between amenable and unamenable nature. Just as disjunctions in a hunter's relationship with the game were often equated with disruptive social events, so |Kaggen by symbolising an animal world seeking to exclude men, could also stand for a de-stabilising element in the social order. The opposition of men and animals involved here with regard to |Kaggen was but one aspect of the broader opposition, nature/culture, to which many of the magico-religious ideas of the |Xam related and which also found correspondences and connections within the social order itself.

Secondly, the reason why !Khwa should not have been open to the same narrative re-interpretation, even though he occupied a similar position on the borderline between culture and unamenable nature, was that !Khwa's sacredness operated specifically in connection with social life. While |Kaggen's narrative activities within the social realm could be observed with levity because his supernatural activities had no connection with them, !Khwa could only be taken in deadly seriousness when social rules were involved.

As one who crossed the boundaries of nature (as a supernatural being) and social boundaries (as a fictional character) |Kaggen may be seen as part of the network of beliefs and symbols which gave definition to |Xam society. By violating social norms within the narratives he re-enforced the 'idea of society' and revealed the dangers lurking at its edges. The need for a prescribed order within society, the division of men and women's roles, the importance of sharing and the regulation, through manners, of social intercourse were all things which |Kaggen made manifest by his violation of them. Furthermore the methods which he employed as a supernatural being, attempting to 'cheat' the hunter of his game by the deception of assuming other forms – louse, hare, puffadder – were also translated into narrative terms when |Kaggen appeared as a trickster continually involved in deceptions of a very similar kind, although at a different level of meaning. In these respects, as a violator of useful order and as a deceiver, |Kaggen's supernatural and narrative characters were unified.

His affinities with other 'boundary' beings may well have given his narrative character submerged resonances for the |Xam, for he operated as part of a logical process relating to order which may be seen at work in several other areas of |Xam magico-religious thought. Indeed in |Kaggen a number of social, religious and conceptual elements converge which may go some way to explaining his popularity amongst the |Xam.

Beneficence

There was another side to |Kaggen which has only been touched on briefly, and that was his 'incidentally and inconsistently beneficent' aspect. This aspect was not revealed in any ceremonial behaviour, although the possibility cannot be ruled out that the song to him, recorded by von Wielligh, was a serious request for help.

That the new moon, |Kaggen's creation, was prayed to for help in hunting while |Kaggen himself was not, is consistent with the incidental character of the other benefits which he was said to have brought about. These benefits fell a long way short of the creation of the world or even of the main natural and celestial phenomena: plains, hills, rivers, *veldkos*, fire, wind, the stars and the sun. The narratives collected by von Wielligh, however, suggest that |Kaggen was indirectly responsible for many of these things, although the re-modelling of the narratives by the collector and the over-neat cosmogony which results from it unfortunately renders these narratives useless as evidence. It might, with caution, be supposed nevertheless that |Kaggen's incidental beneficence extended somewhat further than the texts collected by Bleek and Lloyd indicate.

What certainly was attributed to him was the creation of game, the naming of places and existence of the moon. At most it might be said that part of the present order of the world was believed to be caused by him. In contrast to his anti-human aspect these beliefs do not appear to coalesce with any other beliefs in the powers which might influence the lives of the |Xam. Of the positive forces in nature which were said to aid the |Xam – notably !Gi, the power of shamans, the force known amongst the Zu|wasi as N!ow, the new moon, Canopus, and certain occasional magical practices – only the new moon was connected with |Kaggen.

As will be seen below, in some of the narratives |Kaggen's character was wholly beneficent; he intentionally aided people and showed no sign of being the trickster he was in most of the narratives. The dichotomy in his supernatural personality was, therefore, also paralleled in the narratives, and the problem arises as to how far these aspects can be seen to be unified. The same problem presented itself to Paul Radin in his discussion of the trickster/culture hero of the Winnebago Indians of North America. Radin (1956: 125) wrote:

> Are we dealing here with a disintegration of his creative activities or with a merging of two entirely distinct figures, one a deity, the other a hero? ... Has a hero here been elevated to the rank of a god or was Trickster originally a deity with two sides to his nature, one constructive, one destructive, one spiritual, one material? Or again does Trickster antedate the divine, the animal and the human?

Although no absolute answer to this problem can be given with regard to |Kaggen on the basis of the evidence available, the presence, in many other San groups as well as amongst the Khoe-Khoen, of either two deities, one beneficent the other destructive, or single deities with two natures, points to the fact that |Kaggen's nature is neither exceptional nor impossible to interpret.

Relative to the deities of the Central and Northern San, both beneficence and destructiveness were undeveloped in |Kaggen. His negative aspect was not blamed for illness or death, nor was his positive aspect credited with the creation and maintenance of the world. Both of these aspects, however, clearly possessed the potential for elaborations of these kinds, and in other Southern San groups beliefs about |Kaggen indeed were subjected to such elaborations (Campbell 1822, Vol II, 32f; Arbousset & Daumas, *op. cit.*, 253; Orpen, *op. cit.*, 141ff; Stow, *op. cit.*, 134).

Amongst the Zu|wasi today the principal deity, like |Kaggen, has a cycle of narratives relating to him and, although he is regarded as the greater of two deities, his character in the narratives clearly resembles |Kaggen, the trickster, in the |Xam narratives. Of the rift between the religious and narrative of Gao!na, the Zu|wasi deity, Lorna Marshall (1962: 233) writes:

> The !Kung did not bring up the question as to how his nature came to be changed. I surmise that it may have been when the name of Huwe found

its way from the Bergdamma to the !Kung and the name of Hishe from the Auen that certain elements of the present image came in, changing the earthly old Gao!na into a lofty sky god.

This would seem to be a further example of Radin's problem. However, investigations into a posited 'original' San religion have invariably, and perhaps necessarily, dissolved into speculation which has been at best only plausible (see, e.g., P.W. Schmidt 1929). It is apparent nevertheless that a combination of beneficent and anti-human supernatural beings has long been a feature of San religious thought and that in this respect |Kaggen may be regarded as a typical, if undeveloped, example.

That this division should also be reflected in the narratives further underscores the conceptual unity between |Kaggen's supernatural and narrative characters remarked upon above. As will be seen, however, the interpenetration of beneficence and negativity becomes increasingly complex in some of the most semantically dense narratives, revealing an extension of thought suggestive of mythic expression. This in itself may serve as an index to how far and in what ways the narratives may have been regarded as 'true'.

A note on |Kaggen and the *Mantis religiosa*

The name |Kaggen meant 'mantis' and was translated as such by Bleek and Lloyd, but in recent years much confusion has prevailed over the extent to which |Kaggen should be identified with this insect. Mantids were regarded as oracular creatures by many Khoe and San groups in southern Africa, and in the languages of a large number of those groups the word for mantis is the same as the word for their supreme being. In his book *Von Gelben und Schwarzen Buschmännern*, Martin Gusinde (1966: 68ff) has argued that the importance of the insect *Mantis religiosa* has been greatly exaggerated in the literature dealing with San and Khoe religious beliefs, and that much of this exaggeration was due to white settlers who, wishing to deride the indigenous races, deliberately circulated the idea that the mantis was the 'Hottentot's god'. He argued that while it was true that the name for mantis and the name for the supreme being frequently coincided, the attitude of all Khoe and San peoples to these insects was, and is, always far from reverential.

In a very detailed paper Sigrid Schmidt (1973) reiterates Gusinde's view that the religious significance of the mantis has been exaggerated, but enumerates the various beliefs found in southern Africa concerning mantids and their oracular powers. However, Schmidt further asserts that there was no connection between this insect and the trickster, |Kaggen, of |Xam oral tradition, and that the translation by Bleek of the name '|Kaggen' into 'Mantis' was an error. The same view had previously been put by Harold Pager (1971b: 338), who, also following Gusinde, argued:

> In Bleek's collection the Bushman hero *kaggen* (Mantis) is never described as the insect *Mantis religiosa* ... The Bushmen did not pray to him and there is no sign of Mantis worship in the Bleek collection. If Bleek had called the hero solely by his native name *kaggen* the misunderstanding might have been inconsiderable.

Like Schmidt's account, this dismissal of the *Mantis religiosa* from |Xam belief and literature does not fit with the facts.

There can be no doubt that Bleek and Lloyd were justified in rendering the name '|Kaggen' as 'Mantis', firstly because this was how the narrators themselves rendered it when giving the English equivalents of the names of all the creatures appearing in the stories, and secondly because, contrary to Pager's assertion, a verbal identification of |Kaggen is supplied by |Kaggen himself in a speech contained in *Mantis and His Friends*. In this speech |Kaggen asserts that, although he and the members of his family are now people, some day they will be changed into the creatures whose names they bear. His daughter will become a porcupine and live in a hole; his wife, Dassie, will live in a mountain den because her name is 'Dassie', and, he adds 'I shall have wings, I shall fly when I am green. I shall be a little green thing' (D.F. Bleek 1923: 33). Furthermore, in keeping with this association, |Kaggen's flesh is described as being yellow-green in many of the original texts. There seems, therefore, as much justification for translating the name '|Kaggen' as 'Mantis' in the narratives as there is for translating any of the other animal names into their English equivalents.

There is, however, undoubtedly some confusion in the texts where matters of religious belief are concerned. This confusion is caused by the fact that there appear to have been certain beliefs about mantids held by the |Xam, which ought to be distinguished from beliefs about |Kaggen. There are very few occasions in the texts when the beliefs about mantids are alluded to and none of them is very clear. ||Kabbo was said by |Hang ‡kass'o to be a |kaggen ka !kui, 'mantis man' (D.F. Bleek 1931–36, Part VIII, 143), having a special relationship with mantids in the same way that certain !giten had a special relationship with locusts and game animals (see Appendix B). As there is no evidence that mantids were eaten, it is likely that this relationship involved the use of mantids as oracular creatures, most probably with regard to the movements of game. The possibility of an association of some kind between mantids and game animals is also furthered by comments on Bushman rock paintings copied by Stow which indicate a connection between this insect and the hartebeest (Stow & Bleek, *op. cit.*, texts facing plates 50 and 52).

This much being said, there still remain remarks by informants which indubitably refer to |Kaggen as having a mantis-like appearance, and which cannot be explained away in terms of mistranslation. The most unequivocal remarks are to be found in *Mantis and His Friends* (*op. cit.*, 10) where the head of the hartebeest is said to resemble |Kaggen's head. In another publication it is further explained that this resemblance was due to the fact that the hartebeests' horns turn back like |Kaggen's antennae (Stow & Bleek, *loc. cit.*) In the original text (L. V (6) 4414 rev. 18 rev.) there is no question that this resemblance was simply between a mantis and a hartebeest. The resemblance was offered as a partial explanation for the hartebeests' sense of belonging to |Kaggen.

Although the information concerning the nature of |Kaggen's identification with the *Mantis religiosa* is not detailed, there is certainly sufficient to rule out the possibility of a simple linguistic error by the collectors. However, because |Kaggen was, before all else, a supernatural being of ambivalent form, his name will remain untranslated in this book to avoid over-emphasis on an aspect of the beliefs about him which is certainly in need of further explication.[2]

Notes

1 For a note on this association see 'A note on |Kaggen and the *Mantis religiosa*', page 112.

2 A discussion of why the *Mantis religiosa* might have been an appropriate subject for San religious belief may be found in Holm (1965: 45ff).

7

The |Kaggen narratives (1): characters and content

Of the 21 narratives relating to |Kaggen collected by Bleek and Lloyd, 15 emphasise |Kaggen's quarrelsome, greedy and anti-social nature, while the remaining six portray him as primarily benevolent and helpful. His character in this latter group of narratives most closely resembles the |Kaggen of von Wielligh's collection – that of the benevolent overseer intervening helpfully in the affairs of others. While there are several points of overlap between these two groups, so radical is the difference between the character of |Kaggen in each group, and so different is his role within the narratives, that it is necessary to treat them separately.

Paul Radin discovered a similar dichotomy in the trickster cycle of the Winnebago Indians but regarded it as the intrusion of one distinct group of culture-hero narratives upon another purely trickster-centred cycle (Radin 1956: 155ff). However, given |Kaggen's dual religious nature there are more grounds for assuming that the |Xam narratives reveal a genuine ambiguity concerning |Kaggen's character than that they represent a welding together of disparate groups.

What shall be termed 'Group A' contains the following narratives:[1]

M1. |Kaggen and the Eland (five versions)
M2. |Kaggen and !Goe !kweitəntu (three versions)
M3. A Visit to the Lions (two versions)
M4. |Kaggen and the Cat (two versions)
M5. |Kaggen and the Aard-wolf (two versions)
M6. !Gãunu ts'axau and the Baboons (one version)
M7. |Kaggen and the Magic Bird (two versions)

M8. |Kaggen Takes Away the Ticks' Sheep (three versions)

M9. |Kaggen and ‖Kwai-hɛm (two versions)

M10. |Kaggen and the Elephants (two versions)

M11. |Kaggen, |Kwammang-a and the Dassies (three versions)

M12. |Kaggen and the Koro-twi:tən (one version)

M13. |Kaggen and |Ku-te-!gaua (one version)

M14. |Kaggen Assumes the Form of a Hartebeest (one version)

M15. |Kaggen and the Leopard Tortoise (one version)

Group B contains:

M16. |Kaggen, the |Kain-|kai:n and the Girls (one version)

M17. The Wildebeest, the Mice and the Quaggas (one version)

M18. The Lizard, his Daughter and the Mice (one version)

M19. The Mice and the Beetle (one version)

M20. The Blue Crane's Story (one version)

M21. The Children and the !Khwai-!khwai (one version)[2]

The validity of this division will become more apparent as the discussion proceeds but, apart from the difference in |Kaggen's character in each group, certain other differences may also be mentioned at this stage. All group A narratives situate |Kaggen within the same family unit. This family can best be represented follows:[3]

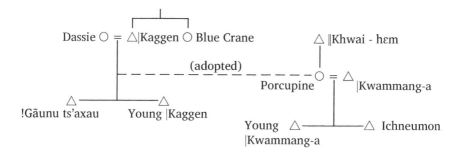

Whenever |Kaggen returns from an adventure it is usually to the lecturing of the Ichneumon, the silent disapproval of |Kwammang-a, and the scorn of the Dassie and the Porcupine. The real father of the Porcupine, ‖Khwai-hɛm, lives elsewhere and Gãunu ts'axau, Young |Kaggen and Young |Kwammang-a each only feature in isolated narratives. A daughter of |Kaggen, called K"we

|nang ‖kain-tu, was also mentioned by one informant but no narratives were collected which feature her. |Kaggen also has another sister who is the mother of a young springbok but again she only features in one narrative and her name is not given. The main part of this family group to feature regularly in the narratives consists of Dassie, |Kaggen, Porcupine, |Kwammang-a and the Ichneumon. In this group of narratives |Kaggen is always the protagonist.

In group B, this family group is rarely mentioned and never has any bearing on the plots, while |Kaggen's role is primarily that of aiding the protagonist who is usually a member of some other family. This lack of emphasis on |Kaggen's character and family life is also a feature of the narratives collected by von Wielligh.

A corollary of the feature of group B is that the absence of an amoral and childlike element in |Kaggen's character rules out the necessity for the moral and practical educative statements, usually made by the Ichneumon for |Kaggen's benefit, which are present in nearly all group A narratives. These educative passages are so much a part of group A that their absence from group B provides further reasons for treating the two groups under separate headings.

Group A

The family

The family unit featured in this group evinces no surprising characteristics *vis-à-vis* what is known of |Xam social structure. The two most dominant characters are |Kaggen and the Ichneumon, who would be in a joking relationship with each other in real life and who, indeed, are clearly in this relationship in the narratives. Their relationship is also strengthened by the fact that whereas |Xam males regarded their fathers' parents as their 'lent' grandparents, they regarded their mothers' parents as their 'real' grandparents. Thus the formal relationship between |Kaggen and the Ichneumon was doubly close. In contrast to this, |Kwammang-a and |Kaggen were in a mutual avoidance relationship and this is emphasised by the necessity for |Kwammang-a to address all of his comments to |Kaggen through his son the Ichneumon. The critical silence of |Kwammang-a, so frequently mentioned in the narratives, forms a strong contrast to the incessant chattering of |Kaggen and the Ichneumon, and further serves to emphasise the impulsive freedoms assumed by |Kaggen, as against the strong and reliable virtues of |Kwammang-a. In one of the narratives |Kaggen refers to |Kwammang-a as 'my sister's son' but as there are no indications given by any of the informants that this was the case, and as the relationship between a man and his sister's son was one of especial closeness in |Xam society, it must be assumed that |Kaggen was, true to character, verbally reversing and, for the audience, drawing attention to, the true state of the case.

In none of the narratives are siblings shown in any kind of relationship together, although the affection between |Kaggen and the Blue Crane is sometimes made explicit. |Kaggen and the Blue Crane are the oldest members of the family and this may have been a reflection of |Xam social organisation for, although very little is known about this aspect of |Xam life, recent studies have shown that in extant San groups the individual camp is founded on a core kin group consisting of siblings, both brothers and sisters, and their offspring of both sexes (Lee 1972d: 351ff).

Relationships between spouses are equally undeveloped in these narratives. Dassie and Porcupine play, for the most part, very minor roles and are seen to be devoted partners. Dassie, however, is not uncritical of |Kaggen for his generally anti-social behaviour. Furthermore, while |Kwammang-a is seen as the model of a good and manly husband, |Kaggen is regarded as constantly failing in his obligations to provide food for his wife. It is the Ichneumon, however, not Dassie, who reprimands |Kaggen for this and berates |Kaggen for continually fighting with people instead of hunting for food. 'We do not eat people but animals,' he asserts. 'How can Dassie cook food if you provide none.' Between parents and children relationships are uniformly conventional. |Kaggen is tender-hearted and protective towards his own offspring if a little feminine in his emotional response to them. |Kwammang-a is more recognisably fatherly, rebuking and silencing the Ichneumon when necessary and approximating more closely than |Kaggen to the ideal father type. |Kaggen does not make the same displays of affection to Porcupine that he does to his natural children although he was said to have adopted her because she found living with her real father, ||Khwai-hɛm, impossible. The Porcupine is, herself, again conventionally close to her own children and prey to |Kaggen's deliberate attempt to frighten her about the Ichneumon's safety in 'A visit to the Lions' (M3) but Dassie is not seen in any context with her own children – a fact which may reflect the weight given to the effeminacy of |Kaggen's parental instincts.

Visits to relatives, a common occurrence in |Xam life, also occur in some of the narratives. These visits are usually initiated by |Kwammang-a.

On every occasion, however, |Kaggen spoils the sociability of the event by being rude or by playing tricks on his hosts, and again the worthy, social virtues of |Kwammang-a are seen in contrast to the unrelenting anti-social behaviour of |Kaggen.

Thus the role of the family in these narratives draws attention to two basic sets of contrasts: the joking and avoidance relationships, and the functioning husband/wife alliance of |Kwammang-a and Porcupine as against the disfunctioning alliance of |Kaggen and Dassie. However, the family group provides the background to – not the centre of – the actions in these narratives, which grow more out of |Kaggen's relationship with the outside world than from his relationship with his family. It is, however, from this home base that |Kaggen sets out on each of his adventures and it is here, too, that he unwillingly receives the knowledge and wisdom of his society. The family functions in these narratives mainly in the contrast between the morality and social norms of |Kaggen's world and his ignorance and violation of them, but it is |Kaggen's response to the world that makes it necessary for the family ideologues to articulate those norms.

The strong educative elements in these narratives might suggest that they were primarily aimed at child audiences. Indeed, a common feature of the educative passages is the emphasis which the Ichneumon places on the fact that he, a child, is teaching an old man who should know better – a reversal of the customary situation which may well have appealed to child audiences. However, amongst the Zu|wasi today narratives containing violations of the social order, which closely resemble |Kaggen's actions, are told to a mainly adult audience and are greatly cherished. Megan Biesele (*op. cit.*, 100) writes:

> The stories are heard with anything but awed reverence. Instead, amazed indignation greets the outrageous or bumbling adventures of the long-ago people. !Kung have no explanation for why their ancestors related to them such absurdities. 'Hey! The doings of the ancient times were foul, I tell you!' was how |asa n!na ended some of her stories.

It is, therefore, worth looking further than the apparent didactic aspect of these narratives to discover something of the emotive and conceptual resonances contained in them. An examination of |Kaggen's character provides a useful starting point.

|Kaggen

Like the trickster of the Winnebago Indians (Radin 1956: 133) |Kaggen is instinctual and undifferentiating. He always acts on impulse, and frequently fails to comprehend not only social mores but also other very basic factors such as the importance of artefacts designed to ensure economic survival. Thus in M12, having been shown how to get at ants' chrysalids with ease, |Kaggen destroys his bow, his arrows and his quiver, breaks his digging-stick and splits the digging-stone weight (an article that takes a great deal of time and effort to produce). He is then without any means of providing food and utterly vulnerable. Indeed, he has no conception of prudence, imagining always that somehow he will be provided for without bothering with practical matters. Unlike the Winnebago trickster, however, his sense of things never improves. His encounters do not teach him anything. There is no gradual journey to maturity and he remains forever a child. It is frequently repeated in the narratives that |Kaggen has 'never grown up' and that he 'does not act like a grown-up person', and in this respect he does not change.

His belligerency, however, is far from childlike. He often picks fights for no reason, and even when he meets someone who offers to help him in some way he manages to offend them and provoke a conflict. He invariably returns home bruised and beaten, and only affects his revenge by applying information given to him by his family, so that, while he is impulsively pugnacious, he is not at all tough or self-sufficient with respect to fighting. In a straight fight he is very vulnerable and it is for this reason that he tries to ensure that no fight is 'straight', taking unfair advantage of his opponents whenever he is able.

One of the most common sources of conflict between |Kaggen and the people he encounters is his greed. What he is not given he attempts to take by force or trickery, and when he is given food he always attempts to take more than his fair share. He has no conception of the proportioning of food – to the |Xam a crucial sense – although he clearly recognizes that others do, for he uses it as an excuse for robbing the Koro-twi:tən and |Ku-te-!gaua (M12 and M13) of their rightful shares, on the grounds that, in each case, they had too much.

This kind of appeal to rights is, however, uncharacteristic. Most of his self-justification in no way exposes contradictions in the moral system or illuminates hypocrisies or discontinuities in the way people were expected to relate to each other. He is constantly self-justificatory but it is most often on the grounds of his anger at certain characters for beating him in fights which he himself had provoked – rarely on the basis of actual injustices. Even when making a major cultural contribution to the San, by stealing the fire, cooking utensils, houses and sheep away from the Ticks (M8) – a feat which he accomplishes with the pronouncement, 'In these pots here shall the Flat People someday cook for they shall have fire' – he ignores the fact that he went among strangers with the intention of taking food and claims instead that 'it seemed right to me because those people attacked me'.

This kind of self-justification is his only defence against criticism but he never feels that he needs any better for he is certain of his own value and importance. Constantly he boasts that he is |Kaggen and no-one is his equal, and, on one occasion, that he is a supernatural being who knows everything. It is this same self-aggrandisement that makes him deny to his enemies that he receives information from his family which enables him to win fights. He cannot bear to be thought of as weak or unresourceful, and he persists in his pretences even in the face of plain refutation. He is content to admit his deceptions to the Ichneumon, however, and chatters boastfully about his follies, impervious to the impression he is making on his listener.

Given |Kaggen's belief in his moral autonomy, it is not surprising to find him being merciless to those weaker than himself or temporarily in his power. When the Elephants leave their child in place of the child which |Kaggen is supposed to be looking after (M10), he clubs it to death before setting off to retrieve his ward. The same thoughtless brutality marks his initial encounter with the child at the Tick's house (M8): 'As for this child, I will first eat till I am satisfied then I will knock him down, for he has no sense', he says. And once he discovers how to combat !Goe !kweitəntu (M2) and the Cat (M4) he is equally relentless.

With all this aggression, greed and self-will he is, in physical terms, defenceless and can be emotionally very tender. Porcupine calls him 'mild', 'cowardly' and 'a runaway'. His attachment to !Gāunu ts'axau in M6 leads him to cry bitterly at his son's fate, in a way that would be impossible for the well-controlled |Kwammang-a, as does his love for his creation, the eland, when it is killed (M1). In this respect, too, he may be regarded as child-like, while at another level he may be seen as the stereotypical weak man, reflecting in his bravado and outward aggressiveness a soft centre.

He does, however, have his own peculiar strengths and is not quite as uniformly cowardly as the Porcupine believes. His encounter with the Elephants is brave, even though his success depends more on trickery than on physical prowess. However, his fighting is usually more the product of foolhardiness and self-overestimation than of courage.

His real strength lies in his magical attributes and he is the only member of his family to possess any. He can acquire wings at will to escape from his enemies; his possessions all have the power of flight, independent movement and speech, and serve him faithfully when he is forced to extricate himself from a difficult or threatening situation.[4] He also changes the world by dreaming. In M14 he changes himself into a hartebeest and thus may be said to have the same formal ambivalence in fiction that he has in the realm of religious belief.

He has great creative powers. He makes an eland out of a piece of |Kwammang-a's shoe. He creates the moon, thus bringing light in the night for all men ever after, and, by dreaming, he conjures the Tick's possessions to rise into the air and come to his home, thus providing the San with all the necessities of daily life. Thus his claim to be a supernatural being with magical powers and omniscience is not at all an idle boast – even if, in mundane, practical matters and social manners he is as unskilled as a child. It is in his very freedom from the practical, mundane world of adults that he finds a realm of possibility for re-arranging the order of things through a spontaneity unrestrained by social and economic obligations, or rational and realistic thought. His weaknesses are, indeed, the source of his strength, for, while |Kwammang-a, the sensible, adult realist, makes a success of being a husband and father, |Kaggen, denied those attributes, transcends the limits of human potential to become a genuinely magical figure while still retaining his humanness.

In connection with |Kaggen's creative powers, it is worth noting that the trace of mild effeminacy in his character, remarked upon above, is not an isolated phenomenon. It is also made plain in the narratives that |Kaggen habitually uses a weighted digging-stick, although amongst the |Xam it was only the women who did this, the men using the stick unweighted. This association of |Kaggen with the female sex is further supported by the fact that he is always said to be left-handed. While this may have been simply another example of his awry relationship with his surroundings, the left hand was regarded by the |Xam as the female hand, and the right hand as the male.[5] A further example of this opposition may be seen in the ceremonial destruction of ‖Khwai-hɛm (M9) where the mild and tearful Young |Kaggen, said to resemble his father, stands to one side of the monster holding a heated spear in his left hand, while brave Young |Kwammang-a, said to resemble his father, stands to the other, holding a heated spear in his right hand. These factors may suggest that the association of |Kaggen with the insect whose name he bears – the female of which, so much larger than the male, devours its sexual partners during intercourse – may not be accidental, and that the sexual ambivalence connected with other trickster figures may also be present in |Kaggen, albeit in unformed or submerged ways. |Kaggen's creative powers may be supported by this feminine association as well as by his freedom from constraints.

|Kaggen as trickster

Given this child-like, willful, anti-social old man with magical powers it is useful to examine the ways in which he can be regarded as a trickster.

Firstly it may be observed that |Kaggen indulges in at least four kinds of tricks. These may be summarized as:

(a) Naughty pranks, used to merely disrupt some normal social situation.
(b) Clever tricks, involving intelligence and resourcefulness.
(c) Strategic tricks, involving a move which anticipates a response of which he intends to, and does, take advantage.
(d) Magical tricks, especially for extrication.

A few examples will serve to clarify these types.

Type a (naughty)

In M3 he knowingly frightens a child, and this angers the child's mother. |Kaggen has to effect his escape. The social ease is disrupted but it has brought no advantage to |Kaggen nor was it intended to.

Type b (clever)

In M10 his quick thinking gains him entrance to the Elephant's stomach where he retrieves the stolen child, injures the Elephant and makes his escape through a crowd of hostile Elephants.

Type c (strategic)

In M6 he uses a strategic trick to retrieve his son !Gãunu ts'axau. He asks if he may join in the catching game which the Baboons are playing with his son's eye (all that remains of his son). He plays for a short while and then manages to hide the eye which he then claims is lost. The Baboons do not believe him and beat him severely but the objective of the strategy is achieved and he escapes with the eye.

Type d (magical)

Magical tricks occur in the majority of narratives in the form of extrication devices but also occasionally in other guises. The elevation and transportation of the Ticks's belongings in M8, and the creation of the moon are both of this kind, (although the latter is also, strictly speaking, an extrication device albeit an atypical one).

Narratives almost always contain magical tricks as well as any of the other trick types, but rarely do trick types (a), (b) and (c) feature in any combination in a single narrative.

Nearly all of the narratives feature |Kaggen attempting to deceive someone, and at the lowest level this takes the form of a blatant lie which no character could fail to see through. Simple lying, cannot, therefore, valuably be included as a trick *per se*, even if it contributes to the trickery. The picking of fights, however, in which |Kaggen commonly indulges, must be included in type (a) naughty, anti-social pranks; although clearly this is a weak form of trick, infrequently involving deception and occasionally only resulting in disaster for |Kaggen.

|Kaggen is not always the only person in the narrative to indulge in tricks. Other characters occasionally use tricks against him. The Aardwolf (M5) does just this, employing a strategic trick against |Kaggen who is trying to take a child away from her. The Ticks (M8) and the Leopard Tortoise (M15) also use deceptions in order to assail him. However, it is |Kaggen whose trickery dominates these narratives, and it is his objectives which govern the plots.

Before discussing distribution of trick-types throughout group A, something should first be said about |Kaggen's objectives, for these do shed light on some of the values which are at stake in the narratives.

Greed and belligerency are the most common features of |Kaggen's interaction with other creatures, and are integral to his objectives in many cases. Robert Plant Armstrong's comparison of Ikto, the trickster of the Dakota Indians of the United States, and Anansi as he appears in the narratives of the Bush Negroes of Paromaribo, Dutch Guiana, shows a contrast which clearly also relates to |Kaggen:

In the Dakota stories, Ikto seems pre-eminently concerned with self-gratification at the expense of those who can be duped. Because of his divine nature, chances of conquest are precluded. Anansi, on the other hand, while undeniably interested in satisfying his desires, seems to be more intrigued with overcoming those more powerful than he.

Specifically, Ikto violates incest taboos which are of great importance amongst the Dakota; Anansi violates the pattern of authority, so important in the African cultures from which these people came, though this violation occurs in the world of perhaps unconscious allegory (Armstrong 1972: 191).

In the case of |Kaggen, both of these objectives – self-gratification and overcoming the powerful – are apparent. Thus one finds M5, M7, M12, and M13 having self-gratification as |Kaggen's objective, and M1, M2, M4, M6, M8, M10, where |Kaggen is predominantly concerned with overcoming those more powerful than himself.

The equation of Anansi and complex authority structures is a suggestive one, yet it is difficult to see how this might apply to |Kaggen, for the |Xam, like all other San groups, are famous for their lack of social stratification. However, in connection with this equation, research by John M. Roberts, Brian Sutton-Smith and Adam Kendon indicates an interesting relationship between games of strategy, folktales with strategic outcomes, and complex societies. Their research showed that:

(a) The strategic mode of competition is modelled in both games and folk tales in a number of cultures; (b) where the strategic mode is modelled in one medium (i.e. games) it is likely to be with both obedience training and cultural complexity (Roberts, Sutton-Smith & Kendon 1972: 206f).

While this research was more conclusive with regard to games than it was to folktales, it would seem valuable to compare the distribution of trick-types in those |Kaggen narratives where the dominant objective is overcoming the powerful, and those where self-gratification is the objective, in order to discover any connection that might obtain between strategy and overcoming the powerful. Under the definition of strategy proposed by Roberts, Sutton-Smith & Kendon (*ibid.*, 201) trick-types (b) and (c) would both be regarded as strategic. The following tables show the distribution of trick types throughout both groups:

Objective: Overcoming the Powerful			Objective: Self-gratification		
Narrative	Trick-Type		Narrative	Trick-Type	
M1	b	D⁶	M5	a	d
M2	a		M7	a	
M4	a	d			
M6	c	D	M12	a	
M8	a	D	M13	a	d
M10	b	d			

(The upper case D indicates tricks other than those used for extrication.) In the remaining narratives, where the objectives are of a different order, the following distribution is found:

Narrative	Trick-Type	
M3	a	d
M9	a	D
M11	a	
M14	c	d
M15	a	d

By aggregating trick-types (b) and (c) in accordance with Roberts, Sutton-Smith and Kendon's definition, the clustering of (b) and (c) within the first group, and the use of special magical effects, seems illuminating *vis-à-vis* the dichotomy indicated by Armstrong. The tables here clearly show how |Kaggen's response to the powerful combines intelligence, strategy and magic. Furthermore in M2 and M4, where this is not the case, |Kaggen's opponents are only more powerful than he by virtue of his ignorance, not by their own innate strength: a situation of which |Kaggen soon learns to take advantage.

However, the majority of these (11 out of 15) involve trick-type (a) and, with the exception of M14, the strategic mode is totally absent. This is, of course, what might be expected of trickster narratives collected from a very weakly stratified society. Here the similarities between Ikto, the Dakota Indian trickster, and |Kaggen become more obvious than they were from the initial simple comparison of objectives. The wide distribution of trick-type (d) provides further grounds for this association for, as Armstrong points out,

Ikto's nature was divine. Furthermore, as 'Ikto violates incest taboos which are of great importance among the Dakota' (Armstrong 1972: 191), the grounds for examining |Kaggen with reference to lateral social constraints becomes increasingly apparent.

The opponents

A consideration of the types of opponent which |Kaggen encounters is instructive in situating his success or failure with these tricks. The conflicts in which |Kaggen places himself are of many kinds but are largely determined by the kind of adversaries or victims which he encounters. These fall broadly into three main groups:

(1) Distant kin (usually represented as groups, e.g. Lions, Dassies).
(2) Creatures encountered on their own while |Kaggen is out supposedly hunting, e.g. Koro-twi:tən, !Ku-te-!gaua.
(3) Strangers who should not be visited, e.g. Ticks, Elephants, Baboons.

These characters, like |Kaggen and his family, are represented as humans but with some of the characteristics of the animals which they will become in time. The Elephants have trunks; the Lions are very menacing; the Ticks hide in the Sheep's wool. In M11 the Dassies are said to live with the Bees, and this is a reflection of the fact that Dassies do burrow in just the kind of rocky hillocks where bees also build their nests. As has been seen in other narratives outside of the |Kaggen group, different groups of animal characters are often said to live together, and the implication seems to be that such groupings represent alliances between different families as they might occur in real life. The world of narratives is, in consequence, a strange mixture of the social and the natural. This ambiguity occasionally makes it difficult to see whether the lesson for |Kaggen, in any narrative, is meant to be concerned with social relationships or with instructions on how to deal with certain animals. In spite of such problems it is generally true that where |Kaggen has dealings with distant kin his ignorance is to be of social behaviour, and where he has dealings with creatures like the Magic Bird (M7) or !Goe !kweitəntu (M2) his ignorance is of practical matters. As for strangers, |Kaggen usually lacks a sense of the danger he places himself in by going amongst them. The lesson which he receives but fails to learn is 'We do not visit strangers' houses'.

|Kaggen's success in his conflicts with these adversaries is very mixed. Some of his distant kin manage to get the better of him and others are bested by him. The same applies to the creatures whom he meets while out hunting. However, when strangers are represented as groups rather than stray individuals, they are always shown as strong and very hostile, and are always bested in some way by |Kaggen. This may reflect something of the |Xam attitude toward their physically powerful neighbours, the Khoe-khoen, the Europeans, and Bantu-speaking peoples. The Ticks in M8, for example, are said to be black people who keep sheep and who are very strong. Their contrasting with |Kaggen and, indeed, in one version, with the San who heard and told these stories, clearly points to an articulation of race conflict situations, and an attempt to preserve racial dignity in the face of physical superiority. Such an emphasis on conflict with other races might also be a reflection of the San's long history of defeat, and may account for the dominance of strategic tricks in those narratives where groups of strangers are represented, for, in some ways, the power of such neighbours has affinities with the vertical power of strongly stratified societies.

|Kaggen and social norms

In pursuing the clue offered by the Dakota Indian trickster-figure, some investigation of social values, the lateral constraints which articulate those values, and |Kaggen, is of considerable importance. Writing of the Zu|wa trickster, Megan Biesele (n.d.) states that

> Stories featuring God ... have to to with the tricks he plays on his wives and has played on him in turn. These stories are bawdy and scatological and are the cause of great hilarity among the Zu|wasi.

However, these same narratives

> explore some of the fundamental problem points of living: sex, excrement, sharing and cooking and eating food, the division of labour and the battle of power between the sexes.

These interests reflect another common aspect of the self-gratifying, foolish trickster-figure which Ruth Finnegan (1970: 352) emphasises when she writes:

(The trickster) can be adapted to express the idea of opposition to the normal world or of the distortion of accepted human and social values. This applies particularly when the trickster-figure is made not only wily but also in some way inordinate and outrageous – gluttonous, uninhibited, stupid, unscrupulous, constantly over-reaching himself. Here the trickster is being represented as a kind of mirror-image of respectable human society, reflecting the opposite of the normally approved or expected character and behaviour.

In the case of the Zu|wa trickster this, indeed, appears to be true, and |Kaggen also evinces just this syndrome. He is predominantly stupid, uninhibited etc., and is most frequently presented as violating social norms. Not only this, but in those narratives where he does not display foolishness, specifically those containing trick-types (b) and (c), the violation of social norms is either weak or absent. (When this equation is transposed to group B it is interesting to find a positive and responsible attitude in |Kaggen combined with wisdom and supernatural knowledge.)

|Kaggen's propensity for anti-social behaviour is founded upon his habitual belligerence and his ignorance not only of how to behave in social situations but also of facts about the habits of other creatures. He does not know how to catch and kill a cat; he does not know that a certain ostrich is magical and should be treated with caution; he does not know that !Goe !kweitəntu's eyes are in his feet, and so on. In all of these matters he has to receive instruction from the Ichneumon. This kind of ignorance is not, of course, anti-social as such but it does stem from a lack of involvement with his society, for knowledge is largely socially owned not acquired by each individual by personal observation. His ignorance of practical matters is a natural consequence of his nonsocial nature.[7]

His belligerence is blatantly anti-social, however, and his tendency to get into trouble is regarded by his family as a misuse of his energies when he should be hunting for food. Not only is his fighting anti-social in its own right but it also shows a disregard for proper responsibility.

In many narratives |Kaggen violates rules which were absolutely fundamental to social life amongst the |Xam. In M12 and M13 his greed leads him to disregard his obligations to share food with those who had helped him to acquire it, and in M5 he attempts to defraud the Aardwolf into giving him more than he could rightfully expect. In a society where food distribution was at the heart of social intercourse, these acts would have been regarded as quite outrageous.

His attitude to kin evinced in his obliviousness to economic responsibilities is equally apparent when he visits other families. In M11, for example, while |Kwammang-a is respectful and reserved when visiting the Dassies, |Kaggen is garrulous and impish. He plays with the children and alarms them. He tells a 'foul' story which offends and angers his hosts, and the consequence of his behaviour is that both he and |Kwammang-a become buried in stones.

Good relations with other bands were of great importance to the |Xam because fluctuating resources of water over a long period meant a band might at any time temporarily join with another band which was better situated. Amongst the Zu|wasi today a network of bonds between even quite distanced groups ensures the long-term survival of all the bands within the area, where over a period of many years rainfall fluctuates and waterholes temporarily dry up (Lee 1972b). Marriage, the exchange of gifts, and friendly visiting provides the social basis for the good relations necessary to such interdependence. It is highly likely that the |Xam had some similar system. Hence |Kaggen's bad social manners would have been felt to be more than simply a playful disrespect of conventions, but an erosion of the bonds which ensured survival.

In M14 |Kaggen does not so much himself contradict expected behaviour as trick others into doing so. This narrative, collected by both Bleek and, apparently separately, von Wielligh (*op. cit.*, Vol 1, 9), has also recently been collected from the Zu|wasi with some interesting modifications. In Bleek's version |Kaggen transforms himself into a dead hartebeest and lies in the path of a group of young girls who are stated to be seeking *gambroo*, a type of cucumber. |Kaggen's intention is that they should cut him up with stone knives – just as in his supernatural role he was said to take the form of a hare so that hunters would kill him. The cutting up of game was, of course, men's work. The girls, by giving up their collection of *veldkos* (women's work), to take advantage of what they believed to be a piece of good fortune, were, therefore, not behaving in accordance with their conventional role.[8]

Having cut up the hartebeest and loaded it onto their backs the girls attempt to carry it home. |Kaggen, however, moves and talks causing the girls to drop the pieces which quickly reassemble in the form of a man who chases them until they are near their home. When they reach home and tell their parents of what happened, the parents tell the children that it was

|Kaggen whom they had cut up. No reprimand is given by the parents and no direct statement is made to the effect that the girls had been doing anything wrong by cutting up the animal. The narrator, however, was at pains to specify that they intended to collect *veldkos* and this would appear to be an important contrast to what actually happened.

That a group of young girls are menaced by a man could suggest that the threat behind |Kaggen's actions was sexual. As only one version of this narrative was taken down by Bleek and von Wielligh's version is given only briefly in Afrikaans, it is impossible to tell if this was so. However the version recently collected by Megan Biesele from the Zu|wasi does describe an explicitly sexual intention on the part of the central character, the God-trickster, Kauha, who again transforms himself into meat with the intention that he should be carried on the back of a young woman who was supposed to be collecting *veldkos* (Biesele 1975: 115f).

Even if Bleek's version of this narrative was not intended to be overtly didactic, the association of females with the cutting up of meat and the subsequent threat, of whatever kind, from |Kaggen would appear to indicate that at least one dynamic of the narrative lies in its contrast of the sexes. Furthermore, the narrator pointed out that as |Kaggen chased the girls he jogged his left shoulder blade because he is a left-handed man (Bleek & Lloyd 1911: 11). Thus while the girls perform an act associated with men, |Kaggen is described in a masculine form but with an emphatic element symbolically associated with the female sex. The boundaries between male and female are therefore undermined at a symbolic level behind the overt drama of the plot. The important point, however, is that |Kaggen wills the whole situation and the responsibility for this confusion of male and female roles is his.

These, then, are some of the ways in which |Kaggen flouts social norms and ignores the constraints which his family wish to apply to him through the traditional socialising devices. The men of his family reprimand him and the women laugh at him but he remains unaltered by both criticism and scorn.

In spite of all |Kaggen's faults, however, he is no unmitigated villain. Our perception of him is also coloured by the tolerance and indulgence of him shown by the Ichneumon, Dassie and the Blue Crane in their pity for him whenever he is injured by his opponents. Like Ture, the Zande trickster, he is an 'engaging rogue' (Evans-Pritchard 1967: 30), and Evans-Pritchard might well have been writing of |Kaggen when he wrote of Ture:

There is another side of his character, which even to us is appealing: his whimsical fooling, recklessness, impetuosity, puckish irresponsibility, his childish desire to show how clever he is ... and his flouting of every convention (*ibid.*, 28).

Like Ture, too, he has an 'endearing innocence' and

One is sorry for him when his cocksureness gets him into trouble, when he overreaches himself and sheds frustrated tears. Then he is pathetic (*ibid.*, 28f).

When Evans-Pritchard suggests that, 'Perhaps Ture also appeals to the Azande because he does what he pleases, what in their hearts they would like to do themselves' (*ibid.*, 29) he also comes close to Dorothea Bleek's opinion of |Kaggen:

|Kaggen seems to me to be just a sort of dream Bushman; and the life he and his people live gives a very good picture of real Bushman family life a century ago, though painted in fanciful tints (D.F. Bleek 1923: vi).

|Kaggen in group A, therefore, is no evil-doer or destroyer. Indeed, his antics, while certainly very anti-social, could never be described as evil. Rather, he is a 'mischief-maker' (D.F. Bleek 1929a: 305), but 'at all times very human' (D.F. Bleek 1923: v); ambiguously of the world yet opposed to its order. It is in this spirit that he violates the norms of |Xam life.

Group B

The six narratives which constitute this group were collected from only one informant, |Hang ǂkass'o, who also gave versions of many narratives from group A. These narratives possess the common feature of showing |Kaggen as a benign and helpful figure as opposed to the trickster he is in group A. Von Wielligh's collection – however poorly authenticated – tends to render it unlikely that this emphasis on |Kaggen's helpfulness and benignity was the exclusive initiative of one man, however.

As has been observed above, these narratives display |Kaggen as a responsible being. M17, M18, and M19 all describe how the Longnosed Mice are duped and killed by someone (a different person in each case). |Kaggen, not situated in his usual family group, dreams that this is happening and informs the Striped Mouse who poses as another victim but manages to overcome the aggressor and secure the revival of the dead Longnosed Mice. The credit for the success of the Striped Mouse goes mainly to |Kaggen, for, as the informant asserts: 'The Striped Mouse was clever but |Kaggen was the one who dreamed of what was happening and told the Striped Mouse about it' (*ibid.*, 59).

All three narratives conclude with the marriage of the Striped Mouse – in M17 and M19 to a Longnosed Mouse, in M18 to the daughter of the aggressor. Thus a situation of conflict is resolved by the intervention of |Kaggen, and concludes with the very social act of marriage.

In M21 |Kaggen is again seen as helpful but here his intervention is both magical (foreknowledge through dreaming) and personal. He appears in this narrative in the role of an old man whose job it is to look after the children during the day while their parents are out searching for food. Again he dreams, this time of a danger to come, and so is able to instruct the children on how to behave when the menacing !Khwai-!Khwai approaches. Thus the !Khwai-!Khwai is defeated and the children are saved. In this narrative the narrator includes a coda plainly intended to relate the benign |Kaggen to his more familiar role as trickster, for it concludes with a speech by |Kaggen which contrasts his actions on this occasion with his wife's usual characterisation of him as childish and lacking in wisdom.

M16, like M21, shows |Kaggen as a protector of vulnerable members of the band, in this case a young girl who is having a menstrual period and who, in consequence, must lie in her hut while the other members of the band are away from the camp collecting food. The girl is approached by a certain bird who intends to stab her and put blood from her nose onto his own nostrils. (This apparently obscure threat does become intelligible in the light of ethnographic information. See Chapter 8 and Appendix A.)

|Kaggen dreams of the bird's approach and warns the other members of the band, telling them that the girl's mother should give the girl a knife with which to protect herself. When the bird approaches the girl produces the concealed knife and stabs him before he has a chance to harm her.

Here again |Kaggen's role is protective, social and wise and, as in M21, much is made of the fact that |Kaggen is not generally regarded as one who tells the truth. Indeed, almost half of the narrative is given over to post-event explications of what had occurred, and |Kaggen's creditable role in contrast to the expectations of many of his fellow band members.

M20 is rather more complex than the other narratives in this group.[9]

However |Kaggen is again seen as helpful – this time to his own sister, Blue Crane, who has been devoured by the two Lions, !Gu and !Hau ta ǂhou, while searching for the husband of her friend the Frog. Although she is captured and eaten by the Lions a small bone survives, and this |Kaggen finds. Apparently he had no dream in this case but had followed the Lions' spoor in search of her. As in M6 (group A), |Kaggen takes the bone to the water where he leaves it to grow and anoints her face with his perspiration. When she has revived and grown to her former size, he brings her clothes and leads her home once more.[10]

This narrative opens with the Blue Crane intervening in the marriage difficulties of the Frog and her husband – indeed in a situation of marital disharmony – and concludes with the Blue Crane's re-inclusion into her own family. The familial inclusion with which this narrative terminates is, in social effect, similar to the inclusions which the marriages of M17, M18 and M19 represent.

Turning briefly to von Wielligh's collection it may be observed that here again |Kaggen is effective in bringing about marriages. He turns his own sons into men who each marry a daughter of Night and Darkness. The marriages are spoiled however, by the indolence of two of the daughters, and by the obsessive industriousness of the third. Furthermore, each couple is assaulted by groups of people wishing to retreive parts of the necklaces given each daughter by their mother Darkness (‖Gaken). |Kaggen, 'sitting on a bush', perceives the assaults and changes his sons and grandsons into various things which allow them to drive away their enemies. In this way |Kaggen is responsible for the creation of fire, wind, rain, echoes, mirages and 'the great water snake'. Two of the wives are so indolent that they sleep forever and become the mountains and the plains, while the third becomes the water, continually on the move as she was in life (von Wielligh, *op. cit.*, Vol 1, *passim*).

The authenticity of these narratives must be doubted. Von Wielligh's intention was not to reproduce precisely the texts which he had collected, and he clearly manipulated the narratives to serve his own aesthetic and educational ends. However, it is likely that the narratives do correspond in many respects to what his |Xam informants told him, and it is unlikely that he totally invented the magical and benign personality of |Kaggen, especially as it appears to accord with the narratives which Lloyd elicited from |Hang ǂkass'o. Von Wielligh's published collection must, therefore, be taken to support the view that the narratives of group B reveal an aspect of |Kaggen's personality which was probably emphasised in more narratives than the handful collected by Lloyd might suggest. What is also clear is that, at least for Bleek and Lloyd's informants, the anti-social aspect of |Kaggen's character was of more interest than was the helpful and benign aspect.

While |Kaggen is a prominent figure in each of the six narratives which constitute group B, he is certainly not the central actor in most of them. Indeed in four out of the six (M16, M17, M18, M19) he could, with very minor modifications, be removed altogether. Rather, he functions as a source of information for the other actors in a way which is similar to the function of the family in some of the narratives of group A. The information he gives, however, is not concerned with social norms and values, although it does serve to avert harm, re-establish stability and bring about social harmony.

As has been observed above, the strongly didactic passages which are a common feature of group A are not present in group B, yet these narratives also deal with threats to social life from characters who are beyond the influence of society: the |Kain |kai:n (M16), the Black Wildebeest (M17), the Lizard (M18), the Beetle (M19), the !Khwai-!khwai (M21) and the two Lions (M20). The threat to society however, stems from the fact that they are first and foremost a threat to life – something which |Kaggen never is. While |Kaggen's anti-social behaviour is frowned upon, it is nevertheless tolerable. The antagonists of group B are not tolerable and are exclusively negative and threatening. |Kaggen is clearly not countering the activities of characters who are similar to himself in social disregard. The threat which they pose is different in kind to the threat which he poses in the narratives of group A. His personality in group B is not, therefore, reversal of his personality in group A, it is, rather, an indication of the limits of his anti-socialness. Where real threats to life are involved he is firmly on the side of life and against destructiveness.

Unlike the narratives of group A, these six narratives are not governed by the nature of |Kaggen's character. The conflicts in them occur on their own account and |Kaggen is not a generative figure as far as plot structure is concerned. In fact, a further distinguishing feature of group B is the very change in plot structure which this shift in theme brings about.[11] The antagonists of group B are not, like |Kaggen, 'marginal' beings, but plainly represent unambiguous threats. By virtue of his marginal and ambiguous status |Kaggen can mediate between the threat and the threatened, and it is in this capacity that he participates in the narratives – almost as an operational principle rather than as an actor.

Each of these narratives concludes with a return to normality and, in three of them, an affirmation of social cohesion through marriage. Thus self-evidently affirmative social behaviour in group B may be said to replace the socially educative statements found in group A. While social affirmation is the ultimate product of |Kaggen's intervention, it is important to note that he himself is not 'on stage' during the final and social affirmative scenes of M16, M17, M18 and M19.

The most obvious feature common to both group A and group B is |Kaggen's magical power, but, as has already been noted, his compassion, seen clearly in group B, is also present at certain times in group A. Likewise his power to restore life (M6) is further employed in M20 and, in M17, M18 and M19, through the agency of the Striped Mouse. This also accords with power to create life (M1). Thus it might be said that his character in general evinces kindness, creativity and magic as well as foolishness, childishness and anti-socialness. It is clear, therefore, that |Kaggen, like many another trickster, is essentially an ambiguous character. The distinction made here between group A and group B, while descriptively useful, also partially serves to mask this essential ambiguity. It is, however, the complex mixing of contradictories that gives these narratives so much of their distinctiveness. |Kaggen is a grandfather but is called a child; he is a man but has feminine associations; he is at once creative and destructive and so on. In this ambiguity much of the power of these narratives resides.

Notes

1   Published versions of most of these narratives may be found in D.F. Bleek's *Mantis and His Friends*. The narratives indicated by the numbers M1–21 in this book (the M, standing for Mantis, differentiates these narratives from the other narratives discussed) may be found in that volume on the following pages: M1, p. 1; M2, p. 13; M3, p. 15; M4, p. 19; M5, p. 21; M7, p. 28; M8, p. 30; M9, p. 34; M10, p. 41; M11, p. 47; M12, p. 50; M13, p. 54; M17, p. 58; M18, p. 60; M19, p. 65; M20, p. 26; M21, p. 45. Versions of M6, M14 and M15 may be found in Bleek & Lloyd (1911: 2ff). Bleek's report of 1875, and Lloyd's of 1889 together provide a complete index to all unpublished versions, giving both notebook and page numbers.

2   The untranslated names appearing in these titles are either the |Xam names for certain unidentified birds or the names of purely fictional creatures. The Korotwi:tən was said to be a small black bird with a red bill and legs; the !Khwai!khwai was a black bird with a white bill. |Ku-te-!gaua was a purely fictional creature said

to be able to enter fire unharmed; !Goe !kweitəntu is the name of another purely fictional character whose eyes were situated between his toes. The latter part of this name meant 'the opening of a penis' but the full meaning of the name is obscure. Narratives concerning this character are numerous in many San traditions, although his name is usually different. The idea of such a character may have been of Khoe origin for Stow reports that there was, 'A tradition among the old Hottentots that there was once a race of men in South Africa who, instead of having eyes in their head, had them placed in their feet, so that it was impossible for anyone to escape from their pursuit on account of their quickness in discovering the trail.' Stow claimed that this notion arose from the San's keenness of sight and unnerving ability to follow trails (Stow, *op. cit.*, 81).

3   Apart from '|Kaggen', the names which can be unambiguously translated into English have been: '‖Khwai-hεm' might mean 'all-devourer' but this is uncertain. In the name '!Gāunu ts'axau', ts'axau means 'eye', and !Gāunu was the name of a certain star which the collectors did not identify. Rather than giving the name half in |Xam and half in English, the full |Xam name is given here. The name '|Kwammang-a' was a personal name, apparently with no meaning. It is not shared with any other fictional or non-fictional character recorded in the collection.

4   Early writers report that on being forced to escape the scene of a battle the San would abandon their weapons to flee unimpeded (see Campbell 1815: 199; Moodie, *op. cit.*, 404; Lichtenstein, *op. cit.*, Vol 2, 331). Perhaps the power possessed by |Kaggen's things to follow after him represents a wishful projection related to this fact.

5   This association is common in Africa and elsewhere (see Wieschhoff 1973).

6   It should be noted that the double trick-types given for this narrative apply to three out of five versions; the remaining two versions contain only trick type D.

7   The social context of knowledge is examined by Berger & Luckman in *The Social Construction of Reality* (1967, *passim*) in a way which also clearly relates to |Kaggen's incapacities with regard to understanding the world.

8   It is likely that it was not taboo for women to handle meat in this way. However, the reason why sex roles are important here is because it was always the men who made the initial distribution of meat. Were a woman to have cut up meat there would have been no rule of distribution that could have been followed.

9   As will be seen in Chapter 8, this narrative is structurally like the majority of group A narratives, but falls within group B in terms of content.

10   See Chapter 9 for further discussion of this motif.

11   This change is discussed in Chapter 8.

8

The |Kaggen narratives (2): sequence and structure

Sequence

Bleek and Lloyd were unable to witness the performance of |Xam narratives to a native audience and furthermore the method of transcription which they employed permitted little indication of the nature of performance to emerge. This has repercussions for any attempt to establish a possible fixed sequence to these narratives. Bleek's main informant, ‖Kabbo, gave the majority of his |Kaggen narratives between September 1871, and January 1872. He often gave two or more versions of each narrative and moved from narrative to narrative, although on many occasions he also wandered from the narrative into accounts of the natural history of various animals or into other non-fictional subjects which interested him. In addition, he sometimes worked with Lloyd on a new narrative, having broken off in the middle of giving a narrative to Bleek on the previous day. These and other factors would inevitably disrupt any sequence which might have been customary. Even by comparing the embedding of narratives where continuing narration occurred, no consistent sequencing emerges; nor do any of the sequences employed by ‖Kabbo coincide with the sequence given by Lloyd's informant |Hang ǂkass'o although ‖Kabbo and |Hang ǂkass'o both progress from M8 to M9. (On other evidence it is also possible to see how these two narratives might have been necessarily linked. See Chapter 10.) Lloyd also felt that the events described by |Hang ǂkass'o in M13 occurred 'later' than those in M12 (Lloyd 1889: 7). This hint of fixed sequence is not corroborated, however, for only single versions of M12 and M13 were collected.

A feature of |Hang ǂkass'o's style is the linking of separate narratives with remarks such as, 'After |Kaggen's recovery from his sufferings (in M10) he went to the Ticks' houses' (M8). Thus the appearance of a fixed sequence is created, although on different occasions, to a native audience, |Hang ǂkass'o may in fact still have varied the sequence while maintaining the appearance of a fixed connection. However, because, for the most part, he only gave single versions of narratives, comparison of sequence is not possible as it is in the case of ‖Kabbo. Dia!kwain did not give a sufficient number of narratives for even a single sequence to be observed.

On the basis of the content of the narratives it is again impossible to see any necessary sequence such as Radin saw in the Winnebago cycle (Radin 1956: 132ff). There is neither a gradual development of |Kaggen's character nor any acquisition of knowledge in one narrative which advances him in any other. Furthermore there is no evidence of any kind that the benign |Kaggen of group B was sequentially prior or posterior to the trickster of group A. Both aspects of his personality appear to have been simultaneously present[1] and, as has been observed, are even described side by side within single narratives.

Hence it appears to be most likely that no fixed sequence obtained with regard to these narratives but that at least M8 and M9 (and possibly other recorded and unrecorded pairs) may have been linked together in performance. Individual narrators may have habitually maintained their own fixed sequences in repeated performances but there is no evidence to suggest that this was so, or indeed that any sequence was more part of the tradition than any other.

Introductory remarks on the structure of the narratives

Before proceeding to discuss the formal properties of the plot structures found in these narratives, some re-statements about the principal characters are useful.

The family group, consisting of Dassie, Porcupine, |Kwammang-a and Ichneumon, are rarely seen doing anything. They are largely perceived through what they say, and what they say usually takes the form of criticisms of |Kaggen, and statements of social norms or socially owned information. Thus the family is always seen to be equated with social values and knowledge, and in opposition to non-social behaviour. In addition to this, to state the obvious, the family lives at |Kaggen's home and it generally features in the narratives actually at home – the place to which |Kaggen returns from his adventures for safety and rest, the place where threatening conflicts do not occur. Thus family, home, and social values/rules are to a large extent equivalent and mutually supportive elements and may be said to 'stand for' social health and safety. Were home or family not to stand for social values and safety the whole nature of the narratives in group A would be changed.

|Kaggen's relationship with his family, as has been seen, is difficult. He is regarded by them as a somewhat unassimilable member and his conversations with them most characteristically take the form of accusation and defence, or educative 'talking down' on the part of the family to |Kaggen, who is far from equal to them in social and practical knowledge. He is, indeed, something of a despised member, although also loved. It is interesting to note, also, that none of the family who appear most regularly in the narratives is actually |Kaggen's blood relative; even Porcupine is said to be an adopted daughter. This is, of course, also true of Dassie but she is firmly in the family circle in other ways. A third factor which separates |Kaggen from the family is his magical power which none of the others possesses. He does not know or accept the rules of behaviour which govern the family's interaction with the world beyond the home, but he does know and use magical principles, semi-magical properties of nature, such as the rejuvenating power of water and perspiration. He knows the principles of the creation of life for he uses honey and water in his creation of the eland. His dreams, too, set him apart from his family as a person supernaturally privileged. In these ways he is a differentiated and marginal member of his own family and is not equated with home and social values as is the family itself.

|Kaggen's adversaries all behave in ways that the family can recognise and cope with, by total avoidance, or by the application of practical knowledge, or by the employment of social rules for good behaviour. When |Kaggen encounters these adversaries, however, and behaves towards them without knowledge of or concern for such principles, they become threatening and respond to his lawless ways in like fashion. In this way |Kaggen taps the potential for social chaos and confusion by initiating the abandonment of rules which govern behaviour. He converts stable situations into chaos. All this takes place away from home in all but one[2] of the group A narratives.

Between the outside world, where the conflicts which |Kaggen induces take place, and the home, where the family and safety are to be found, there is a river where |Kaggen always bathes his wounds, where he washes off the feathers with which his magical powers have provided him in order to escape from his enemies, where he revives himself before walking up to his home. It is this same river in which he revives his son, !Gāunu ts'axau (M6) and his sister, Blue Crane (M20) before leading them fully grown once more and supplied with new clothes, back to the home.

Thus there are in these narratives three worlds with which |Kaggen has contact: (1) The family and home; (2) non-family away from home; (3) a place between home and the arena of conflict, where he magically transforms the conflict and its consequences back into normalcy before returning home. In these narratives he performs two kinds of transformations – one from a manageable situation into a socially bad, chaotic and threatening situation; the other from that state of social break-down into one of safety.

As a marginal member of the family, as a being with magical powers and as one who reveals the underlying possibility of social chaos represented by everything for which the family need to apply rules – i.e. all social intercourse beyond the home – |Kaggen may be seen to relate to three different worlds while never fully being a member of any one. Indeed it is his very marginality which provides the conditions for the transformations which he performs.

In the narratives of group B |Kaggen is again a marginal member of the social groups to which he relates. In M17, M18 and M19 he does not even live with the group which he helps, and in M16 and M21 the communal discussions which follow the action of the narratives reveal that the community does not regard him as a normal member of the group but as set apart by his supernatural knowledge, declared in his predictive dreams, and by his characteristic anti-social behaviour.

The social groups to which he relates in group B are characterised by no special features, except that they are shown as vulnerable; they are no more safe at home than anywhere else; they are not, themselves, possessed of the knowledge necessary to secure their own safety, yet, with |Kaggen's aid, they do manage to overcome the creatures which menace them. There is always one individual, or in M21, one small section of the community, which manages to act on the basis of the information given by |Kaggen, while the rest of the group remain passive either as victims or simply observers.

As has been stated above, the creatures which menace the communities always threaten death. They do not merely disrupt social life; they threaten the community because there are and could be no rules of any kind which might make them manageable. They are simply a naked threat from a world beyond.

|Kaggen has supernatural knowledge of these creatures but he is even less part of their world than he is of the social groups to which he shows responsibility. Again his marginality, his very status as an 'outsider', permits him to mediate these two worlds and initiate the transformations necessary

to convert the threat of death into the actuality of life, and even to effect the resurrection of those already dead.

Thus in group A, where social rules do obtain, the transformations which he performs violate order but do not cause death; in group B, where social rules are irrelevant to the threat, |Kaggen causes transformations which secure life.

It appears to have been a common belief amongst the |Xam, as it is in many cultures, that it was possible for certain sensitive individuals to have dreams which foretold future events (D.F. Bleek 1931–36, Part IV: 326). |Kaggen's predictive dreaming, however, is given much emphasis by all of the narrators and would seem to be of special relevance to his marginality, for dreams, regarded so frequently everywhere as disclosing a 'real' design behind appearances, provide |Kaggen with direct access to the other worlds which impinge upon and sometimes threaten that world to which he physically relates. By being an outsider who nevertheless has such an access to the real shapes behind appearances, he shares something of the position of the blind seer or the hermit magician in the fictions of other cultures. However, his dreams are not just the normal dreams of a peculiarly sensitive person, for they are of such intensity that they can actually move objects in the real world from one place to another (e.g. the tree which |Kaggen conjures out of the ground and which rises taking with it the Meercat's possessions, in one version of M1, and the transportation of the Tick's belongings in M8). Not only do his dreams provide him with special knowledge but they are also an aspect of his grasp of the mysterious power which infuse parts of the natural world – honey, water, perspiration. As was suggested in Chapter 7, these supernatural powers are his substitute for rationality and practical realism, and are the basis for his transformations of the separate worlds described above. They are, as it were, the magical ingredient of the transformations which he effects. This holds true for both groups of narratives.

These magical transformations are effected exclusively from a negative state (i.e. death or conflict) to a positive state (life, safety). The transformations which he performs in the reverse direction, from the world of social order to its negation, are invariably not magical but, at their nodal points, take the form of tricks. Tricks, like jokes, proceed by a kind of semantic reversal: what was thought to be one state suddenly becomes another unexpected state, although still possessing most of the features of the original state. It is as though a different set of relationships were suddenly imposed upon a familiar set of factors. Thus a familiar form of social intercourse is suddenly converted into an unfamiliar form when |Kaggen performs one of his anti-social tricks. The people involved remain the same but the relationships between them are suddenly converted into a different set.

Hence it is possible to be quite precise about the mechanics involved in the transformations effected by |Kaggen: magical transformations convert physically negative states into physically positive states by exposing them to a different and supernatural set of laws; transformations through trickery convert socially positive states into socially negative states by imposing a different set of relationships upon familiar terms.

With these factors in mind it is now possible to examine the syntagmatic structures in these narratives.

Plot structure

For the purposes of this discussion the term 'plot structure' is defined as a pattern of events in temporal sequence seen to recur through a number of narratives. An examination of the 37 versions of the 21 narratives reveals that the majority of narratives of group A share a common plot structure, while the majority from group B share another plot structure different from that of group A. A few narratives remain which show a relation to these structures while not being identical with either of them.

Whereas the definition of units of plot structure might prove problematic within a single narrative, by comparing a number of narratives the plot features which are common to these narratives provide a basis for the isolation of basic units. With the relationships between these units and their capacity for displacement to other parts of the sequence, something of a grammar of composition may be perceived from which particular narratives can be seen to have been generated. Vladimir Propp's 'fundamental components' (Propp 1968: 21) would seem to come sufficiently close to this concept of 'events in temporal sequence' to warrant his term 'function' being applied to these units,[3] for both involve 'an act of a character ... defined from the point of view of its significance for the course of action' (Propp, *loc. cit.*).

In Chapter 7, reference was made to |Kaggen as a 'generative figure' as far as plot structure is concerned, and it is true that all of the events in the majority of group A narratives are initiated by |Kaggen or are causally related to his willed actions. Hence the functions of group A are seen almost exclusively in terms of a single character. However, there are also a few narratives collected by Bleek and Lloyd in which |Kaggen is either not the protagonist, or does not feature at all, but which display the same functions as the |Kaggen narratives of group A.

Functions of 13 group A narratives[4]

A Protagonist departs from his house.

B Protagonist incurs the hostility of another person or other people whom he meets.

C Protagonist becomes involved in either actual or imminently threatening physical conflict with the person(s) he meets.

D Protagonist triumphs over his adversaries.

E Protagonist extricates himself by magical flight.

F Protagonist soothes his wounds in the water near his house.

G Protagonist returns home.

H Protagonist is lectured by members of his family.

In any single narrative certain functions may be omitted. Thus A may be omitted but its existence is necessarily implied in B, and D may render E and/or F unnecessary. These functions are most commonly found in the following two sequences:

$$A \longrightarrow B \longrightarrow G \longrightarrow H; \longrightarrow A \longrightarrow C \longrightarrow E \longrightarrow F \longrightarrow G \longrightarrow H$$
and
$$A \longrightarrow B \longrightarrow C \longrightarrow E \longrightarrow F \longrightarrow G \longrightarrow H; \longrightarrow A \longrightarrow C \longrightarrow D \longrightarrow G \longrightarrow H.$$

Function A would include, '|Kaggen went visiting together with other members of his family', as well as such opening statements as '|Kaggen went out at daybreak', or '|Kaggen went to the Ticks' house'. Function B almost always involves one of the trick-types listed in Chapter 7, thus: '|Kaggen fails to share food with the Koro-twi:tən'; '|Kaggen played a trick on his hosts by telling a foul story'; '|Kaggen was greedy and therefore returned to the Aardwolf's house (and attempted to deceive her.)' Function C would include |Ku-te-!gaua's withdrawal of protection from |Kaggen so that |Kaggen became burnt in the fire (M13) as well as such events as the Ticks' attack on |Kaggen, or |Kaggen's fight with !Goe !kweitəntu (M2). Function D may be |Kaggen's success in a fight, or the besting of an adversary through magical means, e.g. the transportation of the Ticks' belongings (M8) or the success of a strategy, e.g. his escape from the Baboons with the eye of his son (M6). Functions E, F, and G always take the same form.[5] Function H varies according to its position in the sequence. Where it occurs in the middle of a sequence it frequently involves the family giving information relating to the person or creature whom |Kaggen has encountered. Where it occurs at the terminal point of a narrative it tends to involve the statement of social norms and a strong criticism of |Kaggen.

Such a description of the plot structure common to 13 of the 15 narratives of group A does reveal at least some of the formal principles from which narratives were generated. Different narrators used these units in different ways, some giving emphasis to certain sections, other narrators placing the emphasis elsewhere, but the basic structure remains unaltered throughout all versions.

While such uniformity is of great interest in its own right, by looking more carefully at the nature of these functions it is possible to discern other structural co-ordinates which may have been culturally significant. As has been noted, the home is not a place where conflicts occur but is always equated with familiar stability, social knowledge, education and safety. Function H may, therefore, be discriminated by virtue of its semantic significance. Likewise C is an expression of B and these two functions always occur at a place away from the home of |Kaggen's family. Functions D, E, and F can be seen as part of an intermediary state between conflict and safety, E and F actually occurring at an intermediary place between home and the scene of the conflict. Functions A and G are, as it were, moves[6] which set in motion other functions. Hence it is possible to abstract a simplified semantic plot as follows: A $\longrightarrow$ BC $\longrightarrow$ DEF $\longrightarrow$ G $\longrightarrow$ H, where BC = conflict; DEF = intermediary state; H = family, safety, social norms and knowledge. This structure is, however, that of the semantic relationships implicit in the plot functions A to H and does not necessarily relate to the sequence of events in any actual narrative.

It will be observed that this semantic arrangement is closely matched by certain topographical features in this group of narratives: home (standing for safety, norms, etc.); not-home (where a range of disordered events might occur); and an intermediary place, usually containing water (standing between home and not-home and importantly functioning as a condition for |Kaggen's return home).

The topography of these functions may be represented as follows:

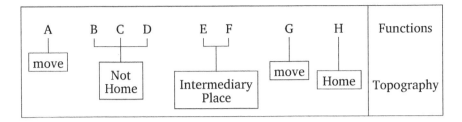

As has been seen above, conflicts represented by functions B and C involve actions by |Kaggen, and then by others, which are not governed by the rules for which the family (H) always stand. These rules are primarily concerned with social behaviour. Thus not-home is always associated with a loss of the rules which govern and create social order. In addition to this, the life-giving and renewing capacity of water (as it operates in these narratives) and the necessary inclusion of magic which takes |Kaggen from danger to safety, suggests that a further structural model can be formulated, the shape of which might be represented thus:

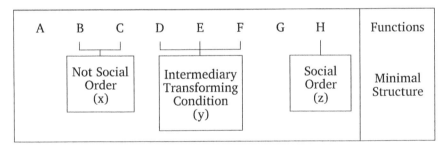

|Kaggen is the only character who may move between (x) and (y) and (z). He may be said to mediate between states on the logical level and to perform transformations between (x) and (z). It must also be stated again that moves A and G are willed by |Kaggen. Importantly, the intermediary condition (y) always involves magic to some degree when the transformation is from (x) to (z) and not when the transformation is from (z) to (x).

While such a model is an abstraction from the narratives, it does help to make |Kaggen's actions intelligible with regard to the overt social content (particularly as evinced in the Ichneumon's speeches) by allowing the underlying ideas and their logic to emerge.

It is possible to see therefore: (1) how |Kaggen was used as an operational principle dealing with the relationship between social order and its negation;

and (2) how such a principle assumed narrative forms which themselves were elaborated at a 'purely' entertainment level by individual performers.

Plot structure of five group B narratives[7]

The functions of group B are fewer than those of group A and are of a different kind in so far as they are not generated exclusively by one character. They are as follows:

I   Non-member of central social group repeatedly kills members of that group.

J |Kaggen discovers this in a dream.

K |Kaggen informs members of the social group of his dream.

L   Member of the group, on the basis of |Kaggen's information defeats threatening non-member.

M   Rebirth of the dead group members and/or survival of the instrumental group member.

N   Social endorsement of success by the group.

In these narratives the threat, which is always of death, may occur either at the home of the social group or elsewhere. Hence the topographical features, which are of semantic significance in group A, are not significant in group B. Nevertheless, looking at the nature of this set of functions, certain semantic groupings can be made.

Functions J and K are appropriated by |Kaggen and here combine to form a source of information (similar to the role of the family in group A). L and M provide the practical application of this information through which the threat represented by I is overcome. N, the social endorsement of success by the group, is not a necessary part of the action but, where it occurs, does so sequentially at the conclusion of all action. Hence I $\longrightarrow$ JK $\longrightarrow$ LM $\longrightarrow$ N is a causal chain wherein I always involves the threat of death; LM always involves either a return to life or the survival of lives; N involves social rituals (marriage) in three out of the five narratives, while the remaining two conclude with a group discussion of the protective role performed by |Kaggen. JK makes the transformation I $\longrightarrow$ MN possible.

These interdependent structures may be represented in the following way:

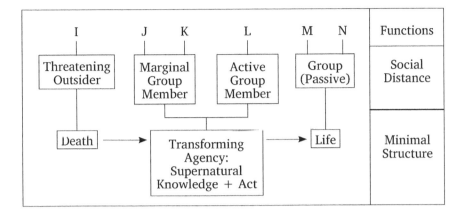

Hence the move from Death to Life, the prominent semantic feature of these narratives, is performed by a combination of supernatural knowledge (|Kaggen) and practical action (Active Group Member). It is important to note that the mediating phase, as in group A when the transformation is from (x) to (z), again involves magic (foreknowledge through dreaming) and that the movement M —→ N is not initiated by |Kaggen – he leaves the centre of the stage as soon as he has performed the task of sharing his supernatural knowledge.

Thus group A may be said, in general terms, to deal with the relationship between social order and its negation, while group B deals with life and death. Although this thematic difference undoubtedly exists and is clearly taken up into the syntagmatic structures of each, the structures themselves do share certain points of similarity. The element of information, falling at the end of the first part of the sequence employed in many of the narratives of group A, corresponds to the information represented by JK in the group B structure. This information follows from the conflict represented by BC in structure A, and I in structure B. Information is followed by a renewed conflict which, in structure B, always results in the success of the differentiated group member, and, in structure A, either results in the protagonist's success, or magical flight and return to safety. In both structures the final functions tend to become an affirmation of social cohesion either through ceremonial inclusion or the expression of socially binding norms. The use of both sets of functions in sequences shows a movement from conflict to information, to conflict renewed, and then to a point of transformation, and, ultimately, to an expression of social cohesion. In structure B, it should be noted, transformation is achieved through the combination of supernatural powers (magical) and individual action (practical). In structure A, positive transformation is achieved through magical practices and occasionally through practical information. Magic is always necessarily involved in positive transformation and often in combination with social practicality.

Of the handful of narratives which display anomalous plot structures, M6, which in terms of content was classified above as belonging to group A, has a structure which combines elements from both groups. (Another such mixed narrative is M9 which is discussed at length in Chapter 10.)

M6 is made up of the following sequence: A $\longrightarrow$ B $\longrightarrow$ C $\longrightarrow$ J; A $\longrightarrow$ C $\longrightarrow$ D $\longrightarrow$ E $\longrightarrow$ F $\longrightarrow$ H $\longrightarrow$ M. This maintains the sequence exactly while moving between both structures. The only deviation being the displacement of H, from its usual terminal point to the penultimate position. However, H has a wide displacement capacity and might appear at any of several points after function C of group A, usually provided that function G precedes it.

Another anomalous narrative, although one which does not display a mixed structure, is M14. In this narrative |Kaggen is found in the position of the non-family member for whom the family employ rules of avoidance. The functions of this narrative follow the sequence A $\longrightarrow$ B $\longrightarrow$ C $\longrightarrow$ E $\longrightarrow$ G $\longrightarrow$ H. Function B, as commonly found, involves a deviation from norms,[8] but E, usually a magical flight, is here merely an escape without magic because it is performed not by |Kaggen but by the girls whom |Kaggen has frightened. However, the magical element always present at this positive transformation stage is again supplied by |Kaggen as he reassembles the parts of the body of the dead hartebeest into the form of a man.

While the functions here are the usual group A functions, they have certain elements missing. Nevertheless, they do conform precisely both to the topography of group A and to the minimal structure. Furthermore, the negative transformation is performed by |Kaggen with the employment of a strategic trick. Again, therefore, at both the positive and negative transformation stages, it is |Kaggen who occupies the governing position.

This general description of the two main structures found in these narratives, and of the minimal structures which can be seen to lie behind the sequence of functions, reveals two important points which are worth re-stating:

(1) Two distinct polarities are important in the |Kaggen narratives: (a) Social/Not Social, (b) Life/Death. These poles are mediated by |Kaggen in differing ways.

(2) When narratives achieve resolution by moving from a negative state to a positive state, some kind of magic is almost always involved.

These observations will be seen to be of relevance to the relationship between the role of |Kaggen as a supernatural being and his character evinced in the oral literature, discussed in Chapter 9.

Before leaving the subject of structure it should be said again that the analysis in this chapter is concerned only with the plots of these narratives and as such leaves aside the structure of any narration as a total performance.[9] In many cases informants would give over more than half of the total narration to amplifying features which they wished to stress, even after the action had been described. These plot structures were only the basic score with which individual narrators worked, a cultural inheritance through which their individual talents expressed themselves.

It should be added that such semantic significance as can be attached to the formal features observed in these narratives in no way limits the range of possible meanings which any given narrative may have possessed. Narratives are structured not only by events but also by the symbols which they employ, i.e. items which either consciously or unconsciously involve what Dmitry Segal has called 'extra mythic elements' (Segal 1972: 217)[10] for their interpretation, knowledge of which may or may not be available to the researcher. In some cases it is possible to semanticise the texts and investigate the significance of elements in such a way that their symbolic weight might be perceived. Such a semanticising may qualify the simple semantic structures described in this chapter or it may amplify them. This fact must be taken into account in any discussion of the possible meaning of any formal attributes of plot structure.

By way of a postscript to this chapter, two summaries of |Kaggen narratives, one from group A (M3) and one from group B (M16) are given below in order to demonstrate in concrete terms some of the structural features that have been described. A brief discussion follows each example.

Example 1

M3. (A visit to the Lions)

One day |Kwammang-a suggested to the Ichneumon that they should both visit the Lions so that they could eat quagga meat with them. |Kaggen overheard the conversation and assumed that he, too, would go. The Ichneumon tried to dissuade him on the grounds that he was always afraid of the Lions and would be likely to be troublesome, but |Kaggen insisted. They set off and soon found the Lions' spoor, but when they saw the Lions themselves |Kaggen became nervous and asked to be hidden in the Ichneumon's bag.

A young Lion cub then came up to |Kwammang-a and the Ichneumon, and saw |Kaggen peeping from the bag. At first he thought that the Ichneumon had brought a hare in the bag and ran nervously back to his mother. He approached again, and again saw |Kaggen's eye peeping out of a hole. Again he returned nervously to his mother. When he approached a third time |Kaggen blinked his eyes and whispered that he would poke out the Lions cub's eye. The Lion cub ran back to his mother crying, and the Lioness became very angry. She walked menacingly up to the party and stood on the bag. |Kaggen then jumped out, magically got feathers and flew off calling to his shoes, quiver, bow, *kaross* and cap to follow him. He flew into the water near his house saying 'See! Our name is |Kaggen! What man is our equal?' His possessions flew onto the opposite bank and there they waited for him. He then emerged from the water, dressed himself and returned home.

When he arrived home he told his wife, who told the Porcupine, that the Lions had killed |Kwammang-a and the Ichneumon. The Porcupine then went out and saw |Kwammang-a and Ichneumon coming carrying quagga meat. Then |Kaggen's wife scolded him for lying to her.

When the Ichneumon arrived, the Porcupine told him that |Kaggen had said they had been killed, and the Ichneumon told the Porcupine at length about |Kaggen's pranks with the lion cub. |Kwammang-a, meanwhile, unpacked the quagga meat in silence because he was so angry about |Kaggen's behaviour. The Porcupine and the Ichneumon continued to discuss |Kaggen's deceitfulness and misbehavior until |Kaggen grew silent with embarrassment and annoyance, and lay down to sleep.

Discussion

In this narrative |Kaggen is seen at his most playful. The visit, suggested by |Kwammang-a, is apparently motivated by the desire to share in the specific food resources of the Lions, and is one in which courtesy should be an essential part. |Kaggen, however, is both afraid of the Lions – as the Ichneumon had said he would be – and quite oblivious both to the social conventions and the pragmatic need to maintain good relations. Once again he disregards the rules which his family employ in their dealings with people, and brings normal social intercourse to the brink of disaster.

The topographical structure of group A is plainly evident in this narrative as is its correlation with the minimal structure. Social orderliness, represented by the conventions surrounding such visits, is converted into its reverse (the angry response of the Lioness who starts to attack |Kaggen) through a trick (type A) performed by |Kaggen. It is possible that the apparent presence of a hare in the Ichneumon's bag might have been intended to suggest that the Lions mistakenly believed that a token gift was going to be made: this would emphasise the anti-socialness of what actually did occur.

|Kaggen's magical flight from the angry lioness and his immersion in the water near his home ensures his own safety once more and, the narrative leaves us to assume, allows |Kwammang-a to patch up the damage done. Doubts about the safety of |Kwammang-a and the Ichneumon – impishly encouraged by |Kaggen – are not dispelled until the visitors have returned home. At this point, disapproval is piled upon |Kaggen by the brooding silence of |Kwammang-a, the Ichneumon's recounting of |Kaggen's wrong-doing, and the Porcupine expressing her embarrassment at being tricked into worrying about the safety of her menfolk.

This simple narrative shows |Kaggen in a very characteristic light. He is cowardly, playful and deceitful but by the end definitely feeling the weight of family criticism. The sequence of functions, each occurring only once, is very straightforward: A —→ B —→ C —→ E —→ F —→ G —→ H.

Example 2

M16. The |Kain |kai:n once went to a girl as she lay 'ill' in her hut, and he told the girl to stand up and touch him. And when the girl had stood up he stabbed her in the breast with a knife. Then blood poured from her nose and this he smelt, smothering his own nose with the blood and making his nostrils red.[11] Then he left the girl lying there and went away with the other |Kain |kai:n birds to look for another girl.

They went to another girl and did the same thing until, eventually, they came near to the place where |Kaggen lived. |Kaggen then dreamed about them and how they went about killing girls as they lay in their huts. Early in the morning |Kaggen went to the people and told them that the mother of the girl who was in isolation should go to her daughter and give her a sharp knife to keep by her as she lay. He told them that he had dreamed that the |Kain |kaːn was going about killing girls and that he would come to their girl the next day.

The girl's mother gave her daughter a sharp knife and instructed her not to play (|kerri) with the |Kain |kaːn because |Kaggen had warned them. Even if she thought that the |Kain |kaːn would not try to smell her, she should not play with him. And so the girl lay down with the knife and, although not looking out for the |Kain |kaːn, listened carefully for any noise. Then she heard him come and he spoke to her and told her to get up and touch him. At that moment she stabbed the |Kain |kaːn, plunging the knife into him, and he crawled away and died.

Then the people came home and saw the |Kain |kaːn lying dead, and knew |Kaggen's dream had been true and that the |Kain |kaːn had waited until they had all gone out to collect food and then flown down. And the people saw the other |Kain |kaːn birds scattering wildly in all directions, as if the girl was stabbing them all. And the people said that they should behave well towards |Kaggen because, although he often teased, he had spoken the truth this time. Usually he teased people and lied but he had not been deceiving anyone over this matter. At night he had dreamed of what would happen, and by the afternoon they had all seen it to be true.

Discussion

Here we see |Kaggen as a guardian of the band, employing his supernatural knowledge to protect a girl who is in a state of vulnerability. Death is threatened but overcome through |Kaggen's foreknowledge and by the girl's own actions (Marginal Group Member + Active Group Member). Just as |Xam girls were warned not to play (|kerri) with young men during a menstrual period in case their menstrual fluid got onto them, so, in this narrative, the girl is told not to play (|kerri) with the |Kain |kaːn because of the danger of which |Kaggen had warned.

The |Kain |kaːn's explicit desire is to put the blood from the girl's nose onto his own nostrils where he can smell it. Blood from the nose, like other kinds of physical emission, was regarded by the |Xam as particularly potent. Mary Douglas has pointed up the symbolic significance of such emissions. She writes:

> All margins are dangerous. If they are pulled this way or that the shape of fundamental experience is altered. Any structure of ideas is vulnerable at

its margins. We should expect orifices of the body to symbolise its specially vulnerable points. Matter issuing from them is marginal stuff of the most obvious kind. Spittle, blood, milk, urine, faeces or tears by simply issuing forth have traversed the boundary of the body. So also have bodily parings, skin, nail, hair clippings and sweat. The mistake is to treat bodily margins in isolation from all other margins (*op. cit.*, 145).

The girl in the narrative is, herself, in a socially marginal position through the separation imposed on her by her condition. The |Kain |kai:n is attracted by her odour and, like !Khwa in the beliefs about menstruation, represents a threat coming from outside of society. The bleeding from the girl's nose may be taken as a cultural symbol of her vulnerability to the dangers which surround her condition. Prior to |Kaggen's intervention, the |Kain |kai:n is successful in molesting young girls. By unopposed assault on these marginal girls, violation of taboo and death occur, and the danger implied by the girls' state becomes realised.

|Kaggen, however, is also a marginal being and as such is capable of activity in this region of ambiguity. His intervention on behalf of Life and against Death transforms the situation completely and achieves the survival of the girl and the eradication of the threat. The |Kain |kai:n is killed and his colleagues disperse in all directions. Here the characteristic group B structures – Threatening Outsider; Marginal Group Member; Active Group Member; Group (Passive) and Death; Transforming Agency; Life – are fleshed out in symbolic terms which are very readily glossed by reference to the customs and belief of the |Xam in regard to menstruation. The structural and symbolic levels are, as it were, saying the same thing.

Here we see |Kaggen's strictly serious side, a side which the narrator, |Hang ǂkass'o is often at pains to stress and relate to the |Kaggen of group A. He does this by putting into the mouths of peripheral characters statements like:

Ng ta u koa: akkən !kõing |Kaggen ta ha a:
ka |kwi |ki ha ǁkaggo-a !k'e, he ha /ne ǂkakka
hi: ĩ:.
(I want you to act nicely to grandfather |Kaggen for he is the one who dreamed about it and told us, for he dreamed about the people and spoke to us about it.)

or:

!K etən ti ta ha ‖khwaija ta ha kwa: ka !ke:i
‖au.
(People say that he lies, but he really told the truth.)
(L. VIII, (3) 6298–6300)

In this way he interprets the two natures of |Kaggen and attempts to emphasise the positive, pro-life aspect and contextualise the negative anti-social aspect. |Kaggen's ambiguous nature must have often presented individual narrators with the task of interpretation and it is illuminating to find |Hang ǂkass'o clearly grappling with this problem.

Notes

1   J.M. Orpen's informant from the Maluti Mountains, however, stated that Cagn (apparently a different spelling of '|Kaggen' less the click) had once been good but became bad as the result of constant fighting (see Orpen, *op. cit.*, 142).

2   The exception is M9, which is discussed at length in Chapter 10.

3   These units come closer to Propp's 'functions' than to Alan Dundes' much less specific 'motifemes' (Dundes 1962, 1965). The analysis of these units, however, does have affinities with the approach to sequential units described in Fischer (1963: 251).

4   The narratives not adequately described by these functions are M9 and M6, both of which combine functions found in group A and group B.

5   A variant of function F is, however, discussed at length in Chapter 9.

6   This term is not used here in the sense intended by Propp (*op. cit.*, 104ff). In this context it means the kind of preparatory move, such as one finds in chess, which is not significant in its own right but which permits important manoeuvres to take place.

7   The exception in this case is M20, which has the structure of a group A narrative, but with the Blue Crane, not |Kaggen, as its protagonist.

8   The confusion of sex roles is described in Chapter 7.

9   For example, the type of analysis suggested by H. Jason (1969), by Fischer (*op. cit.*), by W. Labov & J. Waletsky (1967) and by K.A. Watson (1973).

10 Segal appears to refer these elements only to whole segments of myth but clearly the same tools are necessary for determining the possible meaning of variable symbols which may occur within any given narrative segment.

11 In real life, it will be remembered, this bird has a red bill.

9

|Kaggen in belief, ritual and narrative: a synthesis

In Chapter 6 it was observed how, in the religious beliefs of the |Xam, |Kaggen had a creative aspect which was beneficial to man, and another aspect, opposed the human world, which acted in the interests of various game animals. In his creative aspect he had the attributes of a transformer of the world: he was credited with making the moon, creating the game animals and having named places. His negative aspect was, in part, complementary to this for he protected the animals which he had created and attempted to prevent the |Xam hunters from killing them. However, young mothers and hunters both needed to be guarded against him.

In the narratives these two aspects are also present. |Kaggen, the creative if incidental benefactor, actually helps those whose lives are endangered, both in the narratives of group B and in two narratives of group A (M6, M10). The belief that he created the game animals is given narrative form in M1 where he creates the eland, and the belief that he made the moon is also turned directly into narrative in one conclusion to that same story. In belief and narrative he is always for life even if the order which humans attempt to place on life is anathema to him. His constant fighting, anti-social behaviour, economic irresponsibility and outrageous boastfulness, seen everywhere in group A, are clearly also a reflection of the kind of being he was. Indeed the thematic pairs Life/Death and Social/Non-Social, found in the narratives, may also be seen to be present in the purely religious aspect.

The position ascribed to |Kaggen on the borderline between amenable and unamenable nature was a corollary of his marginality with regard to the moral and empirical universe articulated in the narratives. In religious belief and observance |Kaggen stood for the world of game animals and sought to exclude the influence of men. In other superstitions and religious beliefs of the |Xam the autonomous 'wildness' of game – game acting in strange and unpredictable ways which put them beyond the hunters' skills – was causally related to many disruptive social events, from unruly behaviour in the camp on the part of women and children, illness or a death in the band, to a glance from the eye of a menstruating girl or failure to observe certain eating rules known as !nanna-se (Bleek & Lloyd 1911: 270ff). Because of his singular relationship with the animals, through being both their creator and protector, |Kaggen personified this autonomous wildness and it is therefore fitting that his character in the narratives should possess a distinct moral autonomy which frequently caused disruption to the community and/or economic loss to his family. As was pointed out in Chapter 6, just as disjunctions in a hunter's relationship with the game were often equated with disruptive social events, so |Kaggen, by symbolising an animal world seeking to exclude men, could also represent a de-stabilising element in the social order. Both moral autonomy and the autonomous wildness of game involve that which is non-social and irrational – that which is beyond the power of normal human strategies to control.[1] The combination of these features in the person of |Kaggen indicates a strong consistency in the conceptualisation of this being and pertinent links to the idea of social order amongst the |Xam. Indeed in this complex of related ideas may be seen another example of the way dangers to society were conceived of through animal imagery.

The techniques involved in |Kaggen's autonomous activities also show a uniformity in belief and narrative. It was seen above how |Kaggen's trickery in assuming various forms – louse, hare, puffadder – when attempting to force a hunter into involuntarily relinquishing his quarry, is paralleled in the narratives by the tricks which he employs in gaining his anti-social ends. The uniformity was also apparent to the |Xam themselves for one informant stated that |Kaggen often took the form of a hare

> Because he wants us to kill him so that the gemsbok can live for him, for he remembers that he acted in this way once before – he became a wounded hartebeest because he intended that people should cut him up (L. VIII, (23) 8036 rev.).

Here an explanation of |Kaggen's deceptions in his role as supernatural being is offered with reference to one of the narratives (M14). Furthermore, the words used to describe his deceptive nature – k"eï:jã, ‖khwi:ja, g̠kerru[2] – are common both to narrative and expressions of belief. In both areas |Kaggen may also be seen as a conceptual tool for dealing with the conversion of what was within the ambit of human control into what was beyond that ambit. The possibility of such a conversion was necessarily contained in the |Xam 'idea of society' and reflected in many other areas of |Xam magico-religious thought.

The comparisons between |Kaggen's religious and narrative roles may be summarised as follows:

(1) His creativity and incidental beneficence as a supernatural being is reflected in the narratives when he acts for life and against death (although not on behalf of social order).

(2) His anti-human activities as a protector of game are converted into anti-social behaviour in the narratives.

(3) As a violator of social norms his narrative persona is a corollary of his supernatural position on the borderline between amenable and unamenable nature. He is, in both instances, a marginal being.

(4) His trickery is present in both his religious and his narrative roles and serves to convert socially positive states into socially negative states.

All of this adds up to a very coherent whole. Indeed, so integrated are his actions in the narratives with the religious concept of him that they may well be regarded not so much as fictions but extemporisations on religious themes, if 'religious' can be taken to mean symbolic representations operating together with a certain logic and serving to make the world intelligible at many levels simultaneously (see Berger & Luckman 1967: 122ff).

The explanatory power of the |Kaggen concept, if it may be so called, was nevertheless limited. Other concepts, the most important of which was represented by the figure of !Khwa, were needed to cover other, perhaps more awesome intuitions about the world. The similarities and differences between |Kaggen and !Khwa serve both to underline |Kaggen's nature and, as will be seen, provide further insight into certain structural aspects of the |Kaggen narratives.

|Kaggen and !Khwa

Both |Kaggen and !Khwa were ambivalent beings standing between nature and society, and both represented threats which required ritualistic and magical practices to contain them. |Kaggen could make the game uncontrollable if these practices were not properly adopted and !Khwa could cause cultural reversions of various kinds. However, !Khwa could also unleash rain, thunder and lightning, and cause death, but |Kaggen could do nothing of that degree of destructiveness. Furthermore !Khwa had none of the creative powers of |Kaggen and benefited no-one with his actions. He came as an elemental threat while |Kaggen worked by stealth and trickery. While both |Kaggen and !Khwa shared similar positions on the border between nature and society, they were differentiated by the kinds of threats which they represented and the way in which they represented them. |Kaggen stood for life – but not for socially organised life – while !Khwa actually threatened life. These similarities and differences are seen at work most clearly in the ceremonial practices which involved these beings and especially in the isolation rites for girls experiencing their first menses and hunters who had shot eland, touched upon in Chapter 6.

Ceremonial isolation, like other less extreme forms of social avoidance, was a mechanism for separating certain elements, contact between which might be of danger to society as a whole. The girls' puberty rite marked the passage of a girl into womanhood and conformed precisely to van Gennep's three phases: separation, margin and aggregation (van Gennep 1960: 11). These phases have been usefully summarised by Victor Turner as follows:

> The first phase of separation comprises symbolic behaviour signifying detachment of the individual or group either from an earlier fixed point in the social structure or a set of cultural conditions (a 'state'); during the intervening liminal period, the state of the ritual subject (the 'passenger') is ambiguous; he passes through a realm that has few or none of the attributes of the past or coming state; in the third phase the passage is consummated. The ritual subject, individual or corporate, is in a stable state once more, and, by virtue of this, has rights and obligations of a clearly defined and 'structural' type and is expected to behave in accordance with certain customary norms and ethical standards (Turner 1970: 94).

During the |Xam girls' puberty rites, the isolated girl was thought to be becoming a young woman (!kui |a) and her removal from the isolation hut was followed by her gradual assumption of womanhood. Her physical and social transfromation during the liminal period took place away from contact with the other band members and, provided she performed the necessary ritual actions, hopefully beyond the notice of !Khwa. She was believed to have a potentially harmful effect on hunters if she, directly or through contamination, had contact with them. In fact her position *vis-à-vis* game animals was very similar to that of a hunter who had shot eland or other large game. However, the danger, represented by !Khwa, to herself and the community, required certain ritual acts which were quite distinct from those employed by the isolated eland hunter.

Immediately upon her release from confinement she had to treat all the members of her household with buchu and give the women of the band red haematite with which they were to paint their cheeks and *karosses*. She was also expected to paint haematite stripes like a zebra on the young men of the band to protect them from death by lightning caused by !Khwa. This combination of separation from the community and ritual magic was believed both to distance danger and ensure the ultimate return to normality for the band.

In the case of hunters who had shot eland, isolation was again involved although the magic employed was of a directly sympathetic kind – the hunter mimicking the dying animal while attempting to ignore the tricks played on him by |Kaggen. Both the girls' and the hunters' rites employed the same kind of isolation – the building of a hut between the camp and the bush where the subject would lie in an abject state of apparent illness from which he would in time recover – and both employed magical practices designed to thwart the supernatural beings which threatened them. The very placing of isolation huts beyond the camp was a tangible expression of the liminality of hunters and girls and of their transitional status. As Turner (*ibid.*, 97) points out:

> Transitional beings are neither one thing nor another; or may be both; or neither here nor there; or may even be nowhere (in terms of any recognised cultural topography) and are at the very least 'betwixt and between' all the recognised fixed points in space-time of structural classification.

Something of the intermediary positions of |Kaggen and !Khwa may, perhaps, also be seen as a reflection of this state. However, the differences in the intention behind the kinds of magic employed point to the differences between |Kaggen and !Khwa.

The magic employed by eland hunters was seen as an essential part of the technical business of killing eland and as such fell at a different point on that 'continuous scale' of the sacred and profane described by Leach (1954: 12f):

> At one extreme we have actions which are entirely profane, entirely functional, technique pure and simple; at the other we have actions which are entirely sacred, strictly aesthetic, technically non-functional. Between these two extremes we have the great majority of social actions which partake partly of the one sphere and partly of the other.

In these terms !Khwa was decidedly 'more sacred' than |Kaggen, for the observances relating to |Kaggen were fundamentally integrated with all of the beliefs in sympathetic magic which were so much an indivisible part of hunting practices. On the other hand the magic and symbols which clustered around !Khwa – reptilian imagery, water-flowers, the use of red markings, buchu etc. – had no counterpart in the beliefs concerning |Kaggen. This difference may have been related to the fact that the impetus for the concepts involving !Khwa came directly from social considerations,[3] and indeed the magical acts in the girls' rites were concentrated in the 'aggregation' phase which, as Turner (*op. cit.*, 95) has pointed out, is 'more closely implicated in social structure'. |Kaggen, however, related to the ordered interaction between men and nature and was more technical in application. This technical application is itself in keeping with |Kaggen's role as a transformer of the world.

The ways in which |Kaggen and !Khwa were similar are therefore limited to: (a) their position on the border between nature and society; (b) their formal ambivalence; (c) their capacity to convert the culturally useful into pure nature. These three features were important religious ingredients in the girls' puberty rites and in the hunters' eland rites.

The differences between |Kaggen and !Khwa may be summarised as follows: |Kaggen stood for life, while !Khwa predominantly threatened death; |Kaggen was creative and was a transformer of the world. !Khwa, by contrast, was principally destructive and benefited no living creature – neither men nor animals. In the eland rites the kind of magic employed to counteract the autonomy for which |Kaggen stood was sympathetic and intended to control the animal and ward off |Kaggen. In the girls' puberty ceremony the magic employed was intended to protect the girl, her family and others from death caused by !Khwa. It was not sympathetic magic but involved the use of powerful religious symbols in an attempt to distance danger. This magic was concentrated at the 'aggregation' phase of the rite.

Ritual and narrative

Many writers have drawn attention to the relationship between ritual and myth. The most obvious manifestation of this relationship is where the recital of sacred myths actually accompanies ritual. Thus William Bascom (1965: 4) writes:

> Myths are the embodiment of dogma: they are usually sacred; and they are often associated with theology and ritual.

And as Leach (*op. cit.*, 13) points out:

> The classical doctrine in English Anthropology is that myth and ritual are conceptually separate entities which perpetuate one another through functional interdependence – the rite is a dramatisation of the myth, the myth is the sanction or charter for the rite.

Even in cases where direct empirical association cannot be made, a 'ritual theory of myth' has been put forward by Lord Raglan and others[4] which posits a ritual genesis for all myth. While the claim that all myths have their origin in ritual is plainly well beyond what can, with confidence, be verified, some myths may, indeed, have had such an origin. However, any discovery of the genesis of a myth is highly problematic and inevitably requires a wealth of detailed information if it is to go further than plausible speculation.

In the case of the |Kaggen narratives there is no evidence to suggest either that their performance coincided with any ritual, or that their genesis can be attributed to ritual practices. Nevertheless, certain features of the narratives do appear to be shared with the rites discussed above. These common features cannot be taken to 'prove' anything about either the narratives or the rituals but they are deserving of some attention.

When the differences between the threats posed by |Kaggen and !Khwa are noted, a continuity between the tangible expressions of the liminality of girls/eland hunters and the minimal structures observed in the narratives begins to emerge. It will be remembered that the minimal structure of most of the group A narratives involved a threefold division: Not Social Order; Intermediary Transforming Condition; Social Order. This triad corresponded to certain topographical features, namely: Not Home; Intermediary Place; Home. In these narratives Home is associated with social order and Not Home with a break-down of rules governing behaviour. In the intermediary phase, where |Kaggen effects his magical flight and immerses himself naked in the water standing between Home and Not Home, he transforms the situation of danger and conflict into one of safety. As has been seen, |Kaggen's violation of social norms in the narratives is the social corollary of his protection of the autonomy of game animals. If, on these grounds, a substitution of the terms 'eland within hunter's control' for 'Social Order', and 'eland beyond hunter's control' for 'Not Social Order' is made, the 'Intermediary Transforming Condition' looks very like that liminal state (between camp and bush, home and not-home) in which the secluded eland hunter was placed. In both cases |Kaggen, where he was able, effected transformations from a culturally positive to a culturally negative state, and in both cases some form of magic in combination with isolation was necessary to effect the transformation into the positive state associated with home, social normality and success.

In the narratives, during this intermediary phase, |Kaggen is isolated in the water between home and the place where conflicts occur. He is always naked during his immersion in the water; the signs of his social integration, his clothes and possessions, fly to the other bank and wait for him to emerge transformed into human shape once more. The eland hunter in the |Xam rite was likewise isolated 'betwixt and between' and remained in a sick and abject state in the segregated hut until the magic had worked and the animal was dead. In both narratives and rite, transformations into the negative state are effected by |Kaggen through the use of tricks. Transformation into the positive, socially normal state are effected by magical means.

There are, therefore, these simple broad similarities between the eland rite and topography, content and structure of the majority of group A narratives. These similarities may be represented in diagrammatical form as follows:

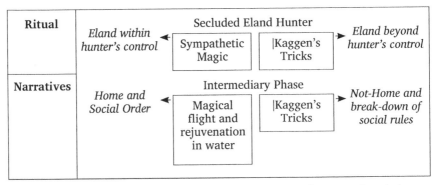

It is not suggested here that the sequence of events in the narratives is in any way similar to the sequence of events in the rite but the fact that the |Xam regarded socially disruptive acts and the uncontrollability of game animals as essentially the same kind of fact makes this juxtaposition of ritual and narrative structure conceptually intelligible. While |Kaggen's trickery is the factor which converts from the left to the right in the diagram above, magic is necessary to convert from the right to the left.

If one looks at those narratives where death is threatened – principally those falling in group B – one finds |Kaggen acting in quite a different manner. He aids people with his supernatural knowledge and with that knowledge opposes the creatures which threaten death. His intervention comes at the intermediary phase of the narratives and is, therefore, interesting *vis-à-vis* the margin phase of the rites discussed above for, atypically for him, he effects the transformation from the negative state into the positive.

Although the topographical features are less obvious in this group of narratives, the threat is always represented as coming from beyond the camp and the victims of the threat are always separate in some way from the rest of the community. As in the other group of narratives, the threat is overcome with the help of magical powers.

If Life and Death may be taken as oppositions, |Kaggen is, in this respect, opposed to !Khwa. |Kaggen is always for Life, while !Khwa predominantly threatens death. In the minimal structure of group B Death, or the possibility of Death, is converted into Life through a combination of |Kaggen's magical foreknowledge and the actions of a differentiated member of the group. The belief structure of the girls' puberty rites may, of course, also be seen in similar terms for !Khwa was believed to threaten death to the girl and the community, and magic, together with seclusion, was again necessary to secure life and safety. Structurally !Khwa occupied a position in ritual identical with that occupied by the various 'threatening outsiders' in the narratives of group B. Indeed, M16 is, in its actual narrative content, concerned explicitly with |Kaggen protecting girls isolated during puberty and assisting in overcoming the threat posed by the |Kain |kai:n bird who, like !Khwa, is attracted by their odour.

With these structural features in mind, one variable of function F (part of the Intermediary Transforming Condition of the minimal structure identified with group A) found in both M6 and M20 stands out as particularly interesting. These two narratives, while being structurally related to group A on the syntagmatic level, both contain the possibility of the death of the central characters. In each narrative the position usually occupied by |Kaggen is occupied by a member of his family. In both of these narratives function F – 'Protagonist soothes his wounds in the water near his house' – not only excludes |Kaggen from the central position, but also includes some additional and suggestive features.

In M6 |Kaggen's son has been almost killed by the Baboons. All that remains of him is his eye, a tiny fragment of life which |Kaggen treats in the following way:

> |Kaggen sat down; he felt inside his bag; he took out the child's eye; he walked on as he held it; he walked, coming up to the grass at the top of the water's bank. He sat down. He exclaimed: 'Oh wi ho' (At the same time putting the first finger of his right hand into his mouth, against his left cheek, and drawing it forcibly out; the eye being meanwhile in the palm of his right hand shut down by his other fingers). He put the child's eye into the water. 'You must grow up so that you may become what you have been', he said. Then he walked on.

|Kaggen then went home where he remained for some time.

> Then he went to look at the place where he had put in the child's eye. And he approached gently because he did not want to make a rustling noise. So he came gently. And the child heard him, because he had not come gently when he was far off; and the child jumped up; it splashed into the water. Then |Kaggen laughed about it because his heart yearned for the child. And he returned.
>
> Then the child grew; it became as it had once been. Then |Kaggen came to look at the child, walking and looking, and he spotted the child while the child was sitting in the sun. Then the child heard him as he came rustling

along. The child sprang up and entered the water. |Kaggen stood looking and then returned. He went to make a front apron for the child and a ‖koroko.[5] He put the things aside then he put the front apron into the bag with the ‖koroko and with these things he left and came to the water. As he approached gently he saw the child lying in the sun opposite the water. So he came gently up to the child. And the child heard his father come gently, and, just as the child was about to get up, |Kaggen sprang forward and caught hold of the child. He anointed the child with his scent.[6] He anointed the child. He said: 'Why are you afraid of me? I am your father. I, |Kaggen, am here. You are my son. You are !Gaūnu ts'axau. I am |Kaggen whose son you are. I am your father.' And the child sat down and |Kaggen took out the front apron and the ‖koroko. He put the front apron onto the child; he put the ‖koroko on the child. Then he took the child with him. In this way they returned and arrived home (Bleek & Lloyd 1911: 31ff).

That narrative was given by ‖Kabbo in 1872. The following narrative, M20, was by |Hang ǂkass'o in 1878. Here the Blue Crane, |Kaggen's sister, has been devoured by two lions, themselves associated elsewhere with threats to a girl following puberty rites (L. VIII, (19) 7643–56; (32) 8852–78). All that remains of her is a single small bone which |Kaggen finds.

He picked it up and went and put it into the water. |Kaggen then went home and stayed at the huts. Then he came out and went to look. The Blue Crane jumped up, up, up and splashed into the water. So |Kaggen turned back, returned home and stayed there.

Once more he went out to look. As he came up he saw the Blue Crane sitting in the sun. She had grown. He turned back without startling her. While the Blue Crane sat basking, he went to make things, clothes which he meant to give to the Blue Crane when she grew up. And he went out again and again saw the Blue Crane sitting in the sun, and he turned and left her in peace for he wished her to sit quietly. He did not startle her; he returned home.

Then he took the clothes, because he thought that the Blue Crane had become a grown person. She seemed to be a young woman. He went out and saw the Blue Crane sitting basking. He put down the things and stole up to her. He caught hold of her. When she tried to get into the water he held her fast and rubbed her face with her perspiration. He made her smell his scent. He told the Blue Crane that he was her brother. It was he the

'Tinderbox' who was holding her. He was her elder brother; she should leave off struggling and sit down.

They the Blue Crane sat down. He covered her with a cap which he had made for her and with a *kaross* and skin apron. The Blue Crane put on the *kaross* and tied on the apron. Then he took Blue Crane with him. They returned home (L. VIII, (32) 8801–11).

The very close similarity between these two passages, given by two different narrators with six years separating their collection, is evidence of the stability of oral tradition. The motif is, apparently, one of significance and is plainly a variant of function F in which usually |Kaggen revives himself in the water and is met by his possessions on the home side of the bank. Certain features of these passages are worthy of special note:

(1) In both accounts the characters are separated from the community and left to grow.
(2) The transformation is represented as a period of physical growth from a small remnant into maturity.
(3) Both |Kaggen's son and his sister are disoriented. They do not know |Kaggen and need to be made to know him. They have no social traits.
(4) In both accounts maturation is followed by the dressing in new clothes and then by the leading of the characters back to their home.
(5) In M20 the phrase, 'Blue Crane had grown up, she seemed to be a young woman' (!kui |a) is identical with the phrases used elsewhere to describe girls during puberty rites.
(6) |Kaggen's actions and speeches are markedly ceremonial.

The emphasis in these passages on the growth of a small part into maturity and the subjects' total lack of social orientation manifests the pre-social nature of the characters prior to their being fully formed and is reminiscent of a common feature of transition rites. Of liminal persona in general Turner writes:

That they are not yet classified is often expressed in symbols modelled in processes of gestation and parturition. The neophytes are likened to or treated as embryos, newborn infants or sucklings by symbolic means which vary from culture to culture (*op. cit.*, 96).

Furthermore Turner (*ibid.*) states that the term 'to grow'

> well expresses how many people think of transition rites … To 'grow' a girl
> into a woman is to effect an ontological transformation; it is not merely to
> convey an unchanging substance from one position to another by a quasi
> mechanical force.

As has been seen, the same words were used in M20 with regard to the
Blue Crane as were commonly used to describe girls during puberty rites. In
addition to this the importance of the characters not seeing |Kaggen might,
besides its overt narrative meaning, reflect the fact that both girls and
hunters were instructed not to look at anyone during their isolation. There is
no evidence that being equipped with new clothes was a feature of any |Xam
rite although Agnes Hoernlé in her investigation of transition rites amongst
groups of Khoe-Khoe who were geographically very close to the |Xam of the
northern Cape, found that a certain stage in the rites was characterised by

> the renunciation of all that represents the old life, after a period, more or
> less prolonged, of complete seclusion. The individual must be reborn. There
> is a special cleansing of the !nau person's body by the individual officiating,
> after which a totally new set of clothing is put on (Hoernlé 1918: 68).

To summarise: there are strong affinities between the minimal structure
identified with the narratives of group A and the belief structure informing
the hunters' eland rites. Furthermore, the narratives and the rites share a
common topography and |Kaggen's role is identical in both cases.

In those narratives where death is threatened, |Kaggen provides the
magic necessary to secure life. In so far as |Kaggen's nature is in contrast
with !Khwa's in a Life/Death opposition, some comparison between these
narratives and the girls' puberty rites suggests itself. In one narrative |Kaggen
does magically intervene on behalf of girls secluded during menses and in
two other narratives a motif occurs as a variant of function F which has a
number of features in common with ideas concerning subjects of transition
rites in general and the |Xam girls' puberty rites in particular.

It is suggested, therefore, that while there are no significant similarities
between the sequence of events in the rites and the sequence of events in the
narratives, a similar way of conceiving of the world is apparent in narrative
and ritual and serves to shape both. In looking at the cultural context of the

|Kaggen narratives this similarity cannot be ignored although its importance with regard to the conscious understanding of the narratives by the |Xam is impossible to estimate.

Narrative humour and its social use

One aspect of the narratives – an aspect which appears to have been fundamental – has not so far been mentioned in relation to the religious and social frame discussed above. This feature is the humour displayed in the narratives. Indeed in analysing the cultural basis of the |Kaggen narratives the humour can be an important index to socio-cultural phenomena. It is, however, more a tool of the individual narrator and less dependent on culturally inherited narrative materials than are plots or the personality features of *dramatis personae*. The humour in a narration may, of course, reside in the situations described, but the way in which those situations are quarried for their humorous content will depend on the innovation and expertise of the narrator himself.

It has been suggested above that by violating social norms in the narratives |Kaggen reinforced the 'idea of society' and revealed some of the dangers lurking at its edges. He achieved this not as part of an unrelenting moral tale but by being the centre of a humorous exposition wherein what was socially dangerous could be held at a distance, encapsulated and enjoyed as slap-stick, at one level unconnected with the real everyday world. The humour, however, was heavily dependent on the assumptions of normality and social order, without which there would be no contrast. It served, therefore, both to entertain and to underline the expected order of social life. The amusement it generated was both a release and an indirect instruction. Here, incidentally, is way in which |Kaggen differed from !Khwa whose religious nature was so uniformly awesome as to exclude him from humorous use in narrative.

Summary

It is now possible to differentiate various levels at which |Kaggen had significance for the |Xam.

(1) At the surface level he provided an opportunity for the reinforcing of social norms simultaneously with a temporary release through humour

from the constrictions of those norms – an entertainment grounded in social life but distanced from quotidian reality by comedy.

(2) He had an aetiological function providing through his life-affirming creativity some explanations for the content of the physical world.

(3) He simultaneously represented the autonomous wildness of game and the possibility of social chaos. He was a marginal being and stood on the boundary of amenable and unamenable nature as a supernatural being, just as he crossed the boundaries of social order in the social context provided for him in the narratives.

(4) At a conceptual level he performed a specific kind of logical operation by being an agent transforming elements from one state into another. This conceptual process was evinced in many other areas of |Xam thought, most notably in the beliefs surrounding certain rituals.

In the person of |Kaggen all of these aspects – humorous, social, religious, conceptual – converge to form a complex capable of a variety of resonances and connections within |Xam life at many different levels: a culturally dense image clustered with diverse significance.

The trickster may be found throughout the world but he is not necessarily, therefore, 'all things to all men' as Radin (1956: 169) suggests. The way in which a trickster is integrated with the ideas and world-view of any society is likely to be specific to that society. In the foregoing chapters an attempt has been made to show some of the ways in which the trickster, |Kaggen, was embedded in and integrated with the ideas and attitudes found in one San group, the |Xam, in one period of their history in so far as those ideas and attitudes are preserved in the collection of |Xam texts made by Bleek and Lloyd.

Notes

1   For a discussion of trickster figures and autonomous psychological states, see J. Layard, review of *The Trickster* by Paul Radin (1957), and Layard (1958).

2   These words, used almost interchangeably, mean 'to tease, lie and deceive'.

3   A connection might be made between the masculinity of !Khwa – who threatened young women once they became capable of child-bearing – and actual or potential in-laws. Some support for this idea may be found in the story of !Haūnū and ǂKagara, a husband and his brother-in-law respectively, who fight over the wife/sister. By

way of a gloss to this narrative the narrator associates !Haūnū the husband, with !Khwa, although he also suggests that !Haūnū may have been a rain !gi:xa.

4   For an historical account of the growth of this theory see S.E. Hyman (1968).

5   The collectors never determined what article of clothing was meant by this word.

6   The |Xam practised anointing with perspiration in contexts where one person wished to transfer certain of his own attributes to another (see D.F. Bleek 1923: 50; 1931–36, Part VIII: 148f).

10

Two |Kaggen narratives: compositional variations

In the foregoing chapters, the |Kaggen narratives were discussed as a group displaying certain thematic, structural and cultural characteristics. Where single versions of narratives are concerned, however, the interplay between a particular story, its cultural density, and the individual narrator, becomes more visible. By comparing different versions of the same narrative the various ways in which narrators used a theme, plot or symbol can be shown. In this chapter two narratives (M1 and M9) are discussed and special attention is paid to the discrepancies between different versions. M1 and M9 are both narratives which, in certain versions, display more complexity than many of the other |Kaggen narratives in the collection. M1 is very well known and has long interested students of San parietal art, since it centrally involves an eland, the antelope which features so prominently in rock painting throughout the Republic of South Africa. M9 has been referred to in passing several times in the previous chapters. Structurally and thematically it is anomalous, and, as will be seen, is also singular in other ways. Versions of both of these narratives were published by Dorothea Bleek (1923: 1ff, 34ff).

|Kaggen and the eland (M1)

In *Mantis and His Friends* Dorothea Bleek presented two versions of a narrative which she entitled 'Mantis makes an eland'. Her 'First version' is a compound summary of three separate narratives, two given by ||Kabbo (B. II, 379–433; L. II, (4) 482–86) and one by Dia!kwain (L. V, (1) 3608–83). Her 'Second version' is a summary of a narrative given by |Hang ‡kass'o

(L. VIII, (6) 6505–83). The title is a little misleading as Dia!kwain's version and one of ‖Kabbo's versions does not include |Kaggen making the eland, and the version given by ‖Kabbo that does include the eland creation has a quite different conclusion from that given in this published 'First version', i.e. it does not conclude with the creation of the moon.

Five versions of a narrative involving |Kaggen and an eland were collected by Bleek and Lloyd, three from ‖Kabbo and one each from Dia!kwain and |Hang ╪kass'o. In addition to these, several other very closely related narratives were also collected, one by Bleek and Lloyd and a few by other writers (L. IV, (2) 3520–33; von Wiellich, *op. cit.*, Vol 1, 97ff; Orpen, *op. cit.*, 143ff; Currlé 1913: 118; Potgieter 1955: 31). While the published 'First version' does pull together interesting elements from all versions and also coincides in part with |Hang ╪kass'o's version, it is a potentially misleading, if elegant, compound.

Before attempting to analyse all or any one of the versions of this narrative it is necessary to separate out the plot elements which appear in various combinations throughout the group. These elements can be placed under three main headings:

(1) *The creation and subsequent death of the eland.* |Kaggen takes a piece of |Kwammang-a's shoe to a pool where it grows into an eland as |Kaggen feeds and rubs it with honey. This honey he should have brought home to feed his family. The Ichneumon discovers what |Kaggen is doing with the honey, whereupon a member of the family, together with a hunting party (Meercats, in most versions), goes to the water, calls the eland out, kills it for food and cuts it up.

(2) *|Kaggen and the meercats.* |Kaggen finds a party of Meercats cutting up an eland. He argues with them but they are much stronger than he and he is forced to escape from them.

(3) *|Kaggen creates the moon.* |Kaggen pierces the eland's gall, which has been hung on a bush, thus causing darkness to blot out the sun. On his way home he creates the moon in order to see his way.

None of the five collected versions contains plot elements relating to all of these headings, although four of the five involve the encounter with the Meercats. This central part of the complex was also collected by Bleek and Lloyd from ╪Kasing as a narrative complete in itself, although featuring the Ichneumon, not |Kaggen, as the protagonist. It was also collected separately by Miss L. Currlé. It can be regarded as the core narrative in this complex and falls soundly within group A under the thematic and structural definitions given in Chapters 8 and 9. Miss Currlé's version is as follows:

> When the devil[1] went out ... he found the meercats following the spoor of a wounded eland which had been wounded by one of the meercats with a poisoned arrow; the devil said in a very contemptuous way, 'What funny people they are, such insignificant-looking people, so small in stature!'
>
> He spoke thus in order to provoke their anger, and to pick a quarrel with them, but the meercats took no notice of all this. They quietly followed the eland's spoor. As the devil could not make them angry, he went and pushed the leader off the spoor and followed the spoor himself, but the meercat came and pushed him off very violently, and said, 'Gar-'argi'-innim', meaning, 'I am a big man, I carry a beard', but the devil pushed him off again. This was done repeatedly until at last they came to blows. The meercat, being a very clever fighter, soon gained the upper hand; in a short time there was nothing left for the devil but flight. The meercats then followed up the spoor of the eland and captured their game without any further disturbance from the devil (Currlé, *loc. cit.*).

Although clearly a curtailed summary, this reported version shows a very strong resemblance to that collected by Bleek and Lloyd from ǂKasing in which an almost identical encounter between the Meercats and the Ichneumon also involves the protagonist insulting the Meercats about their size. The Meercats in ǂKasing's version, however, are not following but cutting up an eland. Two of ǁKabbo's three versions also begin with, and centre upon, a similar encounter with Meercats. In these versions |Kaggen goes to the Meercats while they are cutting up an eland. Because of their superior strength the Meercats command |Kaggen to collect wood for the fire with which they intend to cook the eland meat. There is no suggestion in either of these versions that the eland in question had been created by |Kaggen; it is simply an eland.

An inventory of the main events in this group of narratives and their distribution throughout all versions, brings the out the centrality of this encounter.[2]

		!Kabbo	!Hang ‡kass'o	Dia!kwain	‡Kasing	Currlé
		1	2	3	4	5		
1	!Kaggen makes an eland from !Kwammang-a's shoe		X		X			
2	!Kaggen nurtures the eland on honey		X		X	X		
3	Ichneumon spies on !Kaggen		X		X	X		
4	Ichneumon discovers the eland and tells !Kwammang-a and/or Meercats, who kill it and cut it up		X		X	X		
5	!Kaggen disputes about the eland with							
	(a) the Meercats	X	X	X		X	(X)	X
	(b) !Kwammang-a				X			
6	!Kaggen is physically oppressed by the Meercats	X	X	X		X	(X)	X
7	!Kaggen pierces the gall	X	X	X	X			
8	!Kaggen flees from the Meercats	X	X	X		X	(X)	X
9	!Kaggen creates the moon from							
	(a) his shoe	X		X				
	(b) a feather							
10	!Kaggen magically steals Meercat's belongings		X					

On the basis of Miss Bleek's published 'First version' it would seem that 'the narrative' opens and closes symmetrically with a shoe used in a creative way. Were this to be symbolically interpreted it would not only present great difficulty but would also be quite pointless, as no such narrative actually exists. These versions are too few in number to indicate a very full range of possible combinations of plot elements – although the version compounded by Miss Bleek has strong claims to plausibility – but in looking at the actual materials collected, the most prominent feature, and one supported by ‡Kasing's and Miss Currlé's versions, is the dispute with the Meercats. If one adds to this the belief held by the |Xam that |Kaggen created (a) the bucks and (b) the moon, one has here at least the thematic ground of all the collected versions.

The story of |Kaggen's creation of the moon was, apparently, also capable of sustaining itself outside of the narrative context provided by both the creation of the eland and the dispute with the Meercats, as the following story collected by von Wielligh (*op. cit.*, Vol 1, 97ff) shows:

> |Kaggen made himself a pair of neat shoes with which he was in his element. However, one of the shoes, the right, was hard and chafed him on the right foot. So he told his daughter, the Hammerkop (a bird) to place the shoe in the water to make it soft.
>
> The great Watersnake was enraged by this, because |Kaggen put his dirty shoe in the water. The Watersnake made the water very cold that night so that it was all iced-over by the next morning and the shoe was stuck in the ice.
>
> That morning |Kaggen sent his daughter, the Hammerkop, to fetch the shoe. She brought it with a large piece of shiny ice on it. He was so upset by this that he threw the shoe away, up in the air.
>
> The Hammerkop, who knew the Windbird well, called out: 'Windbird, Windbird take the shoe up, up, up, in the sky so, that we can have light at night!' The shoe with the piece of ice on it then became the moon.

The conclusion to ‖Kabbo's version 2 is also instructive for it is a motif which he uses elsewhere in a quite unconnected narrative (M8). It is clear, therefore, that there is no one authentic version of this story but, rather, a number of combinable elements, many of which came together, at least in this sample, most often around the central core of the identifiably group A story of |Kaggen's encounter with the Meercats.

At this point it is useful to examine this core more closely.

Miss Currlé's version (*op. cit.*, 117) is preceded by an account of |Kaggen which is very recognisable from the Bleek and Lloyd material. She writes:

> (The Bushmen) believe that there was in the early days an evil person or devil who always quarrelled with the others and was always trying to pick a quarrel for the slightest reason.

As examples of his behaviour she then recounts a version of the story of |Kaggen and the Cat (also collected by Bleek and Lloyd in two versions) and follows this with the version of |Kaggen and the Meercats quoted above.

Both of the narratives which she gives open with |Kaggen going out into the veld and close with his flight. In the story of the Cat we are also told about the magical power |Kaggen's possessions had to follow him. No mention is made in either story about |Kaggen's immersion in the water by his home but they are only sketchily reported narratives and it is impossible to tell what details may or may not have been in the stories when first collected. The narrative given by ǂKasing, which is almost identical to that reported by Miss Currlé, does lack a magical flight by the protagonist, the Ichneumon, and at no point does he return home either for information or to be lectured for misbehaviour. Both Miss Currlé's version and ǂKasing's therefore, represent the barest form of the group A structure: A—→ B —→ C —→ (E).³

Turning to Dia!kwain's version, we find again the standard group A topography and a few more of the familiar functions. |Kaggen does return home at the close of the narrative and is lectured, although briefly, by a member of his family, in this case |Kwammang-a. |Kaggen's flight from the Meercats is also magical, although he does not enter the water before proceeding to his home. At the start of the narrative he departs from his home, commits an anti-social act, i.e. collects honey without bringing it back for his family, and returns home several times before his family attempt to discover what he is doing. Therefore, although his anti-social act is perpetrated topographically away from home, its consequences are primarily for his family at home, not for some non-member of the family as is usually the case.

Whereas such creatures as the Cat, the Lions, the Ticks etc., usually physically assail |Kaggen in response to his anti-social behaviour – an option not really open to his family – here the family act to make reparation for their loss of honey by killing the eland for food. Although a logical product of what had gone before, this does present a structural problem in the narrative, and accounts to some extent for the change of attention from the family to the Meercats. To end the narrative with |Kaggen simply returning home having been thwarted by his family would, in terms of the customary narrative structure, be very unsatisfactory. The solution offered in Dia!kwain's version is therefore as follows: A —→ (Protagonist Departs from His Home) B —→ (Incurs hostility of family by 'misusing' honey) G —→ (returns home) —→ (repeat) then: A —→ C (actual conflict: family kill eland but Meercats cut it up and |Kaggen attacks Meercats with arrows which boomerang back at him) ⟶ E (magical flight) ⟶ G (returns home) ⟶ H (lectured by |Kwammang-a).

What is happening in this version, therefore, is that the story of |Kaggen, his family, the honey and the eland, is being joined together with the straightforward story of |Kaggen, the Meercats and the eland, as a way of concluding a structurally difficult plot. This conjunction was not only made by Dia!kwain; it was also made in one other version by ‖Kabbo. The central move which makes this conjunction both possible and intelligible, is that of having a member of the family kill the eland but – as would be the case in real life – giving the job of cutting it up to others, i.e. the Meercats.

The two versions given by ‖Kabbo which open with |Kaggen pestering the Meercats when they were cutting up an eland, like ǂKasing's and Miss Currlé's versions, again conform to a group A structure: A ⟶ B ⟶ C ⟶ F ⟶ G ⟶ H. The magic entailed in |Kaggen's flight is the creation of the moon which, perhaps because the narrator was enthusiastic about the social benefits of this act – it henceforth permits hunting at night etc. – tends to diminish the weight given to the Ichneumon's criticisms of |Kaggen (function H). ‖Kabbo's remaining narrative is very different from his other two in that it describes the stealing of |Kwammang-a's shoe to create an eland, and proceeds, as does Dia!kwain's narrative, to combine the story of |Kaggen's socially irresponsible use of honey with that of |Kaggen and the Meercats. However, |Kaggen is beaten, returns home having only annoyed the Meercats by piercing the gall, and, as in M8, only then triumphs by transporting all of the Meercats' belongings away from them in the night by dreaming that he is doing so. Thus the Meercats are rendered naked, and their arrows, quivers, clothes, plus the eland meat, are carried on a magical tree to where |Kaggen is sleeping.

All of these narratives display various techniques for the construction of a story from fictional materials organised to differing degrees around a familiar structure. The materials used – the plot segments, the motifs, the beliefs about |Kaggen, together with familiar verbal formulae etc. – were apparently the common property of narrators, but their organisation in any given narrative was a matter of individual capacity and taste. |Hang ǂkass'o narrative in this set is particularly interesting from this point of view.

The version of M1 given by |Hang ǂkass'o published by Miss Bleek as the 'Second Version', contains both |Kaggen's creation of the eland and the moon. However, the Meercats do not feature, and this, combined with other features has the effect of completely obliterating the familiar group A structure.

The problem of having |Kaggen meekly returning home, thwarted by his family, is avoided by |Hang ǂkass'o in a way that differs from the strategy employed by Dia!kwain and ‖Kabbo. Rather than transferring the centre of responsibility from the family to the Meercats, |Hang ǂkass'o keeps it all in the family and the resulting narrative is very coherent, if anomalous.

This version also displays |Hang ǂkass'o's tendency to emphasise the creative and benevolent side of |Kaggen's character, for at no point does he mention or even imply that |Kaggen's use of the honey in any way impoverished the family. Furthermore, the eland itself is not made from a shoe stolen from |Kwammang-a, as in ‖Kabbo's version, but from a small piece of leather which |Kwammang-a had cut off and discarded. In no sense, therefore, is |Kwammang-a's killing of the eland a response to any anti-social act by |Kaggen. If anything of this kind has occurred, it is |Kwammang-a who has been crudely pragmatic in his attitude to the eland. To |Kaggen the eland is a beautiful creature; to |Kwammang-a it is simply a tasty meal.

Another way in which |Hang ǂkass'o's version differs from the other versions is that the Ichneumon does not connive with |Kwammang-a to discover what |Kaggen is doing, for he does not suspect that |Kaggen is doing anything. He is invited by |Kaggen to join him on an expedition and is tricked by |Kaggen into sleeping while |Kaggen visits the eland. |Kaggen apparently takes this precaution because he knows that the Ichneumon is liable to tell |Kwammang-a if he sees the eland, and knows, too, the likelihood of |Kwammang-a's unsentimental reaction. However, the Ichneumon does peep out and see the eland. Thus far, at least, this version has none of the characteristics of either a group A or a group B structure.

When the Ichneumon tells |Kwammang-a of |Kaggen's beautiful eland, |Kwammang-a instructs the Ichneumon to guide him and his fellow hunters to it. When the party arrive, |Kwammang-a kills the eland and he and the other hunters (they are called in this text the |Kwammang-agu[4]) cut up the eland. In no way is |Kwammang-a disassociated from the cutting up and no transference of responsibility takes place from the family to another group as in the other versions.

When |Kaggen arrives on the scene he berates |Kwammang-a for not waiting for him to arrive before killing the eland. He cries and insists that only he had the right to allow the eland to be killed. Had this happened then 'his heart would have been comfortable about it' (ha |ī: sing twai-ī, ī:). |Kwammang-a is unmoved by this and tells |Kaggen to stop talking and get on with collecting wood. This |Kaggen does, but, finding his eland's gall on a bush, whispers to it, and it to him, about piercing it and leaping into the darkness which it would emit. As in two of ‖Kabbo's versions, |Kaggen keeps returning to the gall while he is collecting wood, and being scolded by the Ichneumon for tarrying, until |Kwammang-a realises that |Kaggen has seen the gall and is likely to play some kind of trick with it. |Kwammang-a and the Ichneumon then quickly pack the meat into their nets and insist that all depart immediately for home. On the way |Kaggen pretends that he has lost one of his shoes and makes such a fuss about it that |Kwammang-a allows him to return to where they had been cutting up the meat in order to look for it. He runs back, finds the gall, and breaks it. The liquid from the gall covers his head, and his eyes grow large in its darkness. He then gropes around until he finds a feather with which to wipe his eyes. Then he casts the feather into the sky commanding it to become the moon. He says:

'A ku ǂakku !a:ting !gwaxu. A se ‖koaken di !kau!kaura.
Aken a sing |kai au ‖ga:. Asing
|kai|kai, ho oi !kʔe |ho.'
(You shall lie in the sky. You shall completely
become the moon. You must shine at night.
You must take away the darkness by shining for the people.)

His speech to the moon is long and contains instructions on waxing and waning, or, as the text has it 'falling off' (tatten ui) and 'coming to life' (!kauten sa). Then the narrator's own voice concludes the narrative with the statement that when the moon lights up the sky at night, it is because |Kaggen has created it and |Kaggen meant to give light to the people, (|Kaggen a oa |kui koa. |Kakkaken ka, ha koa ǂxi-ja !kʔe). The text then becomes a long description of how the |Xam hunt porcupine at night, a practice made possible by |Kaggen's creation of the moon. This conclusion is very similar to the conclusion to the two versions by ‖Kabbo which also involve the creation of the moon. All three texts emphasise (a) the fact that the moon dies and returns to life, and (b) that the light of the moon is a great benefit to the Bushmen.

No mention is made of |Kwammang-a and the Ichneumon after |Kaggen goes back to the gall, and the sudden darkness created by |Kaggen is not said to have any effect on the others returning home. It seems, therefore, that after his eland is killed, |Kaggen simply wishes to playfully and gratuitously make a darkness with the gall. This action does not appear to be a reprisal against

|Kwammang-a and the Ichneumon for having killed the eland. |Kaggen's actions in this version are all either creative or harmlessly playful.

In abandoning the conventional structures of |Kaggen narratives |Hang ╪kass'o's version is organised more by patterned symbols than by familiarly plotted actions. |Kwammang-a's shoe could have been made from the hide of any animal. The |Xam made shoes from eland, gemsbok, quagga, wildebeest and other animal skins. It was, however, at least dead skin which he made into living flesh. In killing |Kaggen's creation, |Kwammang-a was reversing this process. The feather which |Kaggen used to create the moon, was, according to Miss Lloyd (1889: 5), who collected the version, an ostrich feather, although this is not made explicit in the text. Male ostriches were believed to have the power to resurrect themselves after death. The story, published in *Specimens of Bushman Folklore*, called 'The Resurrection of the Ostrich' (*op. cit.*, 136ff) describes a hunter killing a male ostrich and a single ostrich feather, stained with blood, settling in a pool, and gradually growing to become the same nature ostrich once more which then returns home. W.H.I. Bleek (1875b: 13f) writes:

> The idea of the revival of a dead male ostrich, in and through one of its little feathers, is also mentioned in other places and is compared to the coming to life of the moon; whilst, with the exception of the moon and the Male Ostrich, all other things mortal are said to die outright and not to come to life again.

By using this motif in the conclusion to his version, |Hang ╪kass'o is drawing together two culturally guaranteed symbols of a mediation between Life and Death. From dead skin |Kaggen creates a living eland; the living eland is killed; darkness is generated from its gall, and the moon is created from a feather which both lights the darkness and mediates Life and Death.

It must be assumed that the moon which |Kaggen created was a new moon, arc-shaped like a feather or a curling veld-shoe, and there is no doubt that the |Xam had strong beliefs about the regenerative powers of the new moon. Indeed they even had a ceremony in which the new moon was requested to bestow its revived energies upon them (Bleek & Lloyd 1911: 56ff). Furthermore, the |Xam symbolically associated honey both with the moon and with the revival of dying game animals. It was believed that 'moon water', said to resemble liquid honey, might settle on an animal that was dying from the poison of a hunter's arrow, counteract the poison, and allow the animal to live (*ibid.*, 66ff; von Wielligh, *op. cit.*, Vol. 3, 44). Honey was also believed to have been used by |Kaggen when he gave the bucks their colours.

The gemsbok was given white liquid honey to eat, hence gemsbok are white; the hartebeest was given honeycomb made by young bees because it is red; the springbok was given liquid from the cells of young bees, which is also red, and so on. According to Dia!kwain, |Kaggen gave the eland wasp's honey which is dark, although in the |Hang ǂkass'o narrative, |Kaggen gives his eland honey made from the cells of young bees. There is no doubt, however, that symbolically honey was regarded as a creative substance associated with game animals and with the moon.

It is interesting to note that, in Dia!kwain's version of the story, |Kaggen is alerted to the fact that his eland is dying, by the honey which he is gathering being dry. Characteristic of the sympathy between things in nature, in which the |Xam believed, the state the honey is said to indicate that 'blood is flowing'. |Kaggen then looks for more honey but all the honey which he finds is dry. He then hurries to his eland and discovers drops of eland blood on the hollowed stone in which he has previously been placing the honey for the eland. This motif is only contained in Dia!kwain's version but it is plainly consistent with the association which the |Xam made between game and honey.

By manipulating the conscious symbolic associations of the |Xam, |Hang ǂkass'o's version draws together disparate narrative elements, side-steps the Social/Non-Social opposition posited by the group A structure, and establishes the narrative on a Life/Death axis which is also quite unlike the group B structure usually found in conjunction with that axis. Whether this version was learned from someone else exactly in its collected form – he claimed to have heard it from his mother, |Xabbi-ang – or whether it was composed by him out of familiar motifs, is impossible to tell. Like most of his narratives this text is well organised, with deliberate repetitions and a careful, unhurried movement from beginning to end. In this respect it seems to have a fairly fixed form. Whatever the case, however, it does combine the story of the creation of the eland and the story of the creation of the moon in a most intelligible way. This combination was not attempted in any of the other four versions collected and it stands alone as a uniquely complex version, deeply grounded in the overtly articulated symbolism found in |Xam culture.

|Kaggen and ‖Khwai-hɛm (M9)

The story of |Kaggen and ‖Khwai-hɛm, an all-devouring monster, was collected in two versions, one given by ‖Kabbo (L. II, (33) 2966–3149), the other by |Hang ǂkass'o (L. VIII, (20) 7812–16; (22) 7906–56). On each occasion the story was preceded by a story of |Kaggen's visit to the Ticks (M8) and it is likely that they were usually told in conjunction.

M9 is the only narrative in the collection to show any sign of Bantu influence, and displays, with remarkable clarity the changes that may take place in a narrative when it is transposed from one culture to another. Alice Werner, in her book *Myths and Legends of the Bantu*, describes the large number of Bantu narratives which deal with 'a monster which swallows the population of a village – or, indeed, of the whole country – and is subsequently slain by a boy hero' (Werner 1968: 206). She lists the main points of these stories as follows:

> A whole population is swallowed by a monster. One woman escapes and gives birth to a son. This son kills the monster and releases the people. They make him their chief (*ibid.*).

Clyde Kluckhohn (1965: 163) describes the same theme in very similar terms but adds that the boy 'restores his people – but not his father – and becomes chief'. As the |Xam had no chiefs, it is not surprising to find this aspect of the story absent from the versions given by ‖Kabbo and |Hang ǂkass'o. Briefly, the story is as follows.

> |Kaggen insists that as the family have a large amount of food at their disposal, his adopted daughter, the Porcupine, must go and invite her real father, ‖Khwai-hɛm, to come and share it with them. The Porcupine protests because any contact with her father is very dangerous. She warns that he will eat everything, that his appetite is insatiable and that he rarely travels because of the weight of his massive stomach. |Kaggen, however, insists, and so the Porcupine goes. When she reaches ‖Khwai-hɛm's house she attempts to dissuade him from coming, by saying to him that the food |Kaggen has provided is insufficient. ‖Khwai-hɛm refuses to accept this and insists on taking up the invitation.
>
> When he arrives, |Kaggen places some food out for him which he rapidly devours. |Kaggen then gives him a large pot of soup which he also devours, pot and all. He soon consumes all the food and starts on the bushes, and,

indeed, everything in sight, until the place is quite flat and bare. Finally, he swallows |Kaggen and |Kwammang-a.

The Porcupine is left crying alone but is soon joined by Young |Kaggen, one of |Kaggen's sons. She rather formally interrogates them in turn to discover if they can defeat the monster. She then heats a spear in the fire. Applying it to Young |Kaggen's ear and nostril she says that ‖Khwai-hɛm's tongue is like this. Tears slowly gather in his eyes and she pronounces him a mild person. She repeats the test on Young |Kwammang-a and he does not flinch or cry. Young |Kwammang-a is a brave man, like his father, she declares, while Young |Kaggen is like his father, mild and cowardly. She then gives them each a spear, telling Young |Kwammang-a to hold the spear in his right hand and Young |Kaggen to hold it in his left hand, as his father is left handed.

The two boys then approach ‖Khwai-hɛm. ‖Khwai-hɛm's tongue scorches them both, but, at a signal given by Young |Kwammang-a, they each plunge their spears into his stomach and cut him open. They then run away quickly as all the meat, the sheep |Kaggen had had, the pots, bushes, and |Kaggen and |Kwammang-a pour out. Then ‖Khwai-hɛm doubles up and dies. Later the whole family move to another place where they live in peace.

In terms of plot structure both versions of this narrative are the same. As is the case with group A narratives, |Kaggen invites a conflict by his foolishness. Against the Porcupine's advice he willfully insists that ‖Khwai-hɛm be invited and disaster follows. However, beyond this opening point, it is not |Kaggen but the Porcupine who is the protagonist and it is she who is the agent of function A (protagonist departs from home). From here on the narrative moves rapidly into the conflict phase but, because the conflict is actually at home, as well as having been invited by members of the family – a contradiction in the usual logic of the group A structure – the narrative immediately gives over to a group B structure and proceeds as if dealing with an outsider who threatens death. In this respect it is similar to M6 (!Gāunu ts'axau and the Baboons) – another mixed structure – where |Kaggen sends his son out to collect sticks with which to assail the baboons. In that narrative the positive transformation phase – the gradual resurrection of !Gāunu ts'axau – was, like the equivalent phase in this narrative, highly ceremonial.

The transformation of the situation in M9 is achieved by a combination of an informed member of the community which is under attack (the Porcupine), and two active group members (Young |Kaggen and Young |Kwammang-a). The Porcupine cannot be said to be a marginal group member in the same way that |Kaggen is in the group B narratives, but, like |Kaggen in that group, she does have privileged knowledge of the 'threatening outsider', her real father, and is, perhaps, marginal to some extent by virtue of the fact that she is only an adopted daughter of |Kaggen.

It is especially worthy of attention that function L (Member(s) of the group, on the basis of received information, defeat(s) threatening non-member) here involves a combination of two explicitly differentiated natures: the mild and the brave. These are said to be the respective attributes of |Kaggen, who, as was observed in Chapter 7 has certain female characteristics, and |Kwammang-a, who is always assertively very male. These complementary natures are also here given symbolic representation in the familiar opposition of left and right, for Young |Kaggen is instructed to hold his spear in his left hand and Young |Kwammang-a to hold his spear in his right hand. Among the |Xam, as in many other societies the left was associated with the female sex, the right with the male. Whereas the Porcupine's role in the narrative may well be linked to the woman who 'escapes and gives birth to a son' in the Bantu tradition, this substitute of a complementary male and female monster-defeating instrument for the Bantu son who kills the monster and becomes chief, is a peculiarly San feature. It not only rehabilitates the narrative in a non-stratified social context, but also makes an indirect point about the balanced constitution of San social forces.

The narrative moves logically from function L to M (Rebirth of the dead group members and/or survival of the instrumental group member). As in M19, all the harm done by the 'threatening outsider' is negated and function N (Social endorsement of success by the group) follows, although weakly, in the form of the establishment of a new home where peace continues undisturbed.

It is clear that the basic shape of the Bantu story was suited to being integrated in a |Xam group B structure. Furthermore, in |Hang ‡kass'o's version, the boys hide near ‖Khwai-hɛm's hut by crouching down either side of the entrance and pretending to be stones. The same disguise was used by a woman hiding from a similar monster in a Sesotho narrative of this kind (Werner, *op. cit.*, 208). This motif, the role of the Porcupine, and the omnivorousness of the monster are all plainly retentions from a Bantu source. The way in which the monster was defeated, however, and the reasons for his visit – i.e. the sharing of food are both pure San contributions.

While these features are common to both versions of the narrative, there are considerable differences in the treatment given to the story by ‖Kabbo and |Hang ǂkass'o – particularly in the description of ‖Khwai-hɛm. In ‖Kabbo's version ‖Khwai-hɛm is not only all-devouring but also has many of the attributes of a bush fire. The sky is darkened where he stands; the ground becomes blackened where he has been; he consumes bushes in an instant, and his tongue is like a flame, burning whatever it touches. Indeed the description of his coming to the camp-site of |Kaggen and his family, could well be a literal description of a bush fire.

This feature may have been related to ‖Kabbo's equally distinct treatment of the narrative which immediately preceded this one, M8, in which |Kaggen takes away the Tick's sheep. Both the narrators gave these narratives together; |Hang ǂkass'o concluding M8 (L. VIII, (20) 7790–7811) and then starting M9 as a separate narrative, ‖Kabbo combining M8 (L. II, (32) 2926–65) and M9 into one continuous performance. The narrators differed both in the conclusion which they gave to M8 and in the degree of elaboration given to some of its aspects. As is usual with |Hang ǂkass'o, his version of M8 is well organised and has a clear and simple thrust to the story-line. ‖Kabbo's version, however, while being less single-mindedly concerned with conveying the events clearly, is elaborated and greatly enlivened by images energetically elaborated from the basic features of the plot. Structurally both versions belong to group A.

In |Hang ǂkass'o's version |Kaggen leaves his home and goes to the home of the Ticks. These people are not relatives or friends but 'black people who keep sheep', and he goes not on a social visit, but with the intention of stealing their sheep. The Ticks see him coming and hide in their sheep's wool. When |Kaggen approaches they drop from their hiding-places and beat him severely so that he is forced to escape by magically getting feathers and flying back to his home, his possessions flying faithfully behind him. Having soothed his wounds, he admits to |Kwammang-a where he has been, and |Kwammang-a tells him, through Ichneumon, that the Ticks are dangerous people and not really to be visited. However, |Kwammang-a does give him advice on how he should approach stealing their sheep if this is what he wishes to do. He tells |Kaggen that he should creep up on the Ticks' sheep, pick the Ticks out one by one and drop them in the fire; then he will be free to drive the sheep away. In doing this |Kwammang-a is not acting out of character, for the Ticks, like the Baboons and the Elephants in M6 and M10, are treated as different and menacing racial groups. |Kaggen sleeps overnight and at dawn goes and does just as |Kwammang-a advised. The Ticks argue with him and say that he has learned this method from |Kwammang-a. |Kaggen, true to form, asserts that he had known it himself all along but had simply forgotten on the previous day. He then drives away the sheep and takes them back to his own home.

‖Kabbo's version is far more elaborated. |Kaggen visits the Ticks who see him coming and hide. After a while they drop down one by one, surround him, fiercely beat him with knobkerries, and he escapes in the usual fashion. At this point ‖Kabbo uses the motif he had previously used in one version of M1, i.e. the transportation of his adversaries' belongings, achieved by dreaming that he is doing so. This time it happens on a grand scale for he takes not only all their sheep and all their clothes but also their cooking utensils, their houses and their fire – in fact every material sign of culture. When |Kaggen's family awake in the morning they find a kraal mounted high with sheep, and the Ticks' huts, clothes etc. in their own camp. |Kaggen then delivers a fierce justification of this act, condemning the black people to live evermore without clothing or warmth from a fire, and to eat raw food and drink blood from the ears of hares. The latter part dealing with the drinking of uncooked blood, refers, of course, to the fact that they are ticks, who do feed in this fashion. The whole speech, however, has strong racial overtones and there can be little doubt that the 'black people who we do not visit' refers directly to the Khoe-khoen. Indeed a note relating to this narrative points out that the !Korana were thought of as black because they always seemed to be angry and violent.[5]

What ‖Kabbo's version does is to seize upon the culture/nature opposition implicit in the difference between those who do and do not possess fire, and extrapolate upon this to the extent of overriding the simple basis of the narrative, seen unadorned in |Hang ‡kass'o's version. |Kaggen's speech in self-justification becomes the focus of the narrative, while the actual events at the Ticks' camp are left as the shadowy background. In the speech itself, |Kaggen makes a number of points. Beginning with the fact that the Ticks had made him angry by their treatment of him he declares that henceforth they shall lack those things which provide a material culture, and he lists the ways in which this lack will be felt. They will, he says, eat raw food, not cooked food, because they have no fire; they will also be cold not warm, for the same reason; they will be forced to bite their meat not cut it; they will be naked not clothed; they will have no huts to live in; they will have no animals in their possession; and at night they will be in darkness because they have no fires to provide light.

|Kaggen then goes on to point out that, although for now he and his family have these things because he has taken them away from the Ticks, in time he and the others in his family will become animals and be without them too. Here he predicts that some day the Ichneumon will live in the hills and marry a female Ichneumon; the Porcupine will live in a hole; the Dassie will live in the mountains and he, |Kaggen, will become a little green flying insect. The 'Flat People', i.e. the San from the flat part of the country, will cook in the pots which he has stolen from the Ticks, because they will be the ones who have fire.

In this sense, this narrative becomes a story about the theft of fire, although there is nothing to suggest that |Kaggen and his family did not themselves already possess fire. |Kaggen is mildly berated for his actions by several members of his family, but not only is he unrepentant, he is also very articulate about the benefits of fire and the absolute difference its loss makes.

In elaborating this version from a story about the stealing of sheep, ‖Kabbo is making an implicit association between the keeping of domestic animals and culture – an obvious enough connection but one that is surprising coming from the San who, apart from hunting-dogs, kept no domestic animals. However, this association is likely to have been one result of the cultural contact which ‖Kabbo and the other informants had with non-San societies.

As was observed above, ‖Kabbo's versions of M8 and M9 are continuous. They were given as one narrative. In |Hang ǂkass'o's versions there is a break in the narration. The material justification for linking these narratives is simply that the sheep stolen from the Ticks provided the reason for inviting ‖Khwai-hɛm to visit. However, by making a continuous narrative out of M8 and M9 it appears to be the case that ‖Kabbo was linking these narratives at a symbolic level as well as at the simple level of plot.

If the theme of fire is taken in its different manifestations through ‖Kabbo's M8 and M9, it is evident that fire is established in M8 as a *sine qua non* of culture, but that in M9, in the form of |Khwai-hɛm with his highly destructive bush-fire attributes, the dangers of fire to social life are stressed in contradistinction to its pre-established benefits. In ‖Kabbo's M8, |Kaggen steals Ticks' sheep, cooking utensils, clothes, huts and fires. In M9 ‖Khwai-hɛm does the same thing to |Kaggen and his family. In achieving this symmetry, ‖Kabbo's versions considerably alter both M8 and M9 as given by |Hang ‡kass'o. The symmetry achieved by ‖Kabbo's additions may have been only for aesthetic reasons, but the additions themselves might also have a symbolic weight. The possibility that ‖Kabbo's combined narrative represents an articulation – sub-conscious or otherwise – of how far not to go in the direction of culture as represented by non-San groups, appears to suggest itself, especially as the defeat of the monster is achieved by means which are implicitly assertive about the balanced constitution of |Xam social cohesion. There is, however, no evidence from outside of the narratives that can be appealed to support such an interpretation. Whether actually symbolic or simply aesthetically balanced, ‖Kabbo's compound narrative clearly achieves the same kind of integration of disparate narrative materials and culturally resonant images that |Hang ‡kass'o achieved in his version of '|Kaggen and the eland'.

In the written literatures of advanced industrial societies, the ability to draw upon the culture with insight and depth is one important capacity which may distinguish the good novelist, playwright or poet from the mediocre. All such writers have to use materials which are part of the culture in order to be intelligible, but some do it with a deeper sense of the culture than others. In the above examination of the compositional variations between versions of narratives, it was noted that |Hang ‡kass'o's version of M1 and ‖Kabbo's version of M9 stood out as narratives which uniquely drew upon materials which were resonant with other aspects of |Xam culture at a deep level. Even if this examination were not limited by the slimness of the available ethnographic information, it would still be impossible to assume anything about the aesthetic evaluation of these versions by a native audience on the basis of cultural density. It so happens that, in Western societies, novels deemed to reveal an understanding of the world as complex, or nearly so, as that world in which the critic feels himself to live, are generally regarded as 'great'. But there is no *a priori* reason why cultural depth and complexity should coincide with aesthetic enjoyment. However, there is no doubt that these versions are singular both within the total collection of |Kaggen narratives and by comparison with other versions of 'the same' story. As such they seem to point to a line of enquiry into the relationship between aesthetic evaluations and the cultural density of narratives, which would best be carried out on a living oral literature. It is hoped, however, that the above discussion has found a form of description which can, at least, illuminate both the cultural situation of a particular text and the expressive capacity of individual narrators. In the case of these narratives from an extinct society, further commentary on the relationship between these aspects could only be speculative.

While the discussion of |Xam narratives in this book has centred on theme, plot structure, motif and symbol, and has attempted to see how they were integrated with beliefs, social ideas, and recurrent conceptual frameworks, little has been said about the verbal surface of the texts.[6] This area is far more difficult to discuss than almost any other, primarily because the method of transcription employed by the collectors was such that it was liable to destroy the narrators' verbal flow, and clearly some of the informants managed to adapt better than others to the rather slow dictation method. The following and final chapter will describe some the features of this verbal surface, and, where possible, discriminate the particular styles of the informants.

Notes

1   Although Miss Currlé's informant calls the protagonist 'the devil', there can be no doubt that it is |Kaggen to whom he refers. In a few of Bleek's early transcriptions of narratives given by ‖Kabbo, |Kaggen is also called 'the devil' in the English translations.

2   The versions given by ǂKasing and Miss Currlé are included for comparison. 'X' indicates the presence of the elements listed in the left-hand column. It is bracketed in the case of ǂKasing's version because the protagonist there is the Ichneumon not |Kaggen.

3   Function E is bracketed here because the 'flight' it represents is not magical as is usually the case.

4   The suffix -gu is used to indicate a shared identity. Thus here it means 'those of the |Kwammang-a group'.

5   The same equation of anger and blackness is made elsewhere by ‖Kabbo (B. III, 494–95).

6   The preferences of an audience for particular narrators might well have been bound up with this verbal surface as much as, or even to the exclusion of, any capacity which a narrator might have had for producing performances with strong cultural resonances.

11

The verbal surface: a note on the narrators

Of the six main informants used by Bleek and Lloyd, |A!kungta and ǂKasing gave too few narratives for even the vaguest picture of their styles to emerge, while !Kweiten ta ǁken rarely managed to give a coherent performance in the conditions under which collecting took place. Her narratives are only occasionally free from interjections which run ahead of events in the plot, and it is clear that she found the method of transcription an obstacle to giving narratives animated by any real enthusiasm. The example of her performance of the story of the girl who killed the Waterchildren (mentioned in Chapter 4) is typical of her performance in general. Occasionally showing some engagement with the narrative, isolated passages stand out vividly from a basically perfunctory account of the main events. Little or no elaboration is given and snatches of chant or song are only very rarely included. Her narratives are also amongst the shortest in the collection, only occasionally exceeding 20 pages of manuscript, while some of the other informants gave narratives which run into hundreds of pages.

!Kweiten ta ǁken's performances point out the major problem of discussing the different styles of narration displayed by the various informants, for it is clear that what is available is not how the narrators told stories to |Xam audiences, but how they responded to the particular situation of carefully dictating narratives in a completely alien environment to people of another race and culture. !Kweiten ta ǁken's performances can in no way be taken as indications of how she might have performed to a |Xam audience, and, indeed, the times when she does manage to animate her narratives, suggest that under different circumstances her performance may have been quite different.

The informants who did achieve an ease in their narrations, under these conditions, were Dia!kwain (!Kweiten ta ‖ken's brother), ‖Kabbo, and |Hang ǂkass'o, but even these informants were influenced in various ways by the situation in which they found themselves. Their styles will be discussed below. Before doing so, however, a few points can be made about the verbal techniques which were common to all of the narrators.

While no formal method of introducing a narrative was ever recorded in this collection, a feature which can be observed with some frequency is that of opening a narrative with a brief statement about the central character and how he or she behaved on a certain occasion. Narratives never open with a scene-setting description. Almost always they open with a terse statement which seems to be designed to capture attention and interest immediately. Thus ‖Kabbo opens his version of M2 with the statement:

|Kakkaken a: ka |ku ‖kum !ho !Goe !khwaitən-tu.
(|Kaggen was the one who went to meet !Goe !khwaitan-tu.)

|Hang ǂkass'o opens his version of M1 with:

|Kaggen ‖Kwang |ku a: da: sa:.
(|Kaggen was the one who made an eland.)

And another of his narratives opens with:

!Xwe ‖na s'o !kui ‖kwang ha oa |hang-a ǂNerru.
(A man of the ! Xwe ‖na s'o !kʔe once married a – ǂNerru (bird).)

Often such openings are more lengthy and lead on into the story, but they usually name an important character at the outset and immediately go on to relate that character to some distinctive event.

These opening statements usually involve one of two possibilities. Either they include the relative pronoun a: ('who, which, the one who'), as in the first two examples above, thus forming sentences which seem to suggest that the action is already known to the listener and that its performance should be credited to a certain, usually equally well-known character. Or they include the verb particle oa expressing the distant past, translated as 'once' in the third example above. Another verb particle, also expressing the past, ha, is also sometimes encountered in opening statements of this kind. In these openings the sense shifts to the assumption that the character is already known and that something is about to be revealed concerning him. These alternative forms of initial statements are so common throughout the collection that it is possible that they were employed by narrators performing to |Xam audiences.

Apart from the tendency to conclude a narrative in mid-dialogue, no consistency in methods of termination is observable in the narratives. Connective phrases are, however, commonly used to relate one event to another and to move the narrative forward with a sense of urgency. The phrase most commonly used in this capacity is Hɛ ti hing e: which literally means 'these things they are' but which is really equivalent to 'and so' in English. A similar phrase, Hɛ tiken e: ('these things are') used in the same capacity, also occurs very frequently. In some narratives a heavy reliance is placed upon these phrases and occasionally they are carefully placed at the beginning of each and every new phase of the story, but examples of its use as consistently and predictably applied structural punctuation are rare. The conjunction hɛ (and) is also often used in the same way.

The use of hɛ ti hing e: is not confined to narratives but is also encountered in other types of discourse. However, it is far more heavily used in narrative than elsewhere and, indeed, is employed there to such an extent that it is the most obvious recurrent feature in the purely verbal surface of the narrative texts.

Other features of the texts, such as the marked infrequency of adjectives, and the tendency to repeat sentences and phrases several times with minor modifications in wording, are reflections of |Xam language and speech as a whole and not in any way limited to narration. Indeed, from a purely linguistic point of view, the narratives involve very few special usages by which they can be distinguished. Verbal formulae are, however, a feature of some narratives. These are sometimes peculiar to individual narrators, sometimes not. Those which are common to more than one narrator are confined to the |Kaggen narratives.

The phrase ‖nakka !khe: ‖e ('rattling along'), for example, is very often used to describe |Kaggen when he is hurrying somewhere. It refers to his arrows rattling in their quiver, and is only ever applied to him. Phrases of this kind tend to be associated with certain familiar episodes in the narratives such as |Kaggen's magical escapes or the time between |Kaggen returning home beaten by an adversary, and going out again on the following day. Whenever forced to escape from a beating the words:

|Kakkaken arruko |ki ki ‖gεrri, hang ‖khau !kũi, hang !kwi: !kwa: ka !kauken. '!Kwa:ka !kauken we, |ne o hi iten |ne kho'.

(|Kaggen quickly got feathers. He flew away. He called the hartebeest skin bag. 'Hartebeest children! Leave here! We must go!')

very commonly occur. His triumphant boasts of:

I |ke |kaggen. !kui kua ka-g |ne te:kwa.
(Our name is |Kaggen. What man is our equal!)

and

I |ke-ten !khwaiten !khwaiten. !kui ha i: |ka.

the meaning of which Bleek and Lloyd did not fully unravel but which appears to mean: 'Our name is Penis! The man has done it!' – also occur regularly when he has escaped and flown to the water near his home.

At night, while |Kaggen is waiting to go out on the following morning to meet an enemy for the second time, he characteristically disturbs the Ichneumon, who is trying to sleep. A tuko se a:ke ng ⊙pwõing ('You must really let me sleep!') says the Ichneumon, while |Kaggen 'dreams about the dawn, that it should quickly break for him' (‖kabbo-a !gaue se arruko !khwai:-ja ha). The new day is also commonly introduced with a familiar phrase: |kakkaken |ne koang |hin au !gaue ('|Kaggen rose up at dawn'). |Kaggen narratives also often terminate with the sentence |kakkaken |ne te:n ('|Kaggen lay down') which does provide a link into a new narrative which might open with |Kaggen rising at dawn. It is only here, within a group of narratives that do have familiar episodes, that standardised phrasing occurs. In other narratives, where the thematic materials and plot structures are more varied, such phrases are not found.

The real basis for the discrimination between the styles of the narrators does not reside in the language used, but rather in particular enthusiasms which narrators display in the organisation of their narratives. ‖Kabbo was, perhaps, the most knowledgeable of Bleek and Lloyd's informants, and literally thousands of pages of manuscript contain anecdotes, narratives, accounts of hunting, descriptions of customs and beliefs, and notes on the habits of various animals, given by him. Miss Lloyd wrote of ‖Kabbo that he

> was an excellent narrator, and patiently watched until a sentence had been written down, before proceeding with what he was telling. He much enjoyed the thought that the Bushman stories would become known by means of books (Bleek & Lloyd 1911: x).

He talked about anything that interested him and wandered from natural history into narrative and out again in a kind of 'stream of consciousness' where a word or allusion could spark off a narrative, or a narrative with a certain theme could lead him into a description of some practical activity, such as hunting, for which he had a great relish. On one occasion, for example, he began talking in a factual way about the sun and the moon, and trailed off into an account of why the moon could speak – because it was |Kaggen's creation and all of |Kaggen's things have the power of speech. He then flowed directly into a narrative about |Kaggen and the magic ostrich which included a speech by the Ichneumon on the correct way to collect ostrich eggs. The narrative was then forgotten about as ‖Kabbo continued in his own voice, on the subject of ostrich hunting. While this way of proceeding can often be very difficult to follow, it is helpful in indicating those aspects of narratives which were of special interest to him and which he regarded as important.

He often took a keen interest in practical activities described in the narratives, and this seems to reflect something of his personality. His treatment of the story of |Kaggen and the magic ostrich, for example, with its close attention to details about egg-collecting and ostrich hunting, might be related to his own efficiency in this area. |Hang ǂkass'o, ‖Kabbo's son-in-law, attested to the fact that the pitfalls which ‖Kabbo dug, were 'surpassingly good ones' (*ibid.*, 307). The great attention which he gave to the activity of fire-building, in his versions of M1, also displays again his delight in practical details.

While such things are illuminating *vis-à-vis* ‖Kabbo's personality, they reveal rather less about the narratives than some of his other characteristics. He rarely gave a narrative from beginning to end. Frequently his texts open with an abstract of the plot and then proceed to pick out certain incidents for special attention. Thus he stressed the centres of activity which he found most attractive, and they were often not given in the sequence in which they should have occurred in the story. Among his favourite pieces was |Kaggen's magical flight, and that of his possessions, which ‖Kabbo sometimes repeated time and time again, telling, in reported speech, how |Kaggen commanded his things in turn to follow him, and how they replied or conversed with one another. Or again, |Kaggen's immersion in the water near his home flared ‖Kabbo's imagination, so that the event would be elaborated from every possible point of view: |Kaggen washing off his magical feathers, soothing his wounds, emerging naked on the other side, drying himself, putting on his clothes and picking up his bag and his bow and quiver. ‖Kabbo's capacity for elaborating on such things was quite extraordinary and he would further prompt his imagination by describing the same event from the perspectives of one character after another. Much of this is conducted in reported speech, which itself adds depth to the fiction, as it naturally involves insight into the various characters, how they view |Kaggen, and in what their personalities consist. This ‖Kabbo displayed with great facility.

It is interesting to note that ‖Kabbo also told several whole stories entirely from the Ichneumon's point of view and in the Ichneumon's voice. Here ‖Kabbo seems to have been taking up an aspect of these narratives which is often implicit, i.e. the affection for |Kaggen which all of the narrators clearly felt, simultaneous with a helpless disapproval of him. As |Kaggen's grandson, the Ichneumon has a licence to speak very freely to him, but |Kaggen cannot be controlled, only lectured. At the same time the Ichneumon is always very sorry for |Kaggen when he returns home beaten, even though he has always brought disaster on himself. By giving a story from beginning to end in the Ichneumon's voice, ‖Kabbo seized on both the dramatic aspect of the device and on the fundamentally ambivalent attitude of the |Xam towards this ambiguous being. Thus a drama of pure entertainment is integrated with the more resonant aspect of the narratives at this most playful level of performance.

The banter which goes on between |Kaggen and the Ichneumon was always affectionately described by ‖Kabbo. The following quotation is very typical of the Ichneumon's lecturing at the close of a narrative:

'|Kaggenwe ake |gebbi. Aken !khwi-ja, ng a !khwa;
aken a !kerri. Ng ‖kamma a. Ng a ‖koaka. Ng a
!khwa:. Aken a !kerri. Aken e |gebbi ī: Aken
‖koaka. Aken !khwi-ja'. Hing |kwe-da hing ╪kakkən

‖na. Hi |hang-guken k"we ī. |Niken ‡kaken: 'Kang
‖kowa ka, |Kaggen e |gebbi, hand !khwi-ja'.
('|Kaggen, you are a fool! You are deceitful! I am a child, you are a grown-
up. I teach you! I am your equal. I am a child, you are a grown-up. You
are cunning. You are deceitful.' Thus they talked there. Their womenfolk
laughed at them. The Ichneumon said: 'Don't you agree with me, |Kaggen
is foolish and deceitful.')

The amusement of the womenfolk seems to indicate the habitual nature of
this outspoken but basically affectionate banter.
    ‖Kabbo often seems to take a delight in |Kaggen's outrageousness. In one
passage he even has |Kaggen parodying a |Xam address to the moon:

!Gauewe, arruko !khwai:-ja ki
ng ‖koen ‖gaue au ‖gwatǝn
au ‖kaken kau ng arruko !kauken-a ha |na:.
(Dawn, quickly break for me, so that tomorrow I may look for the Cat, that
I may quickly break his head.)

This passage is very close to the form and sense of all of the 'prayers' collected
as this fragment shows:

Bo, !ka!karrowe ta,
ng se |ka wai
au !gaue.
Ng se ha: wai
au !nwa: a: a.
(Hey! Moon lying there! Let me kill a springbok tomorrow.
Let me eat a springbok from this arrow.)

This kind of emphasis reflects ‖Kabbo's view of |Kaggen and would be very
unlikely to be found taken to such a degree in any of the narratives given
by |Hang ‡kass'o. Not only does |Hang ‡kass'o keep his narratives fairly
unelaborated at the level of dialogue in comparison to ‖Kabbo, he also tends
to play down |Kaggen's outrageousness and stress his creative aspect. It is
not that the stories that |Hang ‡kass'o gave do not show |Kaggen's anti-social
side, but that, where possible, he emphasises the fact that |Kaggen is also
capable of helpfulness and creativity. This much has been noted in passing in

previous chapters, but set in contrast to ‖Kabbo, it is interesting to see how the interpretation of a character can have consequences in the way stories are told.

‖Kabbo and |Hang ǂkass'o were undoubtedly Bleek and Lloyd's best informants. Both of them functioned fluently in dictation, knew a very large number of stories and were clearly used to performing. The differences between their techniques, however, were radical. |Hang ǂkass'o very rarely digressed from a narrative once begun, and tended to structure them in a very patterned way. The most obvious feature of his narratives is the precision with which he repeats recurrent episodes. Where an event happens on several consecutive occasions, his wording changes very little from one account to the next. Furthermore he had a fondness for using the same number of repetitions in different narratives. Frequently he described an event exactly five times, and on the fifth time introduced the next phase of the narrative. He clearly had a very good sense of the overall shape of a narrative – something which must have been difficult to maintain when one story might take many days to dictate. In contrast, ‖Kabbo's sense of the narrative as a complete performance appears to have been very eroded by the slowness of dictation, and to have resulted in his concentrating more on what he was saying at the time than on the need to convey a rounded story. This is not always true of ‖Kabbo; his version of the story of the man who brought home a lion cub, described in Chapter 4, is, as was observed there, a very coherent and well-shaped narrative, even though it took several months to complete. However, that kind of well-ordered narrative is far more characteristic of |Hang ǂkass'o.

Bearing in mind |Hang ǂkass'o's strong sense of narrative shape, one of his narratives stands out from the others as singularly structured. M21 opens with a long description of how the !Khwai!-khwai's – a very menacing character who attacks children – comes to the camp while the adults are out and threatens the children. After a description of the children calling out for help, and the parents hearing their cries from a long way off, |Hang ǂkass'o introduces the sentence,

|Kaggen tatti e: |Kaggen a: ‖kabbo-a ti e:
!Khwai-!khwai a ǂkwai:nja sa ĩ: o !kaukǝn.
(|Kaggen was dreaming that the !Khwai-!khwai had come to molest the children.)

In other words, all that had been described in the opening passages had been the content of |Kaggen's dream. The narrative then continues to show how this dream provided |Kaggen with foreknowledge of the !Khwai-!khwai's actual intentions, and, typically for a group B narrative, the children, on the basis of |Kaggen's information, manage to defeat the !Khwai-!khwai when he really does come.

This device of opening with a dream without letting the audience know that it is a dream until well into the narrative, is unique in the collection. Had the same device been used by ‖Kabbo there would be grounds for thinking that there had been some confusion during transcription, but because it is |Hang ǂkass'o there can be no doubt that this was a deliberate device and one which may well have been used to a native audience.

Another characteristic feature of |Hang ǂkass'o's narratives is his use of chanted phrases and song. He used these more than any of the other narrators and placed them carefully in a narrative to heighten the sense of whatever was taking place at the time. In his version of M6, where the Baboons meet |Kaggen's son !Gāunu ts'axau, and speak in a staccato chant to each other, the chant itself is used to emphasise both the numerousness and the stupidity of the Baboons. Later in the narrative another chant is also used by the Baboons while they play ball with !Gāunu ts'axau's eye:

He ng ǂka-owa hĩ	And I want it.
dekən ta !khume	Whose ball is it?
He ng ǂka-owa hĩ	And I want it.
dekən ta !khume	Whose ball is it?
He ng ǂka-owa hĩ	And I want it.

While the other Baboons replied:

ng ‖k"en ta !khum e	My mate's ball it is,
He n ǂka-owa hĩ	and I want it.
ng ‖k"en ta !khum e	My mate's ball it is,
he n ǂka-owa hĩ	And I want it (*ibid.*, 22).

His use of such chants, particularly in repeated segments, is very characteristic, and his precise placement of them is typical of the care which he brought to his performances and of his keen sense of the centres of dramatic interest, which was remarked upon in Chapter 4.

Dia!kwain was another very good narrator but, for the most part, not as distinctive as ‖Kabbo and |Hang ǂkass'o. He came from the Katkop area, and spoke a slightly different dialect from that of the other two. He is, again, a narrator who often took much care in the construction of his narratives where he felt that narratives and not ethnographic information were of more interest. He clearly knew a great many stories but sometimes gave even the most interesting narratives scant attention if he was using them to demonstrate some aspect of belief. This is particularly a feature of his stories concerning !Khwa. He used them to make points about the sanctions behind the various rules pertaining to puberty, and did know a variety of narratives dealing with these matters, but unfortunately he often trailed off into giving information, and concluded the actual narratives sketchily.

His |Kaggen narratives, although far fewer in number than those contributed by |Hang ǂkass'o and ‖Kabbo, have great energy and, like ‖Kabbo's versions, quarry a lot of interest out of |Kaggen's bantering dialogue with members of his family. His narratives contain no songs or chants, although phrases in dialogue are sometimes reiterated in a patterned way. His interests do not seem to have lain in the more boisterous kind of narrative, however, and his most carefully told stories are two legends concerning encounters with lions. One of these, the story of the young man who was carried off by a lion when asleep on a hill (*ibid.*, 174ff) is, at least to a European taste, one of the most moving pieces in the collection. In very measured stages, it builds up a two-sided perspective in which the lion, having placed the man at the foot of a tree, wishes to go away and drink before eating but suspects the man to be still alive. The man, his face covered with tears of fear, can only peep from below his eyelids to see if the lion had gone yet. The tension between the lion's suspicions and the man's cautious movements is gradually built up until at last the lion goes, and the man is free to escape. Ultimately the lion pursues the man to his home where members of the band fire arrows and throw assegais at it. The lion, however, seems to be impossible to kill, and keeps asking the people for the man whose tears he has licked. Finally, because the lion begins to threaten the whole community the people hand the young man over to him. At the moment at which the young man dies, the lion at last becomes vulnerable to their arrows, and so the story closes with the lion and the man lying dead together. The balance achieved in this narrative, between the opening phase, in which the relationship between the lion and the man is built up, and the conclusion, where the lion seems to volunteer his own death for the sake of having the man, displays an acute sense of the total structure of the narrative which, like many of |Hang ǂkass'o's narratives, was unaffected by the difficulties and duration of the dictation. This narrative is easily Dia!kwain's most impressive performance.

Each of these narrators may have evinced many other individual qualities when performing to a |Xam audience. It is unlikely that ‖Kabbo's practical enthusiasms, his capacity for adopting the voice of many different characters in dialogue, and his emphasis on |Kaggen's outrageousness, would not also be shown in performance amongst his own people. It is certain that |Hang ǂkass'o's sense of a rounded and well-ordered narrative, enlivened by chant and song, and his emphasis on |Kaggen's creativity and helpfulness would be present. Dia!kwain's special capacity for the serious rather than the humorous, may, however, have been influenced by the absence of a full and relaxed audience. Nevertheless, these narrators, who stand out so clearly as individuals, are likely to have had far more distinguishing features than those displayed in the collected texts. What is clear is the thread which leads from such individuating characteristics, through the equally personal selection and use of whole narratives, motifs and symbols owned by the culture, and which ramifies out into that culture at many levels of significance.

Postscript

This examination of |Xam narratives has attempted to reveal the various layers of order which may be present in an individual text or group of texts. Plots, motifs and characters have been described together with the values and conceptual templates which served to shape the narratives. Tragically absent from this examination is any account of the gestural, interactive vitality of living communication. It is hoped, however, that the foregoing discussion has excavated the ground of meaning in which that vitality was once situated, and itself gestured in recognition of the people whose stories cannot again delight the minds of those who knew them best.

Appendix A

Girls' puberty observances of the |Xam

The |Xam did not practice either male or female circumcision and there is nothing in the collected texts to suggest that boys or young men were subjected to any special rite connected with puberty. There were certain foods that young unmarried men should avoid and these were the same as some of those avoided by young girls, notably several reptiles. Young men also had to avoid using the names of certain animals by employing respect words. By contrast, however, girls received a great deal of attention at this time (D.F. Bleek 1931–36, Part VII, p. 303; L. V, (6), pp. 4389 rev.–90 rev.).

At the onset of her first menses a girl's mother would build her a hut (hut-building being a task reserved for the wife/mother of the family);[1] it was set apart from the others and was only large enough to be occupied by one person in a prone position. The girl was taken to the hut by her mother who closed up the entrance upon her. Ritual confinement lasted until the first new moon and although she might leave the hut for defecation she had to avoid contact of any kind with anyone except her mother, keep her eyes downcast and return immediately (L. VIII, (12), pp. 7111 rev.–12 rev.; L. V, (1), pp. 3997–4002; Bleek & Lloyd 1911: 76f).

The girl was brought her food and water by her mother but she was deprived of normal sized rations. Cooked food was taken to her cut up into very small portions and was handed to her through the entrance. Water was also strictly limited. She was handed a perforated ostrich eggshell containing water but the hole was not as large as was usual and furthermore had a very thin reed inserted into it through which she was expected to drink. This greatly limited the amount of water she was able to sip. The water was administered to her as it would be to a very young child and was taken away afterwards not left (L. V, pp. 3875–80).

Not only was her food limited in quantity, it was also limited in kind. Certain edible roots were strictly forbidden her as were some meats and some parts of certain animals. An exhaustive list was not made and only the |Xam names of the vegetable foods were recorded but among the forbidden meats were several reptiles.

Such *veldkos* as she was permitted was gathered exclusively by her mother
and those of her mother's elderly female relatives who were especially
close to her mother. These women, known as xoakengu, the mothers, were
responsible for the enforcement of the rules pertaining to the confinement
and for the instruction of the girl regarding all observances following her
isolation. The only meat she was permitted was non-tabooed game killed by
her father, for it was believed that if she ate game killed by young men her
saliva would enter the flesh and thence into the hands of the young man, the
arrow, and the bow all of which would be made 'cool' and incapable of use
in hunting. Even her father would not hunt for her until she had treated his
hands with buchu, thus 'taking away her saliva from him'. It is not recorded
at what point this treatment of the father's hands took place (L. V, (6), pp.
4392–93; L. II, (28), pp. 2519–20; Bleek & Lloyd 1911: 77ff).

When the father did go hunting a different set of food distribution rules
might be brought to bear from those which usually obtained if his was the
arrow which secured the kill. Instead of the animal being divided between
all of the hunters, any animal from which he wished to feed his daughter
could only also be eaten by the elderly women. At least some of his arrows,
although possibly not all, were recognised as belonging to the girl. Whether
the arrows he used during the hunt were chosen or came to his hand by
chance is not known but the problem of who would hunt with him and how
active a part he would play during the hunt must have been a difficult one
involving often conflicting responsibilities in a situation already fraught with
complex distribution obligations. It is made quite clear in the texts collected
that the girl's family also underwent some reduction in rations during her
isolation and while this may have been part of the confinement rules, it
might also have been influenced by these distribution problems (L. VI, (2),
pp. 4001–2; L. V, (2), pp. 3879–80; D.F. Bleek 1931–36, Part I, p. 175).

The often long confinement was one of great mental and physical hardship
for the girl but on the appearance of the new moon she was taken from the
hut by her xoakengu. At first she looked about her over her mother's hands
after which she was free to look where and as far as she wished once more.
Her release, however, did not represent the removal of all constraints, rather
it was the induction into a new set of observances. She had to treat all the
members of her household with buchu and give the women of the band red
haematite with which they were to paint their cheeks and decorate their
karosses. She was also expected to paint haematite stripes 'like a zebra' on
the young men of the band to protect them from death by lightning caused

by !Khwa. These details might suggest that a dance also occurred at this time as it did with some other San groups but nothing was recorded either way on this matter. Apart from the treatment of members of the band, the water source in current use also had to be thoroughly sprinkled with powdered haematite to appease !Khwa who, it was believed, might cause the pool to dry up completely (L. VI, (2), p. 4001; L. II, (28), p. 2522; L. V, (1), pp. 3970–74).

From the time of her release until her marriage a large number of rules applied exclusively to the girl. Many animals could not be referred to by their usual names but only by respect names. Some animals had several such respect names but it is not recorded what factors, if any, governed the use of any of these. Certain foods continued to be forbidden her. These included certain kinds of *veldkos* as well as reptiles such as the cobra, the puffadder, the tortoise (*Testudo geometrica*) and the water tortoise (*Testudo leopardis*). Any foods gathered by her were eaten only by the elderly people and not given to children in any circumstances. Before her father could eat anything collected by her he would first have to be fumigated by her with the smoke from burning buchu for fear of angering !Khwa. Similarly while she was allowed to gather tortoise for others she could not touch one with her hands but had to put any that she found into her bag with the use of a stick, and this probably applied to any of the other creatures which were believed to be 'put aside as !Khwa's meat' which included those reptiles mentioned above (L. V, (6), pp. 4382–92; L. VIII, (16), p. 7431 rev.).

Domestic duties were also affected by her new status. Cooking for her parents was now regarded as an activity fraught with danger. Whenever she cooked for them she had to sprinkle buchu on the fire so that the cooking pot and its contents would be scented. Failure to do so would again incur the wrath of !Khwa. Similarly, if given responsibility for child-minding, she had first to fumigate the child with buchu to avert the danger to the child which was believed to ensue if her perspiration rubbed off onto it. It is not clear from the texts if these practices operated only during a menstrual period or whether they applied at all times. It seems the most likely, however, that the former was the case (L. V, (6), pp. 4389–93).

Socially she was also restricted. She was discouraged from playing games with young males during a period because of the possibility that menstrual blood might get onto the young men. If she did play with someone whom she knew very well the young man had first to be given buchu to protect him from danger. Fear of the Rain as a supernatural being also involved fear of actual rain. Whenever it rained unmarried girls had to hide silently in their huts and could not play outside until the rain had passed. One of the xoakengu would accompany them, and while they hid, tell them how she had done the same when she was an unmarried woman, and perhaps recount to them some of the stories concerned with !Khwa and disobedient young women (L. V, (6), p. 4392; L. VIII, (23), pp. 8031–32).

Beliefs concerned with her possible adverse effect on hunting still persisted during her adolescence as is shown by a custom observed relating to her father's hunting dog. Game that had been killed by her father's dog and which her mother wished her to eat had first to be used in the following way. A piece of the cooked meat was cut off by the girl and put into her mouth. She then sucked the dirt from her knees and chewed the meat mixing the dirt and saliva together in her mouth. She then asked someone to catch hold of the dog for her and took the chewed meat from her mouth giving it to the dog. She then patted the dog's shoulders saying, 'sa, sa, sa, sa, sa,' as she did so. The word 'sa' probably had no specific meaning in this context but it was the |Xam word for buchu. The important element was the dirt from the girl's knee mixed with the saliva, for had she eaten the meat without first performing this act it was believed that the saliva would, as in the transference to the young men's bows, 'lie on the dog's heart' and undermine the dog's concentration and purpose in the chase. He would 'play with the game, then leave it because the girl had bewitched him, turning his heart from these things by eating.' Once more it should be said that this custom might only have been observed during a menstrual period (L. V, (20), pp. 5592–04).

The responsibility for the enforcement of all these rules, especially those relating to the girl's behaviour immediately following her release from the isolation hut, (known as the house of illness) was that of the xoakengu. Indeed the girl's parents would explicitly request these women to instruct her at this time and this they did supporting their instructions with a wealth of lore relating to the disasters which befell girls who failed to observe the rules. Their influence seems to have been both constant and deeply felt. Exactly who constituted this group remains vague. Dorothea Bleek (1924: 57) only gives the explanation that xoakengu was 'often used where we should say, "the older women" or "mother and her friends"' and as the |Xam followed no strict rule of residence this could have included any of the obvious constellations of older women.

It is unfortunate that certain details, such as the ages at which girls married or the attitude of the |Xam to pre-marital intercourse, are not available. Given the often harsh conditions of their lives, an early marriage and a rule against pre-marital intercourse would seem most likely.[2] However, much information is available relating to the beliefs which supported puberty observances.

A wealth of information was gathered concerning the dangers believed to be incurred if a young girl failed to observe the rules pertaining to puberty and menstruation. While some of this was concerned with the loss of hunting ability by those males with whom she came into contact, the most commonly feared source of danger was !Khwa, whose name, as well as meaning 'water', was also used in one recorded instance, to mean menstrual fluid (L. V, (6), p. 4393). Although the |Xam had but one word for both rain and water, separate words were employed to describe kinds of rain such as drizzle. A further distinction was made between male rain and female rain. Male rain was violent and usually accompanied by thunder and lightning; female rain was gentle and regarded as welcome because it lightly soaked the ground, working its way deep into the earth and nourishing the roots of the plants without bringing attendant dangers from lightning. Female rain is not mentioned at all in the lore relating to puberty and is only encountered as a descriptive term. It was regarded as the most desirable kind of rain for rainmakers to encourage. !Khwa, the supernatural being, was exclusively a male figure who could not only mobilise the harmful aspects of male rain but who might also effect various transformations on disobedient girls and those with whom she came into contact (D.F. Bleek 1931–36, Part V, pp. 279ff).

The punishments administered by !Khwa fall into two main groups, those which were liable to cause death by natural causes, e.g. drought or lightning, and transformations into non-human forms. The haematite zebra markings on young men, the painting of the women with the same substance and the fumigation of the girl's father with buchu were apparently all done to avoid death by lightning caused by the anger of !Khwa. A glance from a girl's eye during the time she was isolated, or the snapping of her fingers at anyone was regarded as highly dangerous and identified with 'rain bolts' which were black pebbles found on the ground and believed to be thrown by !Khwa in his anger. However, transformation into frogs, porcupines or snakes was also liable to follow death (*ibid.*, p. 298).

Something akin to the cultural reversions described in the narratives concerning !Khwa may also be glimpsed in the dangers to hunting which disobedience might unleash. The dangers were twofold. By direct or indirect contact with a girl, a hunter and his weapons and, as seen above, a hunting dog, could lose the ability to kill game. Similarly, if a girl looked at game during her isolation she was liable to make them 'wild'. They would behave in a way which would put them beyond the hunter's powers to influence by his usual means. In both cases the hunter's ability to control the situation through the familiar means was believed to be destroyed and the game placed beyond his influence (Bleek & Lloyd 1911: 77).

While it was believed that effects of this kind could also be caused by other things, the formal reversions wrought by !Khwa were exclusively related to puberty and menstruation rules. It was frequently emphasised by the informants that the odour of the girl was what attracted the attention of !Khwa. Buchu was used to cover this odour. In one narrative !Khwa took the form of a bull and attempted to carry off a younger mother while she lay in her hut during a period. The young woman's use of buchu made !Khwa drowsy and compliant. He eventually fell asleep and she was able to escape. Had she not done so, the narrator explained, she, her xoakengu and her parents would have been killed and transformed into frogs. It would appear from this narrative that even marriage and childbirth was not sufficient to place a woman beyond danger during menses but there is no evidence from outside of the narrative to suggest that married women were subjected to the same elaborated rules as were unmarried women and girls, except, perhaps, an isolated comment, unconfirmed elsewhere, that a certain kind of tortoise said to belong to !Khwa was only given to very old women (L. V, (2), p. 3869; L. VIII, (21), pp. 7843–45; Bleek & Lloyd 1911: 193ff).

Certain elements in these beliefs such as the masculinity of !Khwa, the association of menstruation with cultural reversions and the dominance of reptiles in the imagery employed, seem to suggest a coherent structure of symbolism. The fact that menstrual blood was also referred to by the word which meant water, rain, and the supernatural being, '!khwa' might also be relevant to this structure. It is to be regretted that no more information is apparently available which might further clarify these matters.

Menstruating women were clearly regarded as a source of extreme danger both to life and to the |Xam's power to order the world in useful ways. No social means, except perhaps marriage, could neutralise those dangers and only isolation was really felt to be effective. The role of the xoakengu in perpetuating these ideas was evidently paramount.

Notes

1 Parents and children would occupy one hut until the children became old enough to support themselves by hunting and gathering. When this occurred the children built their own huts next to that of their parents (see Bleek & Lloyd 1911: 307). It is not recorded in the texts at what age the children did this; it is clear that the hut which a girl's mother built for her at the onset of menses was not of this kind but was used to isolate the girl from the community.

2 The recurring emphasis in the texts on the girl's effect on her father's hunting suggests, however, that girls did not marry as young as they do among the Zu|wasi and the G|wi (see L. Marshall 1959: 350; Silberbauer 1963: 15). Silberbauer reports that a girl's first menstrual period forced her husband to stop hunting and remain at the encampment because of the dangers to him. It is, nevertheless, evident from Silberbauer's account that there are many points of similarity between the G|wi and the |Xam customs and beliefs with regard to puberty.

Appendix B

The shamans of the |Xam

During the 1930s a substantial number of texts were published by Miss Dorothea Bleek (1931–36, Parts VI–VIII) in which several |Xam informants, from the Katkop and Strontberg areas of South Africa, described their beliefs and customs with regard to shamans. The |Xam word !giten was originally translated as 'sorcerers' by Miss Bleek's aunt, L.C. Lloyd. Dorothea Bleek herself sometimes used the word 'medicine men' to describe the same people. In the account which follows the published texts have been drawn upon together with the remainder of the unpublished material collected by Bleek and Lloyd, in an attempt to organise what is known of these shamans. The general term used here for them is 'shaman' but the term favoured by Isaac Schapera (1930: 195ff), 'magician', has also been used in places where it makes the sense clearer.

The |Xam had one word, !gi:xa, for people with special 'magical' powers. This applied to rainmakers, medicine men/women and those with a magical influence over certain animals. Rainmakers were said to 'possess' rain and game 'magicians' to 'possess' certain animals. This possession was not exactly one of control, rather it was an ownership of powers capable of influencing these things. While the word !gi:xa was generally used indiscriminately to describe all of these offices, one also finds the word for rain 'magicians' used (!khwa-ka !giten, !giten being the plural form of !gi:xa) or, in the case of game 'magicians', the name of an animal added to !gi:xa (wai-ta !gi:xa, springbok 'magician') as a means of differentiation. Sometimes these offices overlapped and it was usual for game 'magicians' also to be curers (L. II, (37), p. 3337 rev.). Game 'magicians' and curers could be of either sex but rainmakers seem to have been exclusively male.

Rainmakers

Rainmaking was mainly the province of older, experienced men who were requested, usually by a relative, to make rain at certain times. They were free to accept or refuse the request but from the texts they do not appear to have been paid for their services. It was thought good manners, however, to fetch water once for the rainmaker after he had successfully made rain. The people usually asked a member of the band who was in some way close to the rainmaker to make a request on their behalf but occasionally the rainmaker would do his work unprompted. No reference to any rainmaker's initiation ceremony has been recorded but novices did have to undergo a period of training during which they assisted an experienced rainmaker, although very little was recorded of this training.

Rainmaking techniques often varied, depending on the rainmaker concerned but one method which was widely used and was a necessary part of a rainmaker's abilities was that of leading the rain bull or cow across the land so that rain would follow.[1] From evidence in the rock art, hippopotamus seems to have been once used for this in some areas but as these died out, or in areas where they were not found such as those of Bleek and Lloyd's informants, oxen, probably stolen from European farmers were used. Several descriptions of this activity have been collected and the procedure was as follows. The rainmaker and his trainees, or several experienced rainmakers together, would go at night to a deep water-hole with a spring in which the rain animal was believed to live. They would take with them a special leather noose which was used to throw over the animal's head and drag it away from the water. They would approach the water-hole from down wind to avoid alerting the creature to their presence and wait in hiding until the bull emerged from the water to graze. Before it could return to the water they would attempt to capture it with the noose which was secured by the rainmaker in charge of the operation. At that moment all present lent a hand to push and pull the animal away from the water; it was then led across the land. At some point on this journey, possibly close to the *veldkos* source in current use, the animal was killed. Part of the flesh was then broiled (it is not stated whether this was eaten or not) and the remainder, including the ribs which were deliberately broken, strewn on the places where they wanted rain to fall. The blood of the dead animal which soaked into the ground was associated with the rain which was expected to follow (L. II, (25), pp. 2264–19; Bleek & Stow 1930: plts. 34–35; D.F. Bleek 1931–36, Part VI, pp. 378f, 387).

The rain-bull was not feared or respected in itself, although buchu (often used by girls to ward off and pacify !Khwa) was sometimes sprinkled on the bodies or rainmaker novices to make the rain animal more placid. All rainmakers used the act of leading the rain animal as their primary technique but some supplemented this with other methods which could be regarded as personal innovation. The goura was played by one rainmaker in the belief that this caused rain; another would tap upon his bowstring at night while the people slept, so as to bring rain in the morning, and no doubt other rainmakers also had their own techniques (Bleek & Lloyd 1911: 321ff; D.F. Bleek, *op. cit.*, 390). Rainmakers were believed to be able to influence the rain even after death and were prayed to by their children and grandchildren in times of drought. These prayers were personal and couched in much the same kinds of terms as were requests to living rainmakers as the following example shows:

> o !nuing-|kuiten, let the children return to ‖xwa:gen-te, (their father) that he may see the children, for he seems to sit thinking of them. But the children are waiting here with me. Therefore do please cool for them the ground which they must pass on their return (D.F. Bleek 1931–36, Part VII, p. 383).

There seems from the texts to have been no fear of rainmakers, either alive or dead. Unlike medicine men/women they could do no harm to individuals, all they could do was withhold their services and this they sometimes chose to do. The real reasons for them not agreeing to make rain were probably that they knew there was little chance of success, although there is some indication that requests were usually made when there were clouds in the sky which might reasonably be expected to precipitate. Nevertheless the reasons which they gave were of a more moralistic nature, some saying, for example, that they would not make rain because the prosperity following rain brought with it selfishness amongst the band, lack of care for each other and frequent fighting. Despite these deliberately social excuses, rainmakers could be and were accused of callousness and lack of responsibility towards the people, particularly towards the children, in times of drought. The traveller M.H.C. Lichtenstein reported that rainmakers were put to death if their predictions failed and while this is not confirmed elsewhere it does point up the vulnerability of the rainmakers in |Xam society (*ibid.*, pp. 377f; B. XXVII., pp. 2559–86; Lichtenstein 1930, Vol. II, p. 77).

Medicine men/women

The word !gi:xa, when applied to those who were concerned with the cure of illness does not appear to have had any qualifying term attached to it, as it did with game and rain magicians. It shall be used in this section, therefore, to mean medicine men/women only.

!Giten were drawn from both sexes and could be married to another !gi:xa or to someone who was not a !gi:xa. Their services were called upon by their own bands and by units of the band that had temporarily split away from the main group and moved to another part of the hunting territory. They were employed for even minor ailments such as head-ache or ear-ache as well as more acute conditions. A band could contain several !giten and these apparently were elderly or mature members rather than young men and women. There is also a possibility that !giten might have been called in from other nearby bands if a band did not itself contain one, although the evidence on this is insufficient. !Giten were usually paid but a !gi:xa whose abilities were held in low esteem might not receive payment. Nothing is recorded about what kind of articles were thought appropriate as payment but one !gi:xa believed that she should receive a 'real knife' for treating a stomach pain (D.F. Bleek 1931–36, Part VII, pp. 4, 22).

The initiation of !giten took place at a special dance known as the ‖ken dance. It is not recorded how frequently these initiation dances occurred nor how any individual came to be an initiate. The dance was led by an old !gi:xa whose powers were believed to be very strong. He held in his hand a stick of office and started the dance. The initiates would follow him while he instructed them in the movements. All wore caps made from the heads of young gemsbok and some wore horns. They also wore bangles around their arms and legs which were known as the ‖ken's rings. These were made either from the fibrous cortex of a certain edible root or from leather (*ibid.*, pp. 14f; L. V, (10), pp. 4744 rev.–46 rev.).

The function of the initiation dance was to confer healing powers on the initiates. This power was believed to reside in the blood of all !giten and was used when curing took place. An important technique of curing involved the !gi:xa in placing his nose to the ailing part of the patient and making a heavy snoring noise; this snoring was also one of the things which the initiators did to the initiates during the course of the initiation dance. It seems highly likely that the initiator achieved a state of trance through the dance, during which he would snore all the initiates in turn. It was believed that by so doing he was putting the curing power into their blood vessels. During the dance the initiator also suffered a certain amount of bleeding from the nose, possibly consequent upon the violent snoring, but also deliberately encouraged by forced sneezing. The blood expelled was offered to the initiates to smell, this apparently made them retch and this was followed by a feeling of coldness in the throat. The blood of !giten was said to be extremely cold and the initiates would shudder all over upon smelling it. While these things were done to charge the blood of initiates with the power necessary to perform cures, certain (unspecified) things were also given to them to smell which were believed to heighten their sensory awareness, although whether or not this was done during the initiation dance is not clear (D.F. Bleck 1931–36, Part VII, pp. 11ff).

The power and sensory abilities which !giten received at their initiation could weaken after a long time and certain things could also accelerate this weakening. One female !gi:xa complained that a fight with her husband had caused blood to go to her head and this, she believed, had had a weakening effect on her power. Since then she had to be careful only to eat perfectly clean food, uncontaminated with ashes, as not to do so would cause her snoring power to leave her completely (*ibid.*, pp. 20ff).

Whenever a !gi:xa was called in to attend a sick person he would treat the person inside the hut, or outside having covered himself and the patient with his *kaross*. He would then locate the source of the pain by snoring close to the body of the patient. Having located it he would then snore hard at the place in an attempt to draw the sickness out. Many pains were attributed to certain animals entering the body of the sick person; it could be a lion, an owl, a butterfly, a springbok, or some other animal. At the moment of extraction the !gi:xa would utter a loud call – in imitation of the animal extracted. Other pains were caused by other things such as invisible arrows fired by malignant !giten. Having snored the illness out, the !gi:xa would then sniff buchu, given to him by the patient's family, which would make him sneeze, expelling as he did so, a small piece of brightly coloured wood from the inside of his nose. These bits of wood were known as 'harms things' and were believed to have been in the body of the patient (*ibid.*, pp. 1ff; L. V, (4), pp. 4200–30).

Snoring served three main functions. It was initially a means of diagnosis, and a !gi:xa could make a diagnosis in this way but declare that the sickness could not be cured immediately. Secondly, snoring served as a means of extracting the illness by taking it into the nose of the !gi:xa. Thirdly, it was a means of energising a patient who had become weakened by his illness. It was believed that the extraction of some illnesses was done by the !gi:xa's nose penetrating the skin of the patient and entering the flesh at the exact place where the illness was. The skin was then sewn up by the !gi:xa's nose so that it looked untouched. Often the !gi:xa would actually bite at the place, especially if he entered a trance. A state of trance seems to have occurred frequently, but not always during the snoring. The !gi:xa would become violently possessed, beating at the air and biting those attempting to restrain and calm him. The veins of his neck stood out rigid and the tiny hairs on his back stood up. These hairs were known as 'lions hair' and, while the entranced !gi:xa was held down, fat was rubbed into his back to remove them. It was believed that the !gi:xa would turn into a lion and attack them all if these measures were not taken to pacify him. While entranced curing was taking place, the patient, not surprisingly as he may have been severely bitten, was said to feel as if a lion was killing him. Once the !gi:xa had been calmed down and had sneezed the illness from him, the patient was anointed with the blood from the !gi:xa's nose, which apparently always accompanied the sneezing. This was said to aid recovery and give the patient protection from the illness by allowing him to share in the identity of the !gi:xa (D.F. Bleek 1931–36, Part VII, pp. 1ff).

If the curing failed to work, this was accounted for in a number of ways. In some cases the snoring was believed to have a delayed effect but if the illness went away and returned after a short while, this was put down to the work of malignant !giten who had been firing invisible arrows at the patient. If the patient showed no signs of immediate recovery, or even died during the treatment, this was attributed to malignant !giten firing arrows literally 'under the nose of the !gi:xa'. In some cases an illness was blamed on a malignant dead !gi:xa occupying part of the patient's body. When this was diagnosed, the curing !gi:xa would dramatically remove the malignant !gi:xa and pound him with a stone on the ground, saying 'This man has been going about killing people. I will kill him knocking him down, for he is a rascally person. Therefore I will kill him.' When he had beaten him to 'make him soft', he scooped him up with the earth upon which he had been pounding and then 'beat him away'. As he did so, he said, 'May that man go to the spirits who are always killing people. He has only wanted to come here to kill and carry off people' (ibid., pp. 32ff).

The whole curing treatment seems to have been an exhausting affair for the !gi:xa. One !gi:xa spoke of the difficulty of ejecting things from her own body and the pain which it caused her. 'It seems as if my vertebral artery would break, for the thing which I have taken out of the man is really alive', she said. Afterwards the !gi:xa would return to his family who would massage his arteries while singing to him in order to calm him completely and make his arteries lie down. Even at this stage care had to be taken to prevent the !gi:xa from becoming a beast of prey. The patient, too, was taken care of. He was not expected to do any work and was encouraged to rest completely (*ibid.*, p. 2).

!Giten were generally feared and respected by the |Xam. They were thought to be unlike other San and to have access to mysteries that were not available to most men. They were distinguished by their power to trance and by the fact that the payment for their services was an anomaly in |Xam economic and community relations. They were set apart by their appearance, as most of them always wore a *kaross* however hot the weather, because of their extreme coldness, due, it was believed, to their having cold blood. They were apparently also given to fits of shivering in the night which were sometimes explained by the belief that other !giten had come to test them by 'walking on their veins' in order to see if they were great !giten, capable of knowing of the approach of other !giten even while asleep. Some !giten reinforced this separation by forcefully requesting families to part with a child who would then live with them, helping them in the home and collecting wood and food for them. This request could be refused but, if it was, the family would fear that the !giten might take the child from them in some other way, especially through illness (*ibid.*, pp. 5ff).

In the texts collected by Bleek and Lloyd, it is not always clear whether the !giten having dealings with a particular band were from a separated section of that band or from another band altogether. It is not clear, for example, if requests for child-helpers came from within the band or without, or whether a !gi:xa coming to cure was, on occasions, from another band. There is a possibility that the initiation dance was an interband affair and that !giten formed something of a secret society which, in some respects, existed over and above ties within the band. Certainly it was believed that !giten generally knew each other and were connected by their power and knowledge, although the information concerned with this point comes exclusively from informants who were not themselves !giten and may be obscured by an overlay of superstition and hearsay.

!Giten were believed to possess the bodies of certain animals through which they were able to know of events which they themselves did not actually witness – the animals doing the seeing for them. They were also believed to bewitch those who came near them, even people who approached them from behind their line of vision, and were thought to be able to cause illness and death with a glance. They were believed to be particularly hostile to good-looking people whom they would kill if they got a chance, and they were also thought to prowl about at night and attack people.

Comparing these attitudes to !giten in general with attitudes to !giten who were close to the informants, it becomes evident that greater power and malignity were attributed to !giten who were unknown to the informants than to those close to them. Thus while fearing !giten in general, and believing that unknown !giten might fire invisible arrows which cause illness, particular, well known !giten might be estimated with little reference to an undifferentiated and sinister ill-will. This estimation would influence whether or not a !gi:xa would be paid and how effectively he or she was thought to snore people. Anomalous behaviour, such as that by one female !gi:xa who habitually snored people without first covering herself and the patient with a *kaross* might seriously lower the !gi:xa in the estimation of the band. Loss of credibility would be followed by loss of respect and possibly non-payment. The generalised fear of !giten occasionally mitigated this as it was believed that failure to pay might create or activate ill-will in the !gi:xa. When snoring people while suspecting non-payment, !giten were said to do poor work. As one informant put it, 'he becomes a rascal, he merely wants to kill people when he snores. If people cool his heart (by paying him) then it is comfortable, and when he lies snoring a person his heart is quiet. Otherwise when he lies snoring a man, he keeps thinking that he will snore cutting the man's arteries, that he may bring death to the man' (*ibid.*, pp. 21f). There is also a suggestion that !giten might, almost despite themselves, come to be ill-disposed towards people, mobilising small, personal grievances into the vocabulary and belief structure of their role. If this was true it might be related to the nature of the power they were thought to possess. While the trance state was believed to be a manifestation of this power, there were nevertheless degrees of trance believed to be too extreme which were associated with one of the most commonly feared sources of danger – beasts of prey. The nature of this power meant that the !gi:xa could only be of use to the community if he achieved a useful manipulation of this power by harnessing it and not allowing it to completely take him over. If some grievance should make him choose not to do so he was in a position to give shape to that grievance with the use of an analogue drawn from the belief structure which surrounded his role as !gi:xa (*ibid.*, pp. 20f; D.F. Bleek 1931–36, Part VIII, p. 135).

In contrast to this, friendly !giten were believed to be able to transform themselves into their particular animal, say a jackal or a bird, and visit distant friends so as to establish if they were well and contented or if some accident had happened to them. It was believed that the body of the !gi:xa lay sleeping in his hut at night while he went in the form of an animal to investigate. He would return before daybreak and, in the morning, inform the members of that section of the band that their friends were safe and well. Thus a certain protectiveness and general feeling of goodwill towards the community could also be mobilised within the vocabulary of beliefs concerned with !giten (D.F. Bleek 1931–36, Part VII, pp. 15ff). This capacity to protect and guard the community at night, and in the form of an animal, they also shared with rainmakers and game magicians. It is clear that these shamans were of great importance to the |Xam. They had access to sources of power beyond the range of other men; performed important protective services within the band, and articulated, in concrete forms, the dangers that surrounded the band.

Game !giten

These were known under the collective title of ʘpwaiten-ka !giten but were further differentiated by the addition of the name of a specific animal, as with the springbok !giten mentioned above. Also included under this heading will be !giten who had power over certain insects, particularly locusts.

Various people were believed to possess certain creatures; these included the !giten who dealt with sickness, game !giten, those with power over locusts, and, in one recorded instance, a man said to own mantids, insects regarded by the |Xam as favourable to hunting because of their association with |Kaggen. Locusts were believed to be imprisoned in the ground by certain shamans who had placed a spell on them. They were released by these shamans when required and driven among the people who gathered them for food. It was believed that these shamans could perceive through the medium of the locusts and would know and become angry if children threw stones at them. It was also believed by some that, like curers, these men would send invisible arrows which caused illness if this rule was broken. This belief was possibly encouraged to make children respect food and was often blatantly flaunted by the children themselves.

Perhaps the most important kind of shamans with power over animals were the ʘpwaiten-ka !giten proper. These shamans, like the curers, could be of either sex and were believed to have power over specific game animals. Little is known of any techniques which they may have employed but one springbok !giːxa kept a single springbok tied up near her hut and, on occasions, released it to join its fellows in the wild in the belief that it would lead the herd to those people whom she wished to benefit. Two springbok !giten were described in the texts collected by Bleek and Lloyd and both are said to have worn caps made from springbok heads, with springbok ears sewn in place at either side. These caps were apparently regarded as giving the wearer the power to influence the movements of springbok in the wild. As with curers, game !giten occupied an ambiguous position, for they were believed to influence the game in both a beneficent and a negative way. While they were usually thought to help the hunter they could also be blamed for an absence of game and were on occasions accused of an irresponsible use of their powers. One ostrich !giːxa was said to threaten people with an absence of ostriches if he was angered over something. His ability to make good his threat was not doubted but he was openly criticised for the childish misuse of his power. Despite this open criticism, game !giten were often much feared. It was believed that, like curers, they would cause illness and even death in those who displeased them. It is not known if they were approached for help by the community as were rainmakers and curers, or if they were paid (*ibid.*, pp. 35ff).

Game !giten were prayed to after their deaths for they were believed to survive death and live on through their powers. After a period of unsuccessful hunting a prayer might be said accusing the spirits of dead game !giten of turning their backs on the living and was usually of a chiding nature. One short prayer of this kind was accompanied by pounding the ground with a large stone – often the stone used to weight the digging-stick. The action seems to have been an act of symbolic or real violence towards the spirits for the prayer runs: 'The backs of your heads are here! You who are spirit people have turned your backs on me here!' Another long prayer, however, while still accusing the spirits of neglect, is much more explicit about why the request was made. This, too, was accompanied by pounding the ground with a stone. The prayers recorded were said by women and it may have been the case that this kind of prayer was usually done by women on their husband's behalf (*ibid.*, p. 42).

The resemblance between malignant dead !giten and the Zu|wa concept of the ‖Gauwasi is very striking (L. Marshall 1962: 243). However, the power that !giten were believed to possess was not regarded as derived from any deity, as was the power of the ‖Gauwasi and that owned by Zu|wasi medicine men and the emphasis on male curers amongst the Zu|wasi did not exist amongst the |Xam (L. Marshall 1969: 351). Indeed, the collected texts suggest that the incidence of female shamanism was high and, perhaps, more than balanced out any dominance that males might have had through the role of rainmaker. Nothing resembling the great curing dances of the northern San was ever mentioned by Bleek and Lloyd's informants.

Shamanism amongst the |Xam incorporated a greater variety of roles than it does in any other San group that has been investigated. The shamans clearly had much influence on the imagination of the |Xam and their association with beasts of prey was earned both through the extremities of trance and through the occasional practice of forcing parents to part with their children. This latter practice, together with payment for services and the generalised fear of !giten, plainly suggests the conditions for the creation of a power elite. Such elites may well have arisen in some bands and in some areas; there is also good evidence to suggest, however, that !giten by no means always had the upper hand.

Note

1 The |Xam made a distinction between male rain and female rain. Male rain was often violent and might bring dangers from lightning while female rain was gentle. By killing a rain bull they hoped to bring male rain and by killing a rain cow, female rain.

Bibliography

Abott, W.J.L. 1913. 'Pygmy implements from Cape Colony', *Man* 13.

Abrahams, R. 1968. 'Introductory remarks to a rhetorical theory of folk lore', *Journal of American Folklore* 81: 143–158.

Alexander, J.E. 1967. *An Expedition of Discovery into the Interior of Africa.* 2 vols. Cape Town: Struik.

de Almeida, A. 1965. *Bushmen and Other Non-Bantu Peoples of Angola.* (Occasional Papers, 1.) Johannesburg: Institute for the Study of Man in Africa.

Anders, H.D. 1934–35. 'A note on a south-eastern Bushman dialect', *Zeitschrift für Eingeborenen-Sprachen* 25: 81–89.

– 1937. 'Marginal notes to Wikar's journal', *Bantu Studies* 11: 47–52.

Anderson, A.A. 1887. *Twenty-Five Years in a Waggon.* 2 vols. London: Chapman and Hall.

Anthing, L. 1863. 'Cape Parliamentary Papers: Report A 39.' Cape Town: Government House.

Arbousset, T. and F. Daumas. 1846. *Narrative of an Exploratory Tour to the North-East of the Colony of the Cape of Good Hope.* Cape Town: Robertson and Solomon.

Armstrong, R.P. 1972. 'Content analysis in folkloristics', in *Mythology* edited by P. Maranda, pp. 173–193. Middlesex: Penguin.

Arnold, G. and N. Jones. 1918. 'Notes on the Bushman cave at Bambata Motopos', *Proceedings of the Rhodesian Scientific Association* 17: 5–21.

Backhouse, J. 1844. *A Narrative of a Visit to the Mauritius and South Africa.* London: Hamilton Adams.

Bagshawe, F.J. 1924–25. 'The peoples of the Happy Valley', *Journal of the African Society* 24: 25–33, 117–130, 219–227, 328–337.

Baines, T. 1864. *Explorations in South West Africa in the Years 1861 and 1862.* London: Longman.

Balfour, H. 1902. 'The Goura – a stringed wind musical instrument of the Bushmen and Hottentots', *Journal of the Royal Anthropological Institute of Great Britain and Ireland* 32: 156–176.

Barrow, J. 1801. *Travels into the Interior of Southern Africa.* 2 Vols. London: Cadel and Davies.

Bascom, W.R. 1954. 'Four functions of folklore', *Journal of American Folklore* 67, 266: 334–349.

– 1955. 'Verbal art', *Journal of American Folklore* 68, 269: 245–252.

– 1964. 'Folklore research in Africa', *Journal of American Folklore* 77: 12–31.

– 1965. 'The forms of folklore: prose narrative', *Journal of American Folklore* 78: 3–20.

Battis, W. 1945. 'Prehistoric fishing scenes', addendum to 'Sea animals among the prehistoric rock paintings of Ladybrand' (by H. Breuil), *South African Journal of Science* 41.

Beek, J.L.R.W. 1928. 'The Bushman and Zimbabwe', *Native Affairs Department Annual*.

Beidelman, T.O. 1963. 'Further adventures of hyena and rabbit: the folktale as a sociological model', *Africa* 33: 54–69.

– (ed.) 1971. *The Translation of Culture: Essays to E.E. Evans-Pritchard*. London: Tavistock.

Bentjes, B. 1969. *African Rock Art*. London: Dent.

Berger, P.L. 1967. *The Sacred Canopy: Elements of a Sociological Theory of Religion*. New York: Doubleday.

Berger, P.L. and Th. Luckman. 1967. *The Social Construction of Reality*. London: Allen Lane.

Bertin, G. 1886. 'The Bushmen and their language', *Journal of the Royal Asiatic Society of Britain and Ireland* 18, 1: 51–81.

Bicchieri, M.G. (ed.) 1972. *Hunters and Gatherers Today*. New York: Holt, Rinehart and Winston.

Biesele, M. 1971. 'Hunting in semi-arid areas – the Kalahari Bushmen today', *Botswana Notes and Records* (Special Edition No. 1). Gaborone: Government Printer.

– 1972. 'A !Kung Bushman folktale', *Botswana Notes and Records* 4: 133–135.

– 1975. 'Folklore and Ritual of !Kung Hunter-Gatherers.' Ph.D. thesis. Harvard University. Cambridge, Massachusetts.

– 1976. 'Aspects of !Kung folklore', in *Kalahari Hunter-Gatherers: Studies of the !Kung San and their Neighbors*, edited by R.B. Lee and I. DeVore, pp. 302–324. Cambridge and London: Harvard University Press.

Bjerre, J. 1960. *Kalahari*. London: Michael Joseph.

Bleek, D.F. 1921. 'Birds and insects in Bushman folklore', *South Journal of Science* 17: 194.

– 1923. *The Mantis and His Friends: Bushman Folklore*. Cape Town: Maskew Miller.

– 1924. 'Bushman terms of relationship', *Bantu Studies* 2: 57–70.

– 1926. 'Note on Bushman orthography', *Bantu Studies* 2: 71–74.

– 1927. 'The distribution of Bushman languages in South Africa', *Festschrift Meinhof*, pp. 55–64. Hamburg: L. Friedrichsen.

– 1928a. 'Bushmen of central Angola', *Bantu Studies* 3: 105–125.

– 1928b. *The Naron: A Bushman of the Central Kalahari*. Cambridge: University Press.

– 1929a. 'Bushman folklore', *Africa* 2: 302–313.

– 1929b. *Comparative Vocabularies of Bushman Languages*. Cambridge: University Press.

– 1929c. 'Bushman grammar: a grammatical sketch of the language of the |Xam-ka-!k'e',
Zeitschrift für Eingeborenen-Sprachen 19: 81–98.

– 1931. 'The Hadzapi or Watindega of Tanganyika Territory', Africa 4: 273–286.

– 1931–36. 'Customs and beliefs of the |Xam Bushmen; from material collected by
W.H.I. Bleek and L.C. Lloyd between 1870 and 1880', Bantu Studies 5–10.

– 1932. 'A survey of our present knowledge of rock paintings in South Africa', South
African Journal of Science 29: 72–83.

– 1934–35. '!Kung mythology', Zeitschrift für Eingeborenen-Sprachen 25: 261–283.

– 1936. 'Special speech of animals and moon used by the |Xam Bushmen', Bantu Studies
10: 163–199.

– 1937a. '|auni vocabulary', Bantu Studies 11: 259–278.

– 1939–40. 'A short survey of Bushman languages', Zeitschrift für Eingeborenen-Sprachen
30: 52–72.

– 1956. A Bushman Dictionary. (American Oriental Society Series, 41.) New Haven,
Connecticut: American Oriental Society.

Bleek, D.F. and E. Bleek. 1909. 'Notes on the Bushmen', in Bushman Paintings, by M.H.
Tongue. Oxford: University Press.

Bleek, D.F. and A.M. Duggan-Cronin. 1942. The Bushman Tribes of Southern Africa.
Kimberley: Alexander McGregor Memorial Museum.

Bleek D.F. and G.W. Stow. 1930. Rock Paintings in South Africa. London: Methuen.

Bleek, W.H.I. 1851. De nominum generibus linguarum Africae Australis, Copticae,
Semiticarum aliarumque sexualium. Bonn.

– 1862–69. A Comparative Grammar of South African Languages. 2 vols. London:
Trübner.

– 1864. Reynard the Fox in South Africa; or Hottentot Fables and Tales. London: Trübner.

– 1869. 'The Bushman language', in The Cape and Its People, and Other Essays by South
African Writers, edited by R. Noble, pp. 269–284. Cape Town: Juta.

– 1870–74. 'African folklore', Cape Monthly Magazine 1 (July–Dec. 1870), 2 (July–Dec.
1871), 9 (July–Dec. 1874).

– 1873a. 'Report concerning his researches into the Bushman languages and customs',
Cape Parliamentary Papers A 17–'73. Cape Town.

– 1873b. 'Scientific reasons for the study of the Bushman language', Cape Monthly
Magazine 7: 149–153.

– 1874. 'On resemblances in Bushman and Australian mythology', Cape Monthly
Magazine 8: 98–102.

– 1875a. 'Bushman researches', Cape Monthly Magazine 11: 104–115, 150–155.

– 1875b. A Brief Account of Bushman and Other Texts. Cape Town: Juta.

– 1936. 'A fragment: a continuation of "Comparative Grammar of South African Languages"', *Bantu Studies* 10: 1–7.

– 1962. *Wilhelm Heinrich Immanuel Bleek: A Bio-Bibliographical Sketch.* Cape Town: University of Cape Town Libraries.

Bleek, W.H.I. and L.C. Lloyd. 1911. *Specimens of Bushman Folklore.* London: Allen.

– n.d. 'Notebooks.' J.W. Jagger Library, University of Cape Town.

Boas, F. 1916. 'The development of folktales and myths', *Scientific Monthly* 3: 335–343.

– 1940. *Race, Language and Culture.* London: Macmillan.

Bowra, C.M. 1963. *Primitive Song.* London: Weidenfeld and Nicolson.

Breuil, H. 1945. 'Sea animals amongst the prehistoric rock paintings of Ladybrand', *South African Journal of Science* 41: 353–360.

– 1949. 'Some foreigners in the frescoes on rocks in southern Africa', *South African Archaeological Bulletin* 4: 39–50.

– 1954. 'Carbon test and South West African paintings', *South African Archaeological Bulletin* 9: 49.

Breyer-Brandwijk, M.G. 1937. 'A note on the Bushman arrow poison, Diamphidia Simplex Peringeey', *Bantu Studies* 11: 279–284.

Brownlee, F. 1943–44. 'The social organisation of the Kung (!Un) Bushmen of the north-western Kalahari', *Africa* 14: 124–129.

Buchler, I.R. and H.A. Selby. 1968. *A Formal Study of Myth.* Austin: University of Texas Press.

Burchell, W. 1953. *Travels in the Interior of South Africa* (2nd edition). London: Barchwarth.

Burke, K. 1957. *The Philosophy of Literary Form: Studies in Symbolic Action.* New York: Vintage Books.

Burkitt, M.C. 1928. *South Africa's Past in Stone and Paint.* Cambridge: University Press.

Campbell, J. 1815. *Travels in South Africa, Undertaken at the Request of the Missionary Society.* London: Black and Parry.

– 1822. *Travels in South Africa ..., Being a Narrative of a Second Journey into the Interior of that Country.* 2 vols. London: Religious Tract Society.

Campbell, J. 1968. *The Hero with a Thousand Faces.* Princeton: University Press.

Chaplin, J.A. 1959. 'The Munwa Stream rock engravings', *South African Archaeological Bulletin* 14: 28–34.

Chapman, J. 1868. *Travels in the Interior of South Africa.* 2 vols. London: Bell and Daldy, Edward Stanford.

Chatelain, H. 1894. *Folktales of Angola.* Boston: American Folklore Society.

Chatman, S. 1969. 'Analysing narrative structure', *Language and Style* 2: 3–36.

Clark, J.D. 1951. 'Bushmen hunters of the Barotse Forests', *Northern Rhodesia Journal* 1.

– 1958. 'Schematic art', *South African Archaeological Bulletin* 13: 72–74.

– 1970. *The Prehistory of Africa*. London: Thames and Hudson.

Clifford, B.E.A. 1929. 'A journey by motor from Mahalapye through the Kalahari desert', *Geographical Journal* 73.

Colby, B.N. 1965. 'Cultural patterns in narratives', *Science* 151: 798ff.

– 1973 'A partial grammar of Eskimo folktales', *American Anthropologist* 75, 3: 645–662.

Cole, D.T. 1960. 'African linguistic studies, 1943–1960', *African Studies* 19, 4: 219–229.

Collins, R. 1841. *Report upon the Relations between the Cape Colonists and the Kafirs and Bushmen in 1808–9*. London: Robertson and Robertson.

Cooke, C.K. 1963. 'Pomongwe and Tshangula Caves', *South African Archaeological Bulletin* 18: 73–151.

– 1964. 'Animals in southern Rhodesian rock art', *Arnoldia* 1, 13: 1–22.

– 1965. 'Evidence of human migrations from the rock art of southern Rhodesia', *Africa* 35: 263–285.

– 1969. *Rock Art of Southern Africa*. Cape Town: Books of Africa.

Coon, C.S. 1962. *The Story of Man* (Revised edition). New York: Alfred A. Knog.

– 1972. *The Hunting Peoples*. London: J. Cape.

Cowley, C. 1968. *Fabled Tribe*. London: Longmans.

Crosby, O.T. 1931. 'Notes on Bushmen and Ovambo in South West Africa, Part 1', *Journal of the Royal African Society* 30: 344–360.

Currlé, L.C. 1913. 'Notes on Namaqualand Bushmen', *Transactions of the Royal Society of South Africa* 3: 113–120.

Damas, D. (ed.) 1969. *Ecological Essays: Proceedings of the Conference on Cultural Ecology*. Ottawa: National Museum of Canada.

Dart, R.A. 1924. 'A note on Jan, the Bushman', *Bantu Studies* 2: 107–109.

– 1931. 'Rock engravings in southern Africa and some clues to their significance', *South African Journal of Science* 28: 475–486.

– 1937. 'The hut distribution, genealogy and homogeneity of the |'Auni-‡Khomani Bushmen', *Bantu Studies* 11: 159–174.

Davies, O. 1952. *Natal Archaeological Studies*. Pietermaritzburg: Natal University Press.

Deacon, J. 1965. 'Cultural material from the Gamtoos Valley Shelters', *South African Archaeological Bulletin* 20: 193–200.

Doke, C.M. 1923–26. 'An outline of the phonetics of the language of the hu-Bushmen of the north-west Kalahari', *Bantu Studies* 2: 129–165.

– 1925. 'The Qhung Bushmen of the Kalahari', *South African Geographical Journal* 8: 39–44.

– 1928. 'The linguistic situation in South Africa', *Africa* 1: 478–485.

– 1933. 'An alphabetic bibliography of the Bushman language and literature', *Bantu Studies* 7: 34–35.

– 1936. 'An outline of Bushman phonetics', *Bantu Studies* 10: 433–460.

– 1942. 'Native languages of South Africa: a report on their present position with special reference to research and the development of literature', *African Studies* 1: 135–141.

Dornan, S.S. 1909. 'Notes on the Bushmen of Basutoland', *Transactions of the South African Philosophical Society* 18: 437–450.

– 1911. 'The Masarwas and their language', *South African Journal of Science* 8: 218–225.

– 1917. 'The Tati Bushmen (Masarwas) and their language', *Journal of the Royal Anthropological Institute of Great Britain and Ireland* 47: 37–112.

– 1921. 'Tati Bushmen', in *Hastings' Encyclopaedia of Religion and Ethics* 12: 205–208.

– 1922. 'The heavenly bodies in South African mythology', *South African Journal of Science* 18: 430–433.

– 1923a. 'Bushmen of the Kalahari', *Diamond Fields Advertiser*, Kimberley, 7th, 14th, 21st July.

– 1923b. 'Divination and divining bones', *South African Journal of Science* 20: 504–511.

– 1925. *Pygmies and Bushmen of the Kalahari*. London: Seeley, Service & Co.

Dorson, R.M. 1955. 'The eclipse of solar mythology', *Journal of American Folklore* 68: 393–416.

– 1963. 'Current folklore theories', *Current Anthropology* 4: 93–112.

Douglas, M. 1966. *Purity and Danger*. London: Routledge and Kegan Paul.

– 1967a. 'Animals in Lele religious thought', in *Myth and Cosmos*, edited by J. Middleton. New York: Natural History Press.

– 1967b. 'The meaning of myth, with special reference to "La geste d'Asdiwal"', in *Structural Study of Myth and Totemism*, edited by E. Leach. London: Tavistock.

– 1973. *Rules and Meanings*. Middlesex: Penguin.

Drennan, M.R. 1937. 'Finger mutilation in the Bushman', *Bantu Studies* 11: 247–249.

– 1957. 'The principle of change in man and animals and the role of feminism or gynomorphism in it', *South African Archaeological Bulletin* 12: 3–14.

Drury, J. and G. Bloomhill. 1932. 'The Bushman of the Kalahari', *African World Annual* 29: 29ff.

Dundes, A. 1962. 'From etic to emic units in the structural study of folktales', *Journal of American Folklore* 75.

– 1963. 'A structural typology of North American Indian folktales', *Southwestern Journal of Anthropology* 19: 121–130.

– (ed.) 1965a. *The Study of Folklore*. London: Prentice-Hall.

– 1965b. 'The morphology of North American Indian folktales', in *The Study of Folklore*, edited by A. Dundes, pp. 206–215. London: Prentice-Hall.

Dunn, E.J. 1931. *The Bushman*. London: Charles Griffith.

Ellenberger, V. 1953. *La fin tragique des Bushman*. Paris: Amiot Dumont.

Engelbrecht, J. 1936. *The Korana*. Cape Town: Maskew Miller.

England, N. 1967. 'Bushman counterpoint', *Journal of the International Folk Music Council* 19.

Evans-Pritchard, E.E. 1967. *The Zande Trickster*. Oxford: Clarendon.

Farini, G.A. 1886. *Through the Kalahari Desert*. London: Sampson, Low, Marston, Searle and Rivington.

Finnegan, R. 1967. *Limba Stories and Story-Telling*. Oxford: Clarendon.

– 1970. *Oral Literature in Africa*. Oxford: Clarendon.

Fischer, J.L. 1960. 'Sequence and structure in folktales', in *Men and Cultures*, edited by A. Wallace. Philadelphia: Philadelphia Press.

– 1963. 'The sociopsychological analysis of folktales', *Current Anthropology* 4: 235–295.

Fitzsimons, F.W. 1923a. 'The Bushmen of the Zuurberg', *South African Journal of Science* 20: 501–503.

– 1923b. 'The cliff dwellers of Zitzikama', *South African Journal of Science* 20: 541–544.

Fock, G.J. 1966. 'Distribution of animals on rock-engravings in the northern Cape', *Annals of the Cape Province Museum* 5: 85–90.

– 1970. 'The rock art site at Eindgoed', *South African Archaeological Bulletin* 25: 71–72.

Fortes, M. and G. Dieterlen (eds.) 1965. *African Systems of Thought*. Oxford: University Press.

Fourie, L. 1925–26. 'Preliminary notes on certain customs of the Hei-‖om Bushmen', *Journal of the South West African Scientific Society* 1: 49–63.

Frere, Sir H. Bartle. 1883. 'On systems of land tenure among aboriginal tribes in South Africa', *Journal of the Royal Anthropological Institute of Great Britain and Ireland* 12.

Fritsch, G. 1872. *Die Eingeborenen Süd-Afrikas ethnographisch und anatomisch beschrieben*. Breslau.

Fry, R. 1910. 'Bushman paintings', *Burlington Magazine* 14: 333–338.

Gardiner, 1836. *Narrative of a Journey to the Zoolu Country in South Africa*. London: William Crofts.

Gawston, F.G. 1931. 'A consideration of the Bushmen's paintings at Quthing', *South African Journal of Science* 28: 470–471.

Gluckman, M. and E. Devons (eds.) 1964. *Closed Systems and Open Minds*. London: Oliver and Boyd.

Goodall, E. 1946a. 'Domestic animals in rock art', *Proceedings of the Rhodesian Scientific Association* 41.

– 1946b. 'Some observations on rock paintings illustrating burial rites', *Proceedings of the Rhodesian Scientific Association* 41.

Goodwin, A.J.H. 1929. 'The Stone Ages in South Africa', *Africa* 2: 174–182.

– 1936. 'The Bushmen', *African Observer* 5, 5.

– 1946. 'Prehistoric fishing methods in South Africa', *Antiquity* 20.

– 1949. 'A fishing scene from east Griqualand', *South African Archaeological Bulletin* 4: 51–53.

Goodwin, A.J.H. and C. van Riet Lowe. 1929. *The Stone Age Cultures of South Africa*. (Annals of the South African Museum, 27.) Edinburgh: Trustees of the South African Museum.

Greenberg, J.H. 1949–50. 'Studies in African linguistic classification: The click languages', *Southwestern Journal of Anthropology* 6: 223–237.

– 1963. *The Languages of Africa*. The Hague: Mouton.

Greimas, A.J. 1972. 'Comparative mythology', in *Mythology*, edited by P. Maranda, pp. 162–170. Middlesex: Penguin.

Griaule, M. 1950. *Arts of the African Native*. London: Thames and Hudson.

Gusinde, M. 1953. 'Anthropological investigations of the Bushmen of South Africa', *Anthropological Quarterly* 26 (n.s.l), 1: 20–28.

– 1966. *Von gelben und schwarzen Buschmännern. Eine untergehende Altkultur im Süden Afrikas*. Graz: Akademische Druck- und Verlagsanstalt.

Haddon, A.C. 1924. *The Races of Man and Their Distribution*. Cambridge: University Press.

Hahn, T. 1881. *Tsuni-//Goam, the Supreme Being of the Khoi-Khoi*. Cape Town: Trübner.

Hall, I.C. and R.W. Whitehead. 1927. 'A pharmaco-bacteriologic study of African poisoned arrows', *Journal of Infectious Diseases* 41: 51–69.

Hall, R.M. 1912a. 'Bushman paintings in the Madabo Range, southern Rhodesia', *Geographical Journal* 39: 592–596.

– 1912b. 'Antiquity of the Bushman occupation of Rhodesia', *Proceedings of the Rhodesian Science Association* 11: 140–154.

Hansen, J.D.L. 1969. 'The children of hunting and gathering Bushmen', *South African Medical Journal*, 20th September.

Harris, W.C. 1963. *The Wild Sports of Southern Africa.* Cape Town: Struik.

Heinz, H.-J. 1967. 'Conflict, tensions, and release of tensions in a Bushman society.' (Institute for the Study of Man in Africa, Paper No. 23.)

– 1971. 'The ethnobiology of the !Ko Bushmen', *South African Journal of Science* 67: 43–50.

– 1972. 'Territoriality among the Bushmen in general and the !Ko in particular', *Anthropos* 67: 405–416.

Herbst, J.F. 1908. 'Report on Rietfontein Area.' (Cape Parliamentary Papers, G. 53–1908; Colonial Reports, Mise, No. 55.) Cape Town: Government House.

Herskovits, M.J. 1961. 'The study of African oral art', *Journal of American Folklore* 74: 451–456.

Herskovits, M.J. and S. Frances. 1958. *Dahomean Narrative.* (Northwestern University African Studies, 1.) Evanston, Illinois: Northwestern University Press.

Hewitt, J. 1920. 'Notes relating to the aboriginal tribes of the Eastern Province', *South African Journal of Science* 17: 304–321.

Hirschberg, W. 1934. 'The problem of relationship between Pygmies and Bushmen', *Africa* 7: 444–451.

Hodson, A.W. 1912. *Treking the Great Thirst: Travel and Sport in the Kalahari Desert.* London: T. Fisher Unwin.

Hoernlé, A. 1918. 'Certain rites of transition and the conception of !Nau among the Hottentots', *Harvard African Studies* 2: 65–82.

Hoernlé, A.W. 1923. 'South-West Africa as a primitive culture area', *South African Geographical Journal* 6: 14–28.

Holm, E. 1965. *Tier und Gott: Mythik, Mantik und Magie der süd-afrikanischen Urjäger.* Basel – Stuttgart: Schwabe.

Honey, J.A. 1910. *South African Folktales.* New York: Baker and Taylor.

How, M.W. 1962. *The Mountain Bushmen of Basutoland.* Pretoria: Van Schaik.

Hyman, S.E. 1968. 'The ritual view of myth and the mythic', in *Mythology: A Symposium*, edited by Th. A. Sebeok, pp. 136–153. Bloomington: Indiana University Press.

Jacobs, M. 1959. *The Content and Style of Oral Literature: Clackamas Chinook Myths and Tales.* (Viking Fund Publication in Anthropology, 26.)

– 1960a. *The People Are Coming Soon: Analyses of Clackamas Chinook Myths and Tales.* Washington: University Press.

– 1960b. 'Humour and social structure in an oral literature', in *Culture in History: Essays in Honour of Paul Radin*, edited by S. Diamond. New York: Columbia University Press.

Jason, H. 1969. 'A multidimensional approach to oral literature', *Current Anthropology* 10: 413–425.

Johnston, H.H. 1908. 'Man and nature in South-West Africa', *Nature* 77: 385–386.

Jones, J.D. and C.M. Doke (eds.) 1937. *Bushmen of the Southern Kalahari.* Johannesburg: University of the Witwatersrand Press.

Joyce, J.W. 1938. *Report on the Masarwa in the Bomangwato Reserve, Bechuanaland Protectorate.* (League of Nations Publications, 6.)

Kannemeyer, D.R. 1890. 'Stone implements of the Bushmen', *Cape Illustrated Magazine* 1: 120–130.

Kicherer, J. 1803. 'Mr. Kicherer's, etc. mission to South Africa', *Transactions of the London Missionary Society* 1.

Kingon, J.R.L. 1918. 'A survey of aboriginal place-names', *South African Journal of Science* 15: 712–779.

Kirby, P.R. 1936a. 'A study of Bushman music', *Bantu Studies* 10: 205–252.

– 1936b. 'The musical practices of the ǀauni and ǂkhomani Bushmen', *Bantu Studies* 10: 373–431.

– 1958. *Jacob von Reenen and the Grosvenor Expedition of 1790–1.* Johannesburg: Van Riebeeck Society.

Kluckhohn, C. 1953. 'Universal categories of culture', in *Anthropology Today*, edited by A.L. Kroeber. Chicago: University Press.

– 1965. 'Recurrent themes in myths and mythmaking', in *The Study of Folklore*, edited by A. Dundes. London: Prentice-Hall.

Kohler, O. 1963. 'Observations on the Central Khoisan language group', *Journal of African Languages* 2: 227–234.

Kolb, P. 1731. *The Present State of the Cape of Good Hope; or, A Particular Account of the Several Nations of Hottentots.* London.

Labov, W. 1970. 'The study of language in its social context', *Studium Generale* 23: 30–87.

Labov, W. and J. Waletzky. 1967. 'Narrative analysis: oral versions of personal experience', in *Essays on the Verbal and Visual Arts: Proceedings of the 1966 Annual Meeting of the American Ethnological Society*, edited by J. Helm, pp. 12–44. Washington: University Press.

Laing, G.D. 1926. 'The relationship between Boskop Bushman and Negro elements in the formation of the native races of South Africa', *South African Journal of Science* 23: 905–908.

Lanham, L.W. and D.P. Hallowes. 1956a. 'Linguistic relationships and contacts expressed in the vocabulary of Eastern Bushmen', *African Studies* 15: 45–48.

– 1956b. 'An outline of the structure of Eastern Bushman', *African Studies* 15: 98–118.

Larson, Th.J. 1972. *Tales from the Okavango*. Cape Town: Howard Timmins.

Laszlo, A.E. 1955. 'An expedition to rock carvings in southern Angola', *South African Archaeological Bulletin* 10: 128.

Layard, J. 1957. 'Review of *The Trickster*, by Paul Radin', *Journal of Analytical Psychology* 2: 106–111.

– 1958. 'Note on the autonomous psyche and the ambivalence of the trickster concept', *Journal of Analytical Psychology* 3: 21–29.

Leach, E. 1954. *Political Systems of Highland Burma*. London: Bell.

– 1964. 'Anthropological aspects of language: animal categories and verbal abuse', in *New Directions in the Study of Language*, edited by E.H. Lenneberg. Cambridge, Massachusetts: M.I.T. Press.

– 1967. 'Genesis as myth', in *Myth and Cosmos*, edited by J. Middleton. New York: Natural History Press.

– 1970. *Claude Lévi-Strauss*. London: Collins.

– 1972. 'The structure of symbolism', in *The Interpretation of Ritual*, edited by La Fontaine. London: Tavistock.

Lee, D.H. and H.C. Woodhouse. 1964. 'Rock paintings of "Flying Buck"', *South African Archaeological Bulletin* 19: 71–74.

– 1970. *Art on the Rocks of Southern Africa*. Cape Town: Purnell.

Lee, R.B. 1967. 'Trance cure of the !Kung bushmen', *Natural History* (Nov.) 30–37.

– 1968a. 'The sociology of !Kung Bushman trance performances', in *Trance and Possession States*, edited by R. Prince, pp. 35–54. Montreal: R.M. Bucke Memorial Society.

– 1968b. 'What hunters do for a living, or how to make out on scarce resources', in *Man the Hunter*, edited by R.B. Lee and I. DeVore, pp. 30–48. Chicago: Aldine.

– 1969a. 'Eating Christmas in the Kalahari', *Natural History* (Dec.).

– 1969b. '!Kung Bushman subsistence: an input-output analysis', *National Museum of Canada Bulletin* 230: 73–94.

– 1972a. 'The interpretation of social life among the !Kung Bushmen', in *Population Growth: Anthropological Implications*, edited by B. Spooner. Cambridge, Massachusetts: M.I.T. Press.

– 1972b. '!Kung spatial organisation: an ecological and historical perspective', *Human Ecology* 1: 125–147.

– 1972c. 'Population growth and the beginnings of sedentary life among the !Kung Bushmen', in *Population Growth: Anthropological Implications*, edited by B. Spooner. Cambridge, Massachusetts: M.I.T. Press.

– 1972d. 'The !Kung Bushmen of Botswana, in *Hunters and Gatherers Today*, edited by M.G. Bicchieri. New York: Holt, Rinehart and Winston.

Lee, R.B. and I. DeVore (eds.) 1968. *Man the Hunter*. Chicago: Aldine.

Leslie, L. 1830. 'Some remarks on the Bushmen of the Orange river', *South African Quarterly Journal* 1: 79–82.

Le Vaillant, F. 1790. *Voyage dans l'intérieur de l'Afrique par le Cap de Bonne-Esperance dans les années 1780–85.* 2 vols. Paris: Hignou and Comp.

Levine, M.H. 1957. 'Prehistoric art and ideology', *American Anthropologist* 59: 949–964.

Lévi-Strauss, C. 1960. 'Four Winnebago myths: a structural sketch', in *Culture in History: Essays in Honour of Paul Radin*, edited by S. Diamond. New York: Columbia University Press.

– 1970. *The Raw and the Cooked.* London: Cape.

– 1972a. *The Savage Mind.* London: Weidenfeld and Nicolson.

– 1972b. *Structural Anthropology.* London: Penguin University Books.

– 1973. *From Honey to Ashes.* London: Cape.

Levy, L. 1968. *A Preliminary List of Publications Referring to Non-Bantu Click Languages.* (Communications from the School of African Studies, 33.) University of Cape Town.

Lichtenstein, M.H.C. 1930. *Travels in South Africa in the Years 1803–1806.* 2 vols. Cape Town: Van Riebeeck Society.

Lister, M.H. (ed.) 1949. *Journals of Andrew Geddes Bain.* Cape Town: Van Riebeeck Society.

Littleton, C.S. 1965. 'A two-dimensional scheme for the classification of narratives', *Journal of American Folklore* 78: 21–27.

Lloyd, L.C. 1880. 'Bushman folklore', *(South African) Folklore Journal* 2: 39–43.

– 1889. *A Short Account of Further Bushman Material Collected.* London: David Nutt.

Logie, A.C. 1935. 'Preliminary notes on some Bushman arrows from South-West Africa', *South African Journal of Science* 32: 553–559.

Lord, A. 1958. *The Singer of Tales.* Cambridge, Massachusetts: Harvard University Press.

MacCalman, H.R. and B.J. Grobbelaar. 1965. 'Preliminary report on two stone-working Ovatjimba groups in the northern Kaoveld of South West Africa', *Cimbebasia* 13.

MacCrone, I.D. 1937. 'A note on the tsamma and its uses among the Bushmen', *Bantu Studies* 11: 251–252.

Mackenzie, J. 1871. *Ten Years North of the Orange River.* London: Cass.

MacMillan, W.M. 1927. *The Cape Colour Question: A Historical Survey.* London: Faber and Guyer.

Maggs, T.M.O'C. 1967. 'A quantitative analysis of the rock art from a sample area in the Western Cape', *South African Journal of Science* 63: 100–104.

Maingard, L.F. 1931. 'The lost tribes of the Cape', *South African Journal of Science* 28: 487–504.

– 1935. 'The first contacts of the Dutch with the Bushmen until the time of Simon van der Stel (1786)', *South African Journal of Science* 22: 479–487.

– 1937a. 'Notes on health and disease among the Bushmen of the southern Kalahari', *Bantu Studies* 11: 285–294.

– 1937b. 'The ǂkhomani dialect Bushmen: its morphology and other characteristics', in *Bushmen of the Southern Kalahari*, edited by J.D. Rheinaut Jones and C.M. Doke, pp. 237–275. Johannesburg: University of the Witwatersrand Press.

– 1957. 'Three Bushman languages', *African Studies* 16: 37–71.

– 1958. 'The third Bushman language', *African Studies* 17: 100–115.

– 1963. 'A comparative of Naron, Hietshware and Korana', *African Studies* 22: 97–108.

Marais, J.S. 1939. *The Cape Coloured People 1652–1937*. London: Longmans, Green & Co.

Maranda, P. 1967. 'Computers in the bush: tools for the automatic analysis of myths', in *Essays on the Verbal and Visual Arts: Proceedings of the 1966 Annual Meeting of the American Ethnological Association*, edited by J. Helm. Washington: University Press.

– (ed.) 1972. *Mythology*. Middlesex: Penguin.

Maranda, P. and E.K. Maranda-Kongas (eds.) 1971. *Structural Analysis of Oral Tradition*. Philadelphia: University of Pennsylvania.

Markowitz, A. 1971. *The Rebirth of the Ostrich*. Gaborone: National Museum and Art Gallery.

Marks, S. 1972. 'Khoisan resistance to the Dutch in the seventeenth and eighteenth centuries', *Journal of African History* 13: 55–80.

Marshall, J. 1958. 'Man as a hunter', *Natural History* 67,6: 291–309; 67,7: 376–395.

Marshall, L. 1957a. 'N!ow', *Africa* 27: 232–240.

– 1957b. 'The kin terminology system of the !Kung Bushmen', *Africa* 27: 1–24.

– 1959. 'Marriage among the !Kung Bushmen', *Africa* 29: 335–365.

– 1960. '!Kung Bushman bands', *Africa* 30: 325–354.

– 1961. 'Sharing, talking and giving: relief and social tensions among !Kung Bushmen', *Africa* 31: 231–249.

– 1962. '!Kung Bushman religious beliefs', *Africa* 32: 221–252.

– 1965. 'The !Kung Bushmen of the Kalahari desert', in *Peoples of Africa*, edited by J.L. Gibbs Jr. New York: Holt, Rinehart and Winston.

– 1969. 'The medicine dance of the !Kung Bushmen', *Africa* 39: 347–380.

Meinhof, C. 1928–29. 'Versuch einer grammatischen Skizze einer Buschmannsprache', *Zeitschrift für Eingeborenen-Sprachen* 19: 161–188.

Meriggi, P. 1929. 'Versuch einer Grammatik des /xam-Buschmännischen', *Zeitschrift für Eingeborenen-Sprachen* 19: 117–153, 188–205.

Metman, P. 1958. 'The trickster figure in schizophrenia', *Journal of Analytical Psychology* 3: 5–21.

Metschikoff, L. 1889–90. 'Bushmen and Hottentots', *Bulletin de la Société Neuchâteloise de Géographie* 5.

Metzger, F. 1950. *Narro and His Clan.* Windhoek: Meinert.

– 1952. *Und seither lacht die Hyäne.* Windhoek: Meinert.

Middleton, J. (ed.) 1967. *Myth and Cosmos: Readings in Mythology and Symbolism.* New York: American Museum of Natural History.

Moffat, R. 1842. *Missionary Labours and Scenes in South Africa.* London: Missionary Society.

Moodie, D. 1857. *South African Annals – Origin of the Bushmen.* Pietermaritzburg.

– 1860. *The Record; or, a Series of Official Papers Relative to the Condition of the Native Tribes of South Africa.* Cape Town: Balkema.

Mossop, E.E. 1931. *The Journals of Bergh and Schrijver.* Cape Town: Van Riebeeck Society.

Müller, F. 1888. 'Die Sprache der |Kham Buschmänner', in *Grundriß der Sprachwissenschaft,* Vol. 4. Vienna.

Murdock, G.P. 1959. *Africa: Its Peoples and Their Culture History.* New York: McGraw-Hill.

Norton, W.A. 1909. 'Bushmen and their relics near Modderpoort', *South African Journal of Science* 6: 242–244.

– 1919. 'The South-West Protectorate and its native population', *South African Journal of Science* 16: 453–465.

Orpen, J.M. 1874. 'A glimpse into the mythology of the Maluti Bushmen', *Cape Monthly Magazine* 9: 1–13. (Reprinted in *Folklore* 30 (1919) 139–156.)

– 1965. *Reminiscences of Life in South Africa.* Cape Town: C. Struik.

Pager, H. 1971a. 'The rock art of the Ndedema Gorge and neighbouring valleys', *South African Journal of Science.* Special Issue No. 2: 27–33.

– 1971b. *Ndedema: A Documentation of the Rock Paintings of the Ndedema Gorge.* Graz: Akademische Druck-Verlagsanstalt.

Palgrave, W.C. 1877. 'Report ... of his Mission to Damaraland and Great Namaqualand in 1876.' (Cape Parliamentary Papers, G. 50–77.) Cape Town: Government House.

Péringuey, L. 1906. 'On rock engravings of animals and the human figure, the work of South African aborigines', *Transactions of the South African Philosophical Society* 16: 401–412.

– 1909. 'The rock engravings of South Africa', *Transactions of the South African Philosophical Society* 18: 401–419.

– 1911. *The Stone Ages of South Africa*. (Annals of the South African Museum, 8.) Edinburgh: Trustees of the S.A.M.

– 1915. 'The Bushman as Paleolithic Man', *Transactions of the Royal Society of South Africa* 5: 226–236.

Perkins, C.M. and M. Perkins. 1965. *I Saw You from Afar*. New York: Athenaeum.

Planert, W. 1905. 'Über die Sprache der Hottentotten und Buschmänner', *Mitteilungen des Seminars für Orientalische Sprachen zu Berlin* 8 (Abt. 3): 104–176.

Partridge, A.C. 1973. *Folklore of Southern Africa*. Cape Town: Purnell.

Potgieter, E.F. 1955. *The Disappearing Bushmen of Lake Chrissie*. Pretoria: Van Schaik.

Propp, V. 1968. *Morphology of the Folktale*. Austin: University of Texas Press.

Radin, P. 1924. *Monotheism among Primitive Peoples*. London: Allen and Unwin.

– (ed.) 1952. *African Folktales and Sculpture*. New York: Pantheon.

– 1955. 'The literature of primitive peoples', *Diogenes*.

– 1956. *The Trickster*. London: Routledge and Kegan Paul.

Roberts, J.M., B. Sutton-Smith and A. Kendon. 1972. 'Strategy in games and folk tales', *Mythology*, edited by P. Maranda. Middlesex: Penguin.

Roberts, N. 1916. 'Rock paintings of the Northern Transvaal', *South African Journal of Science* 13: 568–573.

Roos, T. 1931. 'Burial customs of the !Kau Bushmen', *Bantu Studies* 5: 81–83.

Rosenthal, E. and A.J.H. Goodwin. 1953. *Cave Artists of South Africa*. Cape Town: A.A. Balkema.

Rudner, I. and J. Rudner. 1959. 'Who were the artists?', *South African Archaeological Bulletin* 14: 106–108.

Rudner, J. 1957. 'Brandberg and its archaeological remains', *Journal of the South-West African Scientific Society* 12: 7–44.

Rudner, J. and I. Rudner. 1970. *The Hunter and His Art*. Cape Town: C. Struik.

Sahlins, M. 1972. *Stoneage Economics*. London: Tavistock.

Schapera, I. 1925a. 'Bushman arrow poisons', *Bantu Studies* 2: 199–214.

– 1925b. 'Some stylistic affinities of Bushman art', *South African Journal of Science* 22: 504–515.

– 1926. 'A preliminary consideration of the relationship between the Hottentots and the Bushmen', *South African Journal of Science* 23: 833–866.

– 1927a. 'The tribal divisions of the Bushmen', *Man* 27: 68–73.

– 1927b. 'Bows and arrows of the Bushmen', *Man* 27: 113–117.

– 1929. Bushman languages', *Encyclopaedia Britannica* (14th edition).

– 1930. *The Khoisan Peoples of South Africa: Bushmen and Hottentots.* London: Routledge and Kegan Paul.

– 1939. 'A survey of the Bushman question', *Race Relations* 6, 2: 68–83.

– 1941. *Select Bibliography of South African Native Life and Problems.* Oxford: University Press.

– 1963. 'The native inhabitants', *The Cambridge History of the British Empire* 8. Cambridge: University Press. (2nd edition.)

Schapera, I. and B. Farrington (eds.) 1933. *The Early Cape Hottentots, Described in the Writings of Olfert Dapper and Willem ten Rhyne (1668) and Johannes Gulielmus de Grevensbroek (1695).* Cape Town: Van Riebeeck Society.

Schmidt, P.W. 1929. 'Zur Erforschung der alten Buschmann-Religion', *Africa* 2: 291–301.

Schmidt, S. 1973. 'Die Mantis Religiosa in den Glaubensvorstellungen der Khoesan-Völker', *Zeitschrift für Ethnologie* 98: 102–127.

– 1975. 'Folktales of the non-Bantu speaking peoples in southern Africa', *Folklore* 86: 99–114.

Schoeman, P. 1957. *Hunters of the Desert Land.* Cape Town: Howard Timmins.

Schönland, S. 1903. 'On some Hottentot and Bushmen pottery in the collection of the Albany Museum', *Records of the Albany Museum (Grahamstown)* 1: 25–32.

– 1904. 'Biological and ethnological observations on a trip to the N.E. Kalahari', *South African Journal of Science* 2: 308–317.

Schoonraad, M. 1962. 'Rock painting depicting prehistoric fishing found near Maclear', *South African Journal of Science* 58: 141–143.

Schoonraad, M. and P. Beaumont. 1968. 'The North Brabant Shelter, N.W. Transvaal', *South African Journal of Science* 64: 319–330.

Schott, R. 1955. 'Die Buschmänner in Südafrika. Eine Studie über Schwierigkeiten der Akkulturation', *Sociologus* N.F. 5: 132–145.

Schwarz, E.H.L. 1927. 'The Bushmen of the Kalahari', *Science Progress* 21: 87–91.

Schweiger, A. 1912. 'The Bushman caves of Keilands', *Catholic Magazine for South Africa* 23.

Sebeok, Th. A. (ed.) 1965. *Myth: A Symposium.* Bloomington: Indiana University Press.

Segal, D.M. 1972. 'The connection between the semantics and the formal structure of a text', in *Mythology* edited by P. Maranda, pp. 215–249. Middlesex: Penguin.

Seubring, G. 1934. 'Three Bushmen and Hottentot tales', *Journal of American Folklore* 47: 329–333.

Shaw, B. 1970. *Memorials of South Africa.* Cape Town: C. Struik.

Silberbauer, G.B. 1961. 'Aspects of the kinship system of the G|wi Bushmen of the Central Kalahari', *South African Journal of Science* 57: 353–359.

– 1963. 'Marriage and the girls' puberty ceremony of the G|wi Bushmen', *Africa* 33: 12–24.

– 1965. *Bushman Survey Report*. Gaberones: Bechuanaland Government Printer.

Silberbauer, G.B. and A. Kuper. 1966. 'Kgalagari masters and Bushman serfs: some observations', *African Studies* 25: 171–179.

Smits, L.G.A. 1971. 'The rock paintings of Lesotho, their content and characteristics', *South African Journal of Science. Special Issue No. 2.* 14–19.

Snyman, J.W. 1970. *An Introduction to the !Xu Language*. Cape Town: A.A. Balkema.

Sollas, W.J. 1911. *Ancient Hunters and Their Modern Representatives*. London: Macmillan.

Sparrman, A. 1785. *A Voyage to the Cape of Good Hope*. 2 vols. London: White.

Spiers, R. 1931–32. 'Bushmen's stock raids in Natal', *Native Teacher's Journal* 11.

Spohr, O. (ed.) 1965. *The Natal Diaries of Dr. W.H.I. Bleek 1855–56*. Cape Town: A.A. Balkema.

Stanford, W.E. 1909. 'Statement of Silayi, with reference to his life among the Bushmen', *Transactions of the Royal Society of South Africa* 1: 435–440.

Stevens, C.M. 1877. 'Remarks on "clicks" with an investigation of the etymon of some South African native geographical names', *Transactions of the South African Philosophical Society* 1: 51–60.

Stopa, R. 1947. *The Hottentots: Their Culture, Language, Folk-Tales and Songs*. London: Lublin.

– 1951. 'Bushman and Hottentot among the isolated languages of Africa', *Rocnik Orientalistyczny Krakow* 17: 351–371.

– 1959. 'Bushman texts', *Folia Orientalia* 1: 105–127.

– 1960. *The Evolution of Click Sounds in Some African Languages*. Cracow.

– 1962. 'Bushman as a language of primitive type', *Folia Orientalia* 4: 187–207.

Story, R. 1958. 'Some plants used by the Bushmen in obtaining food and water, South African Department of Agriculture', *Botanical Survey Memoir* 30.

Stow, G.W. 1873. 'Account of an interview with a tribe of Bushmen in South Africa', *Journal of the Royal Anthropological Institute of Great Britain and Ireland* 3: 244–247.

– 1905. *The Native Races of South Africa*. London: Swan Sonnenschein.

Swierstra, C.J. 1908. 'Note on four rock engravings found in the Transvaal', *Annals of the Transvaal Museum*, pp. 65–70.

Tanaka, J. 1968. 'Bushmen Hunter-Gatherers in the Central Kalahari', *Shizen* 23.

– 1969. 'The ecology and social structure of Central Kalahari Bushmen: a preliminary report', *Kyoto University African Studies* 3: 1–26.

Teixiera, M.A. de Pimental. 1952. 'Rock peckings from Angola', *South African Archaeological Bulletin* 7: 130.

Ten Raa, W.F.E.R. 1963. 'Sandawe musical and other sound producing instruments', *Tanzania Notes and Records* 60: 23–48; 62: 91–93.

– 1969. 'The moon as a symbol of life and fertility in Sandawe thought', *Africa* 39: 24–53.

Theal, G. MacCall. 1886. *Kaffir Folklore*. London: Swan Sonnenschein.

– 1907–10. *History and Ethnography of Africa South of the Zambezi before 1795*. 3 vols. London: Swan Sonnenschein.

– 1910. *The Yellow and Dark-Skinned People of Africa South of the Zambezi*. London: Swan Sonnenschein.

– 1919. *Ethnography and Conditions of Africa South of the Zambezi 1505*. London: Allen and Unwin.

Thomas, E.M. 1959. *The Harmless People*. New York: Knopf.

Thomas, E.W. 1950. *Bushman Stories*. Oxford: University Press.

Thompson, G. 1967. *Travels and Adventures in Southern Africa*. 2 vols. Cape Town: Van Riebeeck Society.

Thompson, S. 1951. *The Folk-Tale*. New York: Dryden.

– 1953. 'The star husband tale', *Studia Septentrionalia* 4: 93–163.

– 1955–58. *Motif-Index of Folk Literature*. Bloomington: Indiana University Press.

Tobias, P.V. 1955. 'Physical anthropology and somatic origins of the Hottentots', *African Studies* 14: 1–15.

– 1956. 'On the survival of the Bushmen', *Africa* 26: 174–186.

– 1957. 'Bushmen of the Kalahari', *Man* 36: 1–8.

– 1959. 'The Nuffield-Witwatersrand University Expeditions to the Kalahari Bushmen, 1958–59', *Nature* 83.

– 1961a. 'Physique of a desert folk', *Natural History* 70, 2: 16–24.

– 1961b. 'New evidence and new views on the evolution of Man in Africa', *South African Journal of Science* 57: 25–38.

– 1962. 'On the increasing stature of the Bushmen', *Anthropos* 57: 801–810.

– 1964. 'Bushman hunter-gatherers: a study in human ecology', in *Ecological Studies in Southern Africa*, edited by D.H.S. Davis. The Hague: Junk.

Tongue, M.H. 1909. *Bushman Paintings*. Oxford: University Press.

Tooke, W.H. 1893. 'The star lore of the South African natives', *Transactions of the South African Philosophical Society* 5.

Townley Johnson, R., H. Rabinowitz and P. Sieff. 1959. *Rock Paintings of the South-West Cape*. Cape Town: Nasimale.

Turner, V. 1960. *The Ritual Process: Structure and Anti-Structure*. Chicago: Aldine.

– 1964a. 'Witchcraft and sorcery: taxonomy versus dynamics', *Africa* 34: 314–324.

– 1964b. 'Symbols in Ndembu ritual', in *Closed Systems and Open Minds*, edited by M. Gluckman. London: Oliver and Boyd.

– 1970. *The Forest of Symbols*. London: Cornell University Press.

Tyler, S. (ed.) 1969. *Cognitive Anthropology*. New York: Holt, Rinehart and Winston.

Ucko, P.J. and A. Rosenfeld. 1967. *Paleolithic Cave Art*. London: World University Library.

Utley, F.L. 1961. 'Folk literature: an operational definition', *Journal of American Folklore* 74: 193–206.

van der Post, L. 1958. *The Lost World of the Kalahari*. London: Hogarth.

– 1961. *The Heart of the Hunter*. London: Hogarth.

van Gennep, A. 1960. *The Rites of Passage*. (Translation by M.B. Vizedom & G.L. Caffee.) London: Routledge and Kegan Paul.

van Riet Lowe, C. 1936. 'Prehistoric art in South Africa', *Official Year Book No. 17 of the Union of South Africa*.

– 1937. 'Prehistoric rock engravings in the Vaal River basin', *Transactions of the Royal Society of South Africa* 24.

– 1945. 'Prehistoric rock engravings in the Krugersdorp–Rustenburg area of the Transvaal', *South African Journal of Science* 41: 329–344.

– 1952. 'The rock engravings of Driekopseiland', *Proceedings of the Second Pan-African Congress on Prehistory, Algiers, 1952*.

van Rippen, B. 1918. 'Notes on some Bushman implements', *Memoirs of the American Anthropological Association* 5: 75–97.

Vansina, J. 1965. *Oral Tradition: A Study in Historical Methodology*. London: Routledge and Kegan Paul.

Vedder, H. 1937. 'Die Buschmänner Südwestafrikas und ihre Weltanschauung', *South African Journal of Science* 34: 416–436.

– 1938. *South West Africa in Early Times*. Oxford: University Press.

Vialis, C.C.C. 1908. 'The Masarwa, or Bushmen of the Kalahari', *African Monthly* 5: 29–33.

Vinnicombe, P. 1960. 'A fishing scene from the Tsoelike River, South-Eastern Basutoland', *South African Archaeological Bulletin* 15: 15–19.

– 1961. 'A painting of a fish-trap on Bamboo Mountain, Underberg District, Southern Natal', *South African Archaeological Bulletin* 16: 114–115.

– 1967. 'Rock painting analysis', *South African Archaeological Bulletin* 22: 129–141.

– 1969. 'Rock painting analysis: preliminary report.' Conference paper, South African Association for the Advancement of Science.

– 1972. 'Myth, motive and selection in Southern African rock art', *Africa* 42: 192–204.

von Wielligh, G.R. 1919–21. *Boesman Stories*. 4 vols. Cape Town: De Nationale Pers.

Walton, J. 1951. 'Kaross-clad figures from South African rock painting', *South African Archaeological Bulletin* 6: 5–8.

– 1954. 'South West African rock paintings and the triple curved bow', *South African Archaeological Bulletin* 9: 131–134.

Waterston, J. 1929. 'The Bushman's arrow-poison beetle and its parasite', *Natural History Magazine* 2: 74–80.

Watson, K.A. 1973. 'A rhetorical and sociolinguistic model for the analysis of narrative', *American Anthropologist* 75: 243–264.

Wehmeyer, A.S. 1969. 'The nutrient composition and dietary importance of some vegetable foods eaten by the !Kung Bushmen', *South African Medical Journal* (20th Dec.).

Wellek, R. and A. Warren. 1970. *Theory of Literature*. Harmondsworth: Penguin Books.

Wellington, J.H. 1955. *Southern Africa: A Geographical Study*. Cambridge: University Press.

Wells, L.H. 1933. 'The archaeology of Cathkin Park', *Bantu Studies* 4: 113–129.

– 1946. 'Marine animals in a rock painting near Fouriesburg', *South African Journal of Science* 42: 236–239.

Werner, A. 1908. 'Some notes on the Bushman race', *Revue des Etudes Ethnographiques et Sociologiques* 1.

– 1909. 'Bushman art', *Anthropos* 4.

– 1925. 'The Bushman languages', in *The Language Families of Africa*, pp. 117–131. London: Routledge and Kegan Paul.

– 1968. *Myths and Legends of the Bantu*. London: Cass.

Wescott, J. 1962. 'The sculpture and myths of Eshu-Elegba, the Yoruba trickster', *Africa* 32: 336–353.

Westphal, E.O.J. 1956. 'The non-Bantu languages of southern Africa', in *The Non-Bantu Languages of North-Eastern Africa*, by A.N. Tucker and M.A. Bryan, pp. 158–173. (Handbook of African Languages, III.) Oxford: University Press.

– 1962a. 'A re-classification of southern African non-Bantu languages', *Journal of African Languages* 1: 1–8.

– 1962b. 'On classifying Bushman and Hottentot languages', *African Language Studies* 3: 30–48.

– 1963. 'The linguistic prehistory of southern Africa: Bush, Kwadi, Hottentot and Bantu linguistic relationships', Africa 33: 237–264.

– 1968. 'Sentence analysis, word categories, and identification in southern African languages', *Taalfasette* 6.

– 1971. 'Click languages of southern and eastern Africa', in *Linguistics in Subsaharan*

Africa, edited by Th.A. Sebeok, pp. 367–420. (Current Trends in Linguistics, 7.) The Hague: Mouton.

Whiteley, W.H. 1964. *African Prose*. Vol. 1. Oxford: Clarendon.

Wieschhoff, H.A. 1973. 'Concepts of right and left in African cultures', in *Right and Left*, edited by R. Needham, pp. 59–73. Chicago: University Press.

Willcox, A.R. 1955. 'The shaded polychrome paintings of South Africa: their distribution, origin and age', *South African Archaeological Bulletin* 10: 10–14.

– 1956a. *Rock Paintings of the Drakensberg*. London: Parrish.

– 1956b. 'Stone cultures and prehistoric art in South Africa', *South African Journal of Science* 53: 68–70.

– 1957. 'The classification of rock paintings', *South African Journal of Science* 54: 417–419.

– 1959. 'Australian and South African rock art compared', *South African Archaeological Bulletin* 16: 97–98.

– 1960. 'Who were the artists? Another opinion', *South African Archaeological Bulletin* 15: 23–25.

– 1962. 'Marine animals in rock paintings', *South African Journal of Science* 58: 6–7.

– 1963a. 'Painted petroglyphs at Balerno in the Limpopo Valley Transvaal', *South African Journal of Science* 59: 108–110.

– 1963b. *The Rock Art of South Africa*. London: Nelson.

– 1965. 'Petroglyphs of domestic animals', *South African Archaeological Bulletin* 20: 214.

– 1971. 'Summary of Dr. Edgar Denninger's reports on the ages of paint samples taken from the rock paintings in South and South West Africa', *South African Journal of Science*. Special Issue No. 2: 84.

Willet, S.M. 1965. *The Bushman: A Select Bibliography 1652–1962*. Johannesburg: University of the Witwatersrand.

Wilman, M. 1910. 'Notes on some Bushman paintings in the Thaba Bosigo District, Basutoland', *South African Journal of Science* 7: 418–421.

– 1933. *The Rock Engravings of Griqualand West and Bechuanaland, South Africa*. Cambridge: University Press.

Wilson, M. and L. Thompson. 1969. *The Oxford History of South Africa*. Vol. 1. Oxford: University Press.

Woldmann, K. 1928a. 'Windmärchen (Buschmann-Mythen)', *Goetheanum* 7, 2: 12–13.

– 1928b. 'Was die Buschmann-Mütter vom Tode erzählen', *Goetheanum* 7, 10: 78–79.

Woodhouse, H.C. 1969. 'Rock paintings of "Eland-fighting" and "Eland-jumping"', *South African Archaeological Bulletin* 94: 63–65.

– 1971. 'Strange relationships between men and eland in the rock paintings of South Africa', *South African Journal of Science* 67: 345–348.

Wuras, C.F. 1920. 'An outline of the Bushman language', *Zeitschrift für Eingeborenen-Sprachen* 10: 81–87.

Wyndham, C.H. and J.F. Morrison. 1956. 'Heat regulation of Masarwa (Bushmen)', *Nature* 178: 869–870.

Yellen, J. and H.C. Harpending. 1972. 'Hunter-gatherer populations and archaeological inference', *World Archaeology* 4.

Index

Printed and bound by CPI Group (UK) Ltd, Croydon, CR0 4YY

09/06/2025

14685819-0003